POETRY & WISDOM

WORLD ENGLISH BIBLE TRANSLATION

Cover illustration: *Job hearing of his ruin* - Gustave Dore, 1885

Cover and icons copyright ©2017 Kris Hull

Book and Jacket design by KR15 Creative Services [KR15.com]
Set in Adobe Garamond & Avenir

ISBN (paperback) 978-0-9910041-5-7

First Edition: November 2017
Printed in the USA

CONTENTS

PREFACE

About this edition

When I told a friend that I was publishing a Bible she said "Why? Don't we have enough Bibles already?" I replied "You can never have too many Bibles!" But the 'why' is a fair question, and I have two answers.

First, I wanted a cheap paperback reader's Bible and I couldn't find one. A "Reader's Bible" is a Bible that has been formatted with none of the usual verse and chapter markers and a minimum of footnotes. This allows the reader to experience the text closer to its original form. A reader's Bible is not meant to be studied line-by-line or to be read by jumping back and forth between verses. A study Bible is great for that. These stripped-down texts are meant to be read straight through. Anything that might be a hindrance has been removed. You experience the text in a different way when you can drink it in one gulp, so to speak.

There are already a lot of wonderful reader's Bibles out there. The problem is that most of them are fancy, precious objects. They cost a lot and they look great on the shelf, but you might not want to throw your $200 hardcover in your bag to read on the bus or by the pool. Some reader's Bibles have stripped out the verse markers but they are still printed on ultra-thin transparent paper in a tiny space-saving typeface.

I wanted a reader's Bible that is small and light enough to take with you, but is set in 11pt. Adobe Garamond on real paper. I also wanted it to be as cheap as possible. The result is that you get a good reading experience but you can take it anywhere and not feel bad about the creases and dog-ears. Just being able to read the Bible in Garamond is reason enough for a new edition. I have also included an estimated time to complete a read through of each book. I have found in my own reading that I am more likely to start if I know what I have signed up for.

The second reason I made this is because I thought it would be fun. I am a graphic artist by trade, and I have spent my career designing all manner of marketing materials, corporate identities, websites, apps, and advertisements. Along the way I have done a little bit of book design and publishing. I have a deep love for the Holy Scriptures and I thought, "Man, wouldn't it be great to design a Bible." Half of the reason I made these volumes was so that I could design the covers and the icons. I initially intended to design one icon for each of the 63 books of the canon (counting Samuel, Kings, and Chronicles as one book each). After I completed the icons for the Torah I realized I would NEVER finish if I tried to design 58 more. I re-aligned my ambitions with reality and designed one more icon for each volume, and ended up with 10 icons.

On a more serious note, one of the ways we respond to the work of the Holy Spirit in our lives is with the desire to use our gifts to honor God or to advance his kingdom in some way. One of the ways that I responded to that desire was to create the book you are holding in your hands. I hope that its accessibility will encourage people who are apprehensive about reading a long and confusing leather-bound tome to dive in and see what the Bible says for themselves.

I also need to give a shout out to Dave Braford. Without his technical expertise, I would not have been able to complete this project. Thanks Dave!

– Kris Hull

ABOUT THE WORLD ENGLISH BIBLE

What is the Holy Bible?

The Holy Bible is a collection of books and letters written by many people who were inspired by the Holy Spirit of God. These books tell us how we can be saved from the evil of this world and gain eternal life that is truly worth living. Although the Holy Bible contains rules of conduct, it is not just a rule book. It reveals God's heart—a Father's heart, full of love and compassion. The Holy Bible tells you what you need to know and believe to be saved from sin and evil and how to live a life that is truly worth living, no matter what your current circumstances may be.

The Holy Bible consists of two main sections: the Old Testament and the New Testament. The Old Testament records God's interaction with mankind before He sent His son to redeem us, while recording prophesy predicting that coming. The New Testament tells us of God's Son and Anointed One, Jesus, and the wonderful salvation that He purchased for us.

The same Holy Spirit who inspired the Holy Bible is living among us today, and He is happy to help you understand what He intended as you study His Word. Just ask Him, and He is more than happy to help you apply His message to your life.

The Old Testament was originally written mostly in Hebrew. The New Testament was originally written mostly in the common street Greek (not the formal Greek used for official legal matters). The Holy Bible is translated into many languages, and being translated into many more, so that everyone may have an opportunity to hear the Good News about Jesus Christ.

Why was the World English Bible translated?

There are already many good translations of the Holy Bible into contemporary English. Unfortunately, almost all of them are restricted by copyright and copyright holder policy. This restricts publication and republication of God's Word in many ways, such as in downloadable files on the Internet, use of extensive quotations in books, etc. The World English Bible was commissioned by God in response to prayer about this subject.

Because the World English Bible is in the Public Domain (not copyrighted), it can be freely copied, distributed, and redistributed without any payment of royalties. You don't even have to ask permission to do so. You may publish the whole World English Bible in book form, bind it in leather and sell it. You may incorporate it into your Bible study software. You may make and distribute audio recordings of it. You may broadcast it. All you have to do is maintain the integrity of God's Word before God, and reserve the name "World English Bible" for faithful copies of this translation.

How was the World English Bible translated?

The World English Bible is an update of the American Standard Version (ASV) of the Holy Bible, published in 1901. A custom computer program updated the archaic words and word forms to contemporary equivalents, and then a team of volunteers proofread and updated the grammar. The New Testament was updated to conform to the Majority Text reconstruction of the original Greek manuscripts, thus taking advantage of the superior access to manuscripts that we have now compared to when the original ASV was translated.

What is different about the World English Bible?

The style of the World English Bible, while fairly literally translated, is in informal, spoken English. The World English Bible is designed to sound good and be accurate when read aloud. It is not formal in its language, just as the original Greek of the New Testament was not formal. The WEB uses contractions rather freely.

The World English Bible doesn't capitalize pronouns pertaining to God. The original manuscripts made no such distinction. Hebrew has no such thing as upper and lower case, and the original Greek manuscripts were written in all upper case letters. Attempting to add in such a distinction raises some difficulties in translating dual-meaning Scriptures such as the coronation psalms.

The World English Bible main edition translates God's Proper Name in the Old Testament as "Yahweh." The Messianic Edition and the British Edition of the World English Bible translates the same name as "LORD" (all capital letters), or when used with "Lord" (mixed case, translated from "Adonai",) GOD. There are solid translational arguments for both traditions. In this printing, the name Yahweh" has been rendered as "YHWH" in small caps reflecting the 4-letter spelling of the name in Hebrew.

Because World English Bible uses the Majority Text as the basis for the New Testament, you may notice the following differences in comparing the WEB to other translations:

- The order of Matthew 23:13 and 14 is reversed in some translations.
- Luke 17:36 and Acts 15:34, which are not found in the majority of the Greek Manuscripts may be included in some other translations.
- Romans 14:24-26 in the WEB may appear as Romans 16:25-27 in other translations.

- 1 John 5:7-8 contains an addition in some translations, including the KJV. Erasmus admitted adding this text to his published Greek New Testament, even though he could at first find no Greek manuscript support for it, because he was being pressured by men to do so, and because he didn't see any doctrinal harm in it. Lots of things not written by John in this letter are true, but we decline to add them to what the Holy Spirit inspired through John.

With all of the above and some other places where lack of clarity in the original manuscripts has led to multiple possible readings, significant variants are listed in footnotes in the full WEB text. *(All footnotes have been omitted from this edition, however).* The reading that in our prayerful judgment is best is in the main text. Overall, the World English Bible isn't very much different than several other good contemporary English translations of the Holy Bible. The message of Salvation through Jesus Christ is still the same. The point of this translation was not to be very different (except for legal status), but to update the ASV for readability while retaining or improving the accuracy of that well-respected translation and retaining the public domain status of the ASV.

More Information

For answers to frequently asked questions about the World English Bible, please visit WorldEnglishBible.org.

THE BOOK OF

JOB

There was a man in the land of Uz, whose name was Job. That man was blameless and upright, and one who feared God, and turned away from evil. There were born to him seven sons and three daughters. His possessions also were seven thousand sheep, three thousand camels, five hundred yoke of oxen, five hundred female donkeys, and a very great household; so that this man was the greatest of all the children of the east. His sons went and held a feast in the house of each one on his birthday; and they sent and called for their three sisters to eat and to drink with them. It was so, when the days of their feasting had run their course, that Job sent and sanctified them, and rose up early in the morning, and offered burnt offerings according to the number of them all. For Job said, "It may be that my sons have sinned, and renounced God in their hearts." Job did so continually.

Now on the day when God's sons came to present themselves before YHWH, Satan also came among them. YHWH said to Satan, "Where have you come from?"

Then Satan answered YHWH, and said, "From going back and forth in the earth, and from walking up and down in it."

YHWH said to Satan, "Have you considered my servant, Job? For there is no one like him in the earth, a blameless and an upright man, one who fears God, and turns away from evil."

Then Satan answered YHWH, and said, "Does Job fear God for nothing? Haven't you made a hedge around him, and around his house, and around all that he has, on every side? You have blessed the work of his hands, and his substance is increased in the land. But stretch out your hand now, and touch all that he has, and he will renounce you to your face."

YHWH said to Satan, "Behold, all that he has is in your power. Only on himself don't stretch out your hand."

So Satan went out from the presence of YHWH. It fell on a day when his sons and his daughters were eating and drinking wine in their oldest brother's house, that there came a messenger to Job, and said, "The oxen were plowing, and the donkeys feeding beside them, and the Sabeans attacked, and took them away. Yes, they have killed the servants with the edge of the sword, and I alone have escaped to tell you."

While he was still speaking, there also came another, and said, "The fire of God has fallen from the sky, and has burned up the sheep and the servants, and consumed them, and I alone have escaped to tell you."

While he was still speaking, there came also another, and said, "The Chaldeans made three bands, and swept down on the camels, and have taken them away, yes, and killed the servants with the edge of the sword; and I alone have escaped to tell you."

While he was still speaking, there came also another, and said, "Your sons and your daughters were eating and drinking wine in their oldest brother's house, and behold, there came a great wind from the wilderness, and struck the four corners of the house, and it fell on the young men, and they are dead. I alone have escaped to tell you."

Then Job arose, and tore his robe, and shaved his head, and fell down on the ground, and worshiped. He said, "Naked I came out of my mother's womb, and naked will I return there. YHWH gave, and YHWH has taken away. Blessed be YHWH's name." In all this, Job didn't sin, nor charge God with wrongdoing.

....

Again, on the day when the God's sons came to present themselves before YHWH, Satan came also among them to present himself before YHWH. YHWH said to Satan, "Where have you come from?"

Satan answered YHWH, and said, "From going back and forth in the earth, and from walking up and down in it."

YHWH said to Satan, "Have you considered my servant Job? For there is no one like him in the earth, a blameless and an upright man, one who fears God, and turns away from evil. He still maintains his integrity, although you incited me against him, to ruin him without cause."

Satan answered YHWH, and said, "Skin for skin. Yes, all that a man has he will give for his life. But stretch out your hand now, and touch his bone and his flesh, and he will renounce you to your face."

YHWH said to Satan, "Behold, he is in your hand. Only spare his life."

So Satan went out from the presence of YHWH, and struck Job with painful sores from the sole of his foot to his head. He took for himself a potsherd to scrape himself with, and he sat among the ashes. Then his wife said to him, "Do you still maintain your integrity? Renounce God, and die."

But he said to her, "You speak as one of the foolish women would speak. What? Shall we receive good at the hand of God, and shall we not receive evil?"

In all this Job didn't sin with his lips. Now when Job's three friends heard of all this evil that had come on him, they each came from his own place: Eliphaz the Temanite, Bildad the Shuhite, and Zophar the Naamathite; and they made an appointment together to come to sympathize with him and to comfort him. When they lifted up their eyes from a distance, and didn't recognize him, they raised their voices, and wept; and they each tore his robe, and sprinkled dust on their heads toward the sky. So they sat down with him on the ground seven days and seven nights, and no one spoke a word to him, for they saw that his grief was very great.

....

After this Job opened his mouth, and cursed the day of his birth. Job answered:
"Let the day perish in which I was born,
*   the night which said, 'There is a boy conceived.'*
Let that day be darkness.
*   Don't let God from above seek for it,*
*   neither let the light shine on it.*
Let darkness and the shadow of death claim it for their own.
*   Let a cloud dwell on it.*
*   Let all that makes black the day terrify it.*
As for that night, let thick darkness seize on it.
*   Let it not rejoice among the days of the year.*
*   Let it not come into the number of the months.*
Behold, let that night be barren.
*   Let no joyful voice come therein.*
Let them curse it who curse the day,
*   who are ready to rouse up leviathan.*
Let the stars of its twilight be dark.
*   Let it look for light, but have none,*
*   neither let it see the eyelids of the morning,*
because it didn't shut up the doors of my mother's womb,
*   nor did it hide trouble from my eyes.*

"Why didn't I die from the womb?
*   Why didn't I give up the spirit when my mother bore me?*
Why did the knees receive me?
*   Or why the breast, that I should nurse?*

For now should I have lain down and been quiet.
   I should have slept, then I would have been at rest,
with kings and counselors of the earth,
   who built up waste places for themselves;
or with princes who had gold,
   who filled their houses with silver:
or as a hidden untimely birth I had not been,
   as infants who never saw light.
There the wicked cease from troubling.
   There the weary are at rest.
There the prisoners are at ease together.
   They don't hear the voice of the taskmaster.
The small and the great are there.
   The servant is free from his master.

"Why is light given to him who is in misery,
   life to the bitter in soul,
Who long for death, but it doesn't come;
   and dig for it more than for hidden treasures,
who rejoice exceedingly,
   and are glad, when they can find the grave?
Why is light given to a man whose way is hidden,
   whom God has hedged in?
For my sighing comes before I eat.
   My groanings are poured out like water.
For the thing which I fear comes on me,
   That which I am afraid of comes to me.
I am not at ease, neither am I quiet, neither have I rest;
   but trouble comes."

....

Then Eliphaz the Temanite answered,
   "If someone ventures to talk with you, will you be grieved?
   But who can withhold himself from speaking?
Behold, you have instructed many,
   you have strengthened the weak hands.
Your words have supported him who was falling,
   You have made firm the feeble knees.
But now it has come to you, and you faint.
   It touches you, and you are troubled.

Isn't your piety your confidence?
Isn't the integrity of your ways your hope?

"Remember, now, whoever perished, being innocent?
Or where were the upright cut off?
According to what I have seen, those who plow iniquity,
and sow trouble,
reap the same.
By the breath of God they perish.
By the blast of his anger are they consumed.
The roaring of the lion,
and the voice of the fierce lion,
the teeth of the young lions, are broken.
The old lion perishes for lack of prey.
The cubs of the lioness are scattered abroad.

"Now a thing was secretly brought to me.
My ear received a whisper of it.
In thoughts from the visions of the night,
when deep sleep falls on men,
fear came on me, and trembling,
which made all my bones shake.
Then a spirit passed before my face.
The hair of my flesh stood up.
It stood still, but I couldn't discern its appearance.
A form was before my eyes.
Silence, then I heard a voice, saying,
'Shall mortal man be more just than God?
Shall a man be more pure than his Maker?
Behold, he puts no trust in his servants.
He charges his angels with error.
How much more, those who dwell in houses of clay,
whose foundation is in the dust,
who are crushed before the moth!
Between morning and evening they are destroyed.
They perish forever without any regarding it.
Isn't their tent cord plucked up within them?
They die, and that without wisdom.'

....

"Call now; is there any who will answer you?
To which of the holy ones will you turn?
For resentment kills the foolish man,
and jealousy kills the simple.
I have seen the foolish taking root,
but suddenly I cursed his habitation.
His children are far from safety.
They are crushed in the gate.
Neither is there any to deliver them,
whose harvest the hungry eats up,
and take it even out of the thorns.
The snare gapes for their substance.
For affliction doesn't come out of the dust,
neither does trouble spring out of the ground;
but man is born to trouble,
as the sparks fly upward.

"But as for me, I would seek God.
I would commit my cause to God,
who does great things that can't be fathomed,
marvelous things without number;
who gives rain on the earth,
and sends waters on the fields;
so that he sets up on high those who are low,
those who mourn are exalted to safety.
He frustrates the plans of the crafty,
So that their hands can't perform their enterprise.
He takes the wise in their own craftiness;
the counsel of the cunning is carried headlong.
They meet with darkness in the day time,
and grope at noonday as in the night.
But he saves from the sword of their mouth,
even the needy from the hand of the mighty.
So the poor has hope,
and injustice shuts her mouth.

"Behold, happy is the man whom God corrects.
Therefore do not despise the chastening of the Almighty.
For he wounds and binds up.

He injures and his hands make whole.
He will deliver you in six troubles;
*   yes, in seven no evil will touch you.*
In famine he will redeem you from death;
*   in war, from the power of the sword.*
You will be hidden from the scourge of the tongue,
*   neither will you be afraid of destruction when it comes.*
You will laugh at destruction and famine,
*   neither will you be afraid of the animals of the earth.*
For you will be allied with the stones of the field.
*   The animals of the field will be at peace with you.*
You will know that your tent is in peace.
*   You will visit your fold, and will miss nothing.*
You will know also that your offspring will be great,
*   Your offspring as the grass of the earth.*
You will come to your grave in a full age,
*   like a shock of grain comes in its season.*
Look at this. We have searched it. It is so.
*   Hear it, and know it for your good."*

....

Then Job answered,
*   "Oh that my anguish were weighed,*
*   and all my calamity laid in the balances!*
For now it would be heavier than the sand of the seas,
*   therefore have my words been rash.*
For the arrows of the Almighty are within me.
*   My spirit drinks up their poison.*
The terrors of God set themselves in array against me.
*   Does the wild donkey bray when he has grass?*
Or does the ox low over his fodder?
*   Can that which has no flavor be eaten without salt?*
Or is there any taste in the white of an egg?
*   My soul refuses to touch them.*
They are as loathsome food to me.

*   "Oh that I might have my request,*
*   that God would grant the thing that I long for,*
even that it would please God to crush me;

that he would let loose his hand, and cut me off!
Let still be my consolation,
    yes, let me exult in pain that doesn't spare,
    that I have not denied the words of the Holy One.
What is my strength, that I should wait?
    What is my end, that I should be patient?
Is my strength the strength of stones?
    Or is my flesh of bronze?
Isn't it that I have no help in me,
    That wisdom is driven quite from me?

"To him who is ready to faint, kindness should be shown from his friend;
    even to him who forsakes the fear of the Almighty.
My brothers have dealt deceitfully as a brook,
    as the channel of brooks that pass away;
Which are black by reason of the ice,
    in which the snow hides itself.
In the dry season, they vanish.
    When it is hot, they are consumed out of their place.
The caravans that travel beside them turn away.
    They go up into the waste, and perish.
The caravans of Tema looked.
    The companies of Sheba waited for them.
They were distressed because they were confident.
    They came there, and were confounded.
For now you are nothing.
    You see a terror, and are afraid.
Did I say, 'Give to me?'
    or, 'Offer a present for me from your substance?'
or, 'Deliver me from the adversary's hand?'
    or, 'Redeem me from the hand of the oppressors?'

"Teach me, and I will hold my peace.
    Cause me to understand my error.
How forcible are words of uprightness!
    But your reproof, what does it reprove?
Do you intend to reprove words,
    since the speeches of one who is desperate are as wind?
Yes, you would even cast lots for the fatherless,

and make merchandise of your friend.
Now therefore be pleased to look at me,
for surely I will not lie to your face.
Please return.
    Let there be no injustice.
    Yes, return again.
    My cause is righteous.
Is there injustice on my tongue?
    Can't my taste discern mischievous things?

....

"Isn't a man forced to labor on earth?
    Aren't his days like the days of a hired hand?
As a servant who earnestly desires the shadow,
    as a hireling who looks for his wages,
so am I made to possess months of misery,
    wearisome nights are appointed to me.
When I lie down, I say,
    'When will I arise, and the night be gone?'
    I toss and turn until the dawning of the day.
My flesh is clothed with worms and clods of dust.
    My skin closes up, and breaks out afresh.
My days are swifter than a weaver's shuttle,
    and are spent without hope.
Oh remember that my life is a breath.
    My eye will no more see good.
The eye of him who sees me will see me no more.
    Your eyes will be on me, but I will not be.
As the cloud is consumed and vanishes away,
    so he who goes down to Sheol will come up no more.
He will return no more to his house,
    neither will his place know him any more.

"Therefore I will not keep silent.
    I will speak in the anguish of my spirit.
    I will complain in the bitterness of my soul.
Am I a sea, or a sea monster,
    that you put a guard over me?
When I say, 'My bed will comfort me.

My couch will ease my complaint;'
then you scare me with dreams,
*   and terrify me through visions:*
so that my soul chooses strangling,
*   death rather than my bones.*
I loathe my life.
*   I don't want to live forever.*
*   Leave me alone, for my days are but a breath.*
What is man, that you should magnify him,
*   that you should set your mind on him,*
that you should visit him every morning,
*   and test him every moment?*
How long will you not look away from me,
*   nor leave me alone until I swallow down my spittle?*
If I have sinned, what do I do to you, you watcher of men?
*   Why have you set me as a mark for you,*
*   so that I am a burden to myself?*
Why do you not pardon my disobedience, and take away my
iniquity?
*   For now will I lie down in the dust.*
*   You will seek me diligently, but I will not be."*

....

Then Bildad the Shuhite answered,
"How long will you speak these things?
*   Shall the words of your mouth be a mighty wind?*
Does God pervert justice?
*   Or does the Almighty pervert righteousness?*
If your children have sinned against him,
*   he has delivered them into the hand of their disobedience.*
If you want to seek God diligently,
*   make your supplication to the Almighty.*
If you were pure and upright,
*   surely now he would awaken for you,*
and make the habitation of your righteousness prosperous.
*   Though your beginning was small,*
yet your latter end would greatly increase.

"Please inquire of past generations.
*   Find out about the learning of their fathers.*

(For we are but of yesterday, and know nothing,
*   because our days on earth are a shadow.)*
Shall they not teach you, tell you,
*   and utter words out of their heart?*

"Can the papyrus grow up without mire?
*   Can the rushes grow without water?*
While it is yet in its greenness, not cut down,
*   it withers before any other reed.*
So are the paths of all who forget God.
*   The hope of the godless man will perish,*
Whose confidence will break apart,
*   Whose trust is a spider's web.*
He will lean on his house, but it will not stand.
*   He will cling to it, but it will not endure.*
He is green before the sun.
*   His shoots go out along his garden.*
His roots are wrapped around the rock pile.
*   He sees the place of stones.*
If he is destroyed from his place,
*   then it will deny him, saying, 'I have not seen you.'*
Behold, this is the joy of his way:
*   out of the earth, others will spring.*

"Behold, God will not cast away a blameless man,
*   neither will he uphold the evildoers.*
He will still fill your mouth with laughter,
*   your lips with shouting.*
Those who hate you will be clothed with shame.
*   The tent of the wicked will be no more."*

....

Then Job answered,
*   "Truly I know that it is so,*
*   but how can man be just with God?*
*   If he is pleased to contend with him,*
*   he can't answer him one time in a thousand.*
*   God who is wise in heart, and mighty in strength:*
*   who has hardened himself against him and prospered?*
*   He removes the mountains, and they don't know it,*

when he overturns them in his anger.
He shakes the earth out of its place.
   Its pillars tremble.
He commands the sun and it doesn't rise,
   and seals up the stars.
He alone stretches out the heavens,
   and treads on the waves of the sea.
He makes the Bear, Orion, and the Pleiades,
   and the rooms of the south.
He does great things past finding out;
   yes, marvelous things without number.
Behold, he goes by me, and I don't see him.
   He passes on also, but I don't perceive him.
Behold, he snatches away.
   Who can hinder him?
   Who will ask him, 'What are you doing?'

"God will not withdraw his anger.
   The helpers of Rahab stoop under him.
How much less will I answer him,
   And choose my words to argue with him?
Though I were righteous, yet I wouldn't answer him.
   I would make supplication to my judge.
If I had called, and he had answered me,
   yet I wouldn't believe that he listened to my voice.
For he breaks me with a storm,
   and multiplies my wounds without cause.
He will not allow me to catch my breath,
   but fills me with bitterness.
If it is a matter of strength, behold, he is mighty!
   If of justice, 'Who,' says he, 'will summon me?'
Though I am righteous, my own mouth will condemn me.
   Though I am blameless, it will prove me perverse.
I am blameless.
   I don't respect myself.
   I despise my life.

"It is all the same.
   Therefore I say he destroys the blameless and the wicked.
If the scourge kills suddenly,

he will mock at the trial of the innocent.
The earth is given into the hand of the wicked.
*   He covers the faces of its judges.*
*   If not he, then who is it?*

"Now my days are swifter than a runner.
*   They flee away. They see no good.*
They have passed away as the swift ships,
*   as the eagle that swoops on the prey.*
If I say, 'I will forget my complaint,
*   I will put off my sad face, and cheer up;'*
I am afraid of all my sorrows,
*   I know that you will not hold me innocent.*
I will be condemned.
*   Why then do I labor in vain?*
If I wash myself with snow,
*   and cleanse my hands with lye,*
yet you will plunge me in the ditch.
*   My own clothes will abhor me.*
For he is not a man, as I am, that I should answer him,
*   that we should come together in judgment.*
There is no umpire between us,
*   that might lay his hand on us both.*
Let him take his rod away from me.
*   Let his terror not make me afraid;*
then I would speak, and not fear him,
*   for I am not so in myself.*

....

"My soul is weary of my life.
*   I will give free course to my complaint.*
*   I will speak in the bitterness of my soul.*
I will tell God, 'Do not condemn me.
*   Show me why you contend with me.*
Is it good to you that you should oppress,
*   that you should despise the work of your hands,*
*   and smile on the counsel of the wicked?*
Do you have eyes of flesh?

Or do you see as man sees?
Are your days as the days of mortals,
    or your years as man's years,
that you inquire after my iniquity,
    and search after my sin?
Although you know that I am not wicked,
    there is no one who can deliver out of your hand.

"'Your hands have framed me and fashioned me altogether,
    yet you destroy me.
Remember, I beg you, that you have fashioned me as clay.
    Will you bring me into dust again?
Haven't you poured me out like milk,
    and curdled me like cheese?
You have clothed me with skin and flesh,
    and knit me together with bones and sinews.
You have granted me life and loving kindness.
    Your visitation has preserved my spirit.
Yet you hid these things in your heart.
    I know that this is with you:
if I sin, then you mark me.
    You will not acquit me from my iniquity.
If I am wicked, woe to me.
    If I am righteous, I still will not lift up my head,
    being filled with disgrace,
    and conscious of my affliction.
If my head is held high, you hunt me like a lion.
    Again you show yourself powerful to me.
You renew your witnesses against me,
    and increase your indignation on me.
    Changes and warfare are with me.

"'Why, then, have you brought me out of the womb?
    I wish I had given up the spirit, and no eye had seen me.
I should have been as though I had not been.
    I should have been carried from the womb to the grave.
Aren't my days few?
    Stop!
Leave me alone, that I may find a little comfort,
    before I go where I will not return from,

to the land of darkness and of the shadow of death;
the land dark as midnight,
of the shadow of death,
without any order,
where the light is as midnight.'"

....

Then Zophar, the Naamathite, answered,
"Shouldn't the multitude of words be answered?
Should a man full of talk be justified?
Should your boastings make men hold their peace?
When you mock, will no man make you ashamed?
For you say, 'My doctrine is pure.
I am clean in your eyes.'
But oh that God would speak,
and open his lips against you,
that he would show you the secrets of wisdom!
For true wisdom has two sides.
Know therefore that God exacts of you less than your iniquity
deserves.

"Can you fathom the mystery of God?
Or can you probe the limits of the Almighty?
They are high as heaven. What can you do?
They are deeper than Sheol. What can you know?
Its measure is longer than the earth,
and broader than the sea.
If he passes by, or confines,
or convenes a court, then who can oppose him?
For he knows false men.
He sees iniquity also, even though he doesn't consider it.
An empty-headed man becomes wise
when a man is born as a wild donkey's colt.

"If you set your heart aright,
stretch out your hands toward him.
If iniquity is in your hand, put it far away.
Don't let unrighteousness dwell in your tents.
Surely then you will lift up your face without spot;
Yes, you will be steadfast, and will not fear:

for you will forget your misery.
*   You will remember it like waters that have passed away.*
Life will be clearer than the noonday.
*   Though there is darkness, it will be as the morning.*
You will be secure, because there is hope.
*   Yes, you will search, and will take your rest in safety.*
Also you will lie down, and no one will make you afraid.
*   Yes, many will court your favor.*
But the eyes of the wicked will fail.
*   They will have no way to flee.*
*   Their hope will be the giving up of the spirit."*

....

Then Job answered,
"No doubt, but you are the people,
*   and wisdom will die with you.*
But I have understanding as well as you;
*   I am not inferior to you.*
*   Yes, who doesn't know such things as these?*
I am like one who is a joke to his neighbor,
*   I, who called on God, and he answered.*
*   The just, the blameless man is a joke.*
In the thought of him who is at ease there is contempt for misfor-
tune.
*   It is ready for them whose foot slips.*
The tents of robbers prosper.
*   Those who provoke God are secure,*
*   who carry their god in their hands.*

"But ask the animals, now, and they will teach you;
*   the birds of the sky, and they will tell you.*
Or speak to the earth, and it will teach you.
*   The fish of the sea will declare to you.*
Who doesn't know that in all these,
*   YHWH's hand has done this,*
in whose hand is the life of every living thing,
*   and the breath of all mankind?*
Doesn't the ear try words,
*   even as the palate tastes its food?*
With aged men is wisdom,

in length of days understanding.

"With God is wisdom and might.
    He has counsel and understanding.
Behold, he breaks down, and it can't be built again.
    He imprisons a man, and there can be no release.
Behold, he withholds the waters, and they dry up.
    Again, he sends them out, and they overturn the earth.
With him is strength and wisdom.
    The deceived and the deceiver are his.
He leads counselors away stripped.
    He makes judges fools.
He loosens the bond of kings.
    He binds their waist with a belt.
He leads priests away stripped,
    and overthrows the mighty.
He removes the speech of those who are trusted,
    and takes away the understanding of the elders.
He pours contempt on princes,
    and loosens the belt of the strong.
He uncovers deep things out of darkness,
    and brings out to light the shadow of death.
He increases the nations, and he destroys them.
    He enlarges the nations, and he leads them captive.
He takes away understanding from the chiefs of the people of the earth,
    and causes them to wander in a wilderness where there is no way.
They grope in the dark without light.
    He makes them stagger like a drunken man.

....

"Behold, my eye has seen all this.
    My ear has heard and understood it.
What you know, I know also.
    I am not inferior to you.

"Surely I would speak to the Almighty.

I desire to reason with God.
But you are forgers of lies.
You are all physicians of no value.
Oh that you would be completely silent!
Then you would be wise.
Hear now my reasoning.
Listen to the pleadings of my lips.
Will you speak unrighteously for God,
and talk deceitfully for him?
Will you show partiality to him?
Will you contend for God?
Is it good that he should search you out?
Or as one deceives a man, will you deceive him?
He will surely reprove you
if you secretly show partiality.
Shall not his majesty make you afraid,
and his dread fall on you?
Your memorable sayings are proverbs of ashes.
Your defenses are defenses of clay.

"Be silent!
Leave me alone, that I may speak.
Let come on me what will.
Why should I take my flesh in my teeth,
and put my life in my hand?
Behold, he will kill me.
I have no hope.
Nevertheless, I will maintain my ways before him.
This also will be my salvation,
that a godless man will not come before him.
Listen carefully to my speech.
Let my declaration be in your ears.
See now, I have set my cause in order.
I know that I am righteous.
Who is he who will contend with me?
For then would I hold my peace and give up the spirit.

"Only don't do two things to me,
then I will not hide myself from your face:
withdraw your hand far from me,

and don't let your terror make me afraid.
Then call, and I will answer,
    or let me speak, and you answer me.
How many are my iniquities and sins?
    Make me know my disobedience and my sin.
Why do you hide your face,
    and consider me your enemy?
Will you harass a driven leaf?
    Will you pursue the dry stubble?
For you write bitter things against me,
    and make me inherit the iniquities of my youth:
You also put my feet in the stocks,
    and mark all my paths.
    You set a bound to the soles of my feet,
though I am decaying like a rotten thing,
    like a garment that is moth-eaten.

....

"Man, who is born of a woman,
    is of few days, and full of trouble.
He grows up like a flower, and is cut down.
    He also flees like a shadow, and doesn't continue.
Do you open your eyes on such a one,
    and bring me into judgment with you?
Who can bring a clean thing out of an unclean?
    Not one.
    Seeing his days are determined,
    the number of his months is with you,
    and you have appointed his bounds that he can't pass;
Look away from him, that he may rest,
    until he accomplishes, as a hireling, his day.

"For there is hope for a tree if it is cut down,
    that it will sprout again,
    that the tender branch of it will not cease.
Though its root grows old in the earth,
    and its stock dies in the ground,
yet through the scent of water it will bud,

and sprout boughs like a plant.
But man dies, and is laid low.
   Yes, man gives up the spirit, and where is he?
As the waters fail from the sea,
   and the river wastes and dries up,
so man lies down and doesn't rise.
   Until the heavens are no more, they will not awake,
   nor be roused out of their sleep.

"Oh that you would hide me in Sheol,
   that you would keep me secret until your wrath is past,
   that you would appoint me a set time and remember me!
If a man dies, will he live again?
   I would wait all the days of my warfare,
   until my release should come.
You would call, and I would answer you.
   You would have a desire for the work of your hands.
But now you count my steps.
   Don't you watch over my sin?
My disobedience is sealed up in a bag.
   You fasten up my iniquity.

"But the mountain falling comes to nothing.
   The rock is removed out of its place;
The waters wear the stones.
   The torrents of it wash away the dust of the earth.
   So you destroy the hope of man.
You forever prevail against him, and he departs.
   You change his face, and send him away.
His sons come to honor, and he doesn't know it.
   They are brought low, but he doesn't perceive it of them.
But his flesh on him has pain,
   and his soul within him mourns."

....

Then Eliphaz the Temanite answered,
   "Should a wise man answer with vain knowledge,
      and fill himself with the east wind?
   Should he reason with unprofitable talk,

or with speeches with which he can do no good?
Yes, you do away with fear,
    and hinder devotion before God.
For your iniquity teaches your mouth,
    and you choose the language of the crafty.
Your own mouth condemns you, and not I.
    Yes, your own lips testify against you.

"Are you the first man who was born?
    Or were you brought out before the hills?
Have you heard the secret counsel of God?
    Do you limit wisdom to yourself?
What do you know that we don't know?
    What do you understand which is not in us?
With us are both the gray-headed and the very aged men,
    much elder than your father.
Are the consolations of God too small for you,
    even the word that is gentle toward you?
Why does your heart carry you away?
    Why do your eyes flash,
That you turn your spirit against God,
    and let such words go out of your mouth?
What is man, that he should be clean?
    What is he who is born of a woman, that he should be righ-
        teous?
Behold, he puts no trust in his holy ones.
    Yes, the heavens are not clean in his sight;
how much less one who is abominable and corrupt,
    a man who drinks iniquity like water!

"I will show you, listen to me;
    that which I have seen I will declare
(which wise men have told by their fathers,
    and have not hidden it;
to whom alone the land was given,
    and no stranger passed among them):
the wicked man writhes in pain all his days,
    even the number of years that are laid up for the oppressor.
A sound of terrors is in his ears.
    In prosperity the destroyer will come on him.

He doesn't believe that he will return out of darkness.
He is waited for by the sword.
He wanders abroad for bread, saying, 'Where is it?'
He knows that the day of darkness is ready at his hand.
Distress and anguish make him afraid.
They prevail against him, as a king ready to the battle.
Because he has stretched out his hand against God,
and behaves himself proudly against the Almighty,
he runs at him with a stiff neck,
with the thick shields of his bucklers,
because he has covered his face with his fatness,
and gathered fat on his thighs.
He has lived in desolate cities,
in houses which no one inhabited,
which were ready to become heaps.
He will not be rich, neither will his substance continue,
neither will their possessions be extended on the earth.
He will not depart out of darkness.
The flame will dry up his branches.
He will go away by the breath of God's mouth.
Let him not trust in emptiness, deceiving himself;
for emptiness will be his reward.
It will be accomplished before his time.
His branch will not be green.
He will shake off his unripe grape as the vine,
and will cast off his flower as the olive tree.
For the company of the godless will be barren,
and fire will consume the tents of bribery.
They conceive mischief, and produce iniquity.
Their heart prepares deceit."

Then Job answered,
"I have heard many such things.
You are all miserable comforters!
Shall vain words have an end?
Or what provokes you that you answer?
I also could speak as you do.
If your soul were in my soul's place,

I could join words together against you,
and shake my head at you,
but I would strengthen you with my mouth.
The solace of my lips would relieve you.

"Though I speak, my grief is not subsided.
Though I forbear, what am I eased?
But now, God, you have surely worn me out.
You have made all my company desolate.
You have shriveled me up. This is a witness against me.
My leanness rises up against me.
It testifies to my face.
He has torn me in his wrath and persecuted me.
He has gnashed on me with his teeth.
My adversary sharpens his eyes on me.
They have gaped on me with their mouth.
They have struck me on the cheek reproachfully.
They gather themselves together against me.
God delivers me to the ungodly,
and casts me into the hands of the wicked.
I was at ease, and he broke me apart.
Yes, he has taken me by the neck, and dashed me to pieces.
He has also set me up for his target.
His archers surround me.
He splits my kidneys apart, and does not spare.
He pours out my bile on the ground.
He breaks me with breach on breach.
He runs at me like a giant.
I have sewed sackcloth on my skin,
and have thrust my horn in the dust.
My face is red with weeping.
Deep darkness is on my eyelids.
Although there is no violence in my hands,
and my prayer is pure.

"Earth, don't cover my blood.
Let my cry have no place to rest.
Even now, behold, my witness is in heaven.
He who vouches for me is on high.
My friends scoff at me.

My eyes pour out tears to God,
that he would maintain the right of a man with God,
of a son of man with his neighbor!
For when a few years have come,
I will go the way of no return.

....

"My spirit is consumed.
My days are extinct,
and the grave is ready for me.
Surely there are mockers with me.
My eye dwells on their provocation.

"Now give a pledge. Be collateral for me with yourself.
Who is there who will strike hands with me?
For you have hidden their heart from understanding,
Therefore you will not exalt them.
He who denounces his friends for plunder,
Even the eyes of his children will fail.

"But he has made me a byword of the people.
They spit in my face.
My eye also is dim by reason of sorrow.
All my members are as a shadow.
Upright men will be astonished at this.
The innocent will stir himself up against the godless.
Yet the righteous will hold to his way.
He who has clean hands will grow stronger and stronger.
But as for you all, come back.
I will not find a wise man among you.
My days are past.
My plans are broken off,
as are the thoughts of my heart.
They change the night into day,
saying 'The light is near' in the presence of darkness.
If I look for Sheol as my house,
if I have spread my couch in the darkness,
if I have said to corruption, 'You are my father;'
to the worm, 'My mother,' and 'My sister,'

where then is my hope?
 as for my hope, who will see it?
Shall it go down with me to the gates of Sheol,
 or descend together into the dust?"

··

Then Bildad the Shuhite answered,
 "How long will you hunt for words?
  Consider, and afterwards we will speak.
Why are we counted as animals,
 which have become unclean in your sight?
You who tear yourself in your anger,
 will the earth be forsaken for you?
  Or will the rock be removed out of its place?

"Yes, the light of the wicked will be put out.
 The spark of his fire won't shine.
The light will be dark in his tent.
 His lamp above him will be put out.
The steps of his strength will be shortened.
 His own counsel will cast him down.
For he is cast into a net by his own feet,
 and he wanders into its mesh.
A snare will take him by the heel.
 A trap will catch him.
A noose is hidden for him in the ground,
 a trap for him on the path.
Terrors will make him afraid on every side,
 and will chase him at his heels.
His strength will be famished.
 Calamity will be ready at his side.
The members of his body will be devoured.
 The firstborn of death will devour his members.
He will be rooted out of the security of his tent.
 He will be brought to the king of terrors.
There will dwell in his tent that which is none of his.
 Sulfur will be scattered on his habitation.
His roots will be dried up beneath.
 His branch will be cut off above.

His memory will perish from the earth.
He will have no name in the street.
He will be driven from light into darkness,
and chased out of the world.
He will have neither son nor grandson among his people,
nor any remaining where he lived.
Those who come after will be astonished at his day,
as those who went before were frightened.
Surely such are the dwellings of the unrighteous.
This is the place of him who doesn't know God."

....

Then Job answered,
"How long will you torment me,
and crush me with words?
You have reproached me ten times.
You aren't ashamed that you attack me.
If it is true that I have erred,
my error remains with myself.
If indeed you will magnify yourselves against me,
and plead against me my reproach,
know now that God has subverted me,
and has surrounded me with his net.

"Behold, I cry out of wrong, but I am not heard.
I cry for help, but there is no justice.
He has walled up my way so that I can't pass,
and has set darkness in my paths.
He has stripped me of my glory,
and taken the crown from my head.
He has broken me down on every side, and I am gone.
He has plucked my hope up like a tree.
He has also kindled his wrath against me.
He counts me among his adversaries.
His troops come on together,
build a siege ramp against me,
and encamp around my tent.

"He has put my brothers far from me.
My acquaintances are wholly estranged from me.

My relatives have gone away.
My familiar friends have forgotten me.
Those who dwell in my house and my maids consider me a stranger.
I am an alien in their sight.
I call to my servant, and he gives me no answer.
I beg him with my mouth.
My breath is offensive to my wife.
I am loathsome to the children of my own mother.
Even young children despise me.
If I arise, they speak against me.
All my familiar friends abhor me.
They whom I loved have turned against me.
My bones stick to my skin and to my flesh.
I have escaped by the skin of my teeth.

"Have pity on me. Have pity on me, you my friends;
for the hand of God has touched me.
Why do you persecute me as God,
and are not satisfied with my flesh?

"Oh that my words were now written!
Oh that they were inscribed in a book!
That with an iron pen and lead
they were engraved in the rock forever!
But as for me, I know that my Redeemer lives.
In the end, he will stand upon the earth.
After my skin is destroyed,
then I will see God in my flesh,
whom I, even I, will see on my side.
My eyes will see, and not as a stranger.

"My heart is consumed within me.
If you say, 'How we will persecute him!'
because the root of the matter is found in me,
be afraid of the sword,
for wrath brings the punishments of the sword,
that you may know there is a judgment."

Then Zophar the Naamathite answered,
"Therefore my thoughts answer me,
    even by reason of my haste that is in me.
I have heard the reproof which puts me to shame.
    The spirit of my understanding answers me.
Don't you know this from old time,
    since man was placed on earth,
that the triumphing of the wicked is short,
    the joy of the godless but for a moment?
Though his height mount up to the heavens,
    and his head reach to the clouds,
yet he will perish forever like his own dung.
    Those who have seen him will say, 'Where is he?'
He will fly away as a dream, and will not be found.
    Yes, he will be chased away like a vision of the night.
The eye which saw him will see him no more,
    neither will his place see him any more.
His children will seek the favor of the poor.
    His hands will give back his wealth.
His bones are full of his youth,
    but youth will lie down with him in the dust.

"Though wickedness is sweet in his mouth,
    though he hide it under his tongue,
though he spare it, and will not let it go,
    but keep it still within his mouth;
yet his food in his bowels is turned.
    It is cobra venom within him.
He has swallowed down riches, and he will vomit them up again.
    God will cast them out of his belly.
He will suck cobra venom.
    The viper's tongue will kill him.
He will not look at the rivers,
    the flowing streams of honey and butter.
He will restore that for which he labored, and will not swallow it down.
    He will not rejoice according to the substance that he has gotten.
For he has oppressed and forsaken the poor.
    He has violently taken away a house, and he will not build it

up.

"*Because he knew no quietness within him,*
    he will not save anything of that in which he delights.
There was nothing left that he didn't devour,
    therefore his prosperity will not endure.
In the fullness of his sufficiency, distress will overtake him.
        The hand of everyone who is in misery will come on him.
When he is about to fill his belly, God will cast the fierceness of his
wrath on him.
        It will rain on him while he is eating.
He will flee from the iron weapon.
        The bronze arrow will strike him through.
He draws it out, and it comes out of his body.
        Yes, the glittering point comes out of his liver.
        Terrors are on him.
All darkness is laid up for his treasures.
        An unfanned fire will devour him.
        It will consume that which is left in his tent.
The heavens will reveal his iniquity.
        The earth will rise up against him.
The increase of his house will depart.
        They will rush away in the day of his wrath.
This is the portion of a wicked man from God,
    the heritage appointed to him by God."

....

Then Job answered,
    "*Listen diligently to my speech.*
        Let this be your consolation.
    Allow me, and I also will speak;
        After I have spoken, mock on.
    As for me, is my complaint to man?
        Why shouldn't I be impatient?
    Look at me, and be astonished.
        Lay your hand on your mouth.
    When I remember, I am troubled.
        Horror takes hold of my flesh.

    "*Why do the wicked live,*

become old, yes, and grow mighty in power?
Their child is established with them in their sight,
    their offspring before their eyes.
Their houses are safe from fear,
    neither is the rod of God upon them.
Their bulls breed without fail.
    Their cows calve, and don't miscarry.
They send out their little ones like a flock.
    Their children dance.
They sing to the tambourine and harp,
    and rejoice at the sound of the pipe.
They spend their days in prosperity.
    In an instant they go down to Sheol.
They tell God, 'Depart from us,
    for we don't want to know about your ways.
What is the Almighty, that we should serve him?
    What profit should we have, if we pray to him?'
Behold, their prosperity is not in their hand.
    The counsel of the wicked is far from me.

"How often is it that the lamp of the wicked is put out,
    that their calamity comes on them,
    that God distributes sorrows in his anger?
How often is it that they are as stubble before the wind,
    as chaff that the storm carries away?
You say, 'God lays up his iniquity for his children.'
    Let him recompense it to himself, that he may know it.
Let his own eyes see his destruction.
    Let him drink of the wrath of the Almighty.
For what does he care for his house after him,
    when the number of his months is cut off?

"Shall any teach God knowledge,
    since he judges those who are high?
One dies in his full strength,
    being wholly at ease and quiet.
His pails are full of milk.
    The marrow of his bones is moistened.
Another dies in bitterness of soul,
    and never tastes of good.

They lie down alike in the dust.
    The worm covers them.

"Behold, I know your thoughts,
    the plans with which you would wrong me.
For you say, 'Where is the house of the prince?
    Where is the tent in which the wicked lived?'
Haven't you asked wayfaring men?
    Don't you know their evidences,
that the evil man is reserved to the day of calamity,
    That they are led out to the day of wrath?
Who will declare his way to his face?
    Who will repay him what he has done?
Yet he will be borne to the grave.
    Men will keep watch over the tomb.
The clods of the valley will be sweet to him.
    All men will draw after him,
    as there were innumerable before him.
So how can you comfort me with nonsense,
    because in your answers there remains only falsehood?"

....

Then Eliphaz the Temanite answered,
    "Can a man be profitable to God?
        Surely he who is wise is profitable to himself.
Is it any pleasure to the Almighty that you are righteous?
        Or does it benefit him that you make your ways perfect?
Is it for your piety that he reproves you,
        that he enters with you into judgment?
Isn't your wickedness great?
        Neither is there any end to your iniquities.
For you have taken pledges from your brother for nothing,
        and stripped the naked of their clothing.
You haven't given water to the weary to drink,
        and you have withheld bread from the hungry.
But as for the mighty man, he had the earth.
        The honorable man, he lived in it.
You have sent widows away empty,
        and the arms of the fatherless have been broken.
Therefore snares are around you.

Sudden fear troubles you,
or darkness, so that you can not see,
    and floods of waters cover you.

"Isn't God in the heights of heaven?
    See the height of the stars, how high they are!
You say, 'What does God know?
    Can he judge through the thick darkness?
Thick clouds are a covering to him, so that he doesn't see.
    He walks on the vault of the sky.'
Will you keep the old way,
    which wicked men have trodden,
who were snatched away before their time,
    whose foundation was poured out as a stream,
who said to God, 'Depart from us;'
    and, 'What can the Almighty do for us?'
Yet he filled their houses with good things,
    but the counsel of the wicked is far from me.
The righteous see it, and are glad.
    The innocent ridicule them,
saying, 'Surely those who rose up against us are cut off.
    The fire has consumed their remnant.'

"Acquaint yourself with him, now, and be at peace.
    By it, good will come to you.
Please receive instruction from his mouth,
    and lay up his words in your heart.
If you return to the Almighty, you will be built up,
    if you put away unrighteousness far from your tents.
Lay your treasure in the dust,
    the gold of Ophir among the stones of the brooks.
The Almighty will be your treasure,
    and precious silver to you.
For then you will delight yourself in the Almighty,
    and will lift up your face to God.
You will make your prayer to him, and he will hear you.
    You will pay your vows.
You will also decree a thing, and it will be established to you.
    Light will shine on your ways.
When they cast down, you will say, 'be lifted up.'

He will save the humble person.
He will even deliver him who is not innocent.
Yes, he will be delivered through the cleanness of your hands."

....

Then Job answered,
"Even today my complaint is rebellious.
His hand is heavy in spite of my groaning.
Oh that I knew where I might find him!
That I might come even to his seat!
I would set my cause in order before him,
and fill my mouth with arguments.
I would know the words which he would answer me,
and understand what he would tell me.
Would he contend with me in the greatness of his power?
No, but he would listen to me.
There the upright might reason with him,
so I should be delivered forever from my judge.

"If I go east, he is not there;
if west, I can't find him;
He works to the north, but I can't see him.
He turns south, but I can't catch a glimpse of him.

But he knows the way that I take.
When he has tried me, I will come out like gold.
My foot has held fast to his steps.
I have kept his way, and not turned away.
I haven't gone back from the commandment of his lips.
I have treasured up the words of his mouth more than my
necessary food.
But he stands alone, and who can oppose him?
What his soul desires, even that he does.
For he performs that which is appointed for me.
Many such things are with him.
Therefore I am terrified at his presence.
When I consider, I am afraid of him.
For God has made my heart faint.
The Almighty has terrified me.
Because I was not cut off before the darkness,

neither did he cover the thick darkness from my face.

....

"Why aren't times laid up by the Almighty?
  Why don't those who know him see his days?
There are people who remove the landmarks.
  They violently take away flocks, and feed them.
They drive away the donkey of the fatherless,
  and they take the widow's ox for a pledge.
They turn the needy out of the way.
  The poor of the earth all hide themselves.
Behold, as wild donkeys in the desert,
  they go out to their work, seeking diligently for food.
The wilderness yields them bread for their children.
  They cut their food in the field.
They glean the vineyard of the wicked.
  They lie all night naked without clothing,
and have no covering in the cold.
  They are wet with the showers of the mountains,
and embrace the rock for lack of a shelter.
  There are those who pluck the fatherless from the breast,
and take a pledge of the poor,
  So that they go around naked without clothing.
  Being hungry, they carry the sheaves.
They make oil within the walls of these men.
  They tread wine presses, and suffer thirst.
From out of the populous city, men groan.
  The soul of the wounded cries out,
  yet God doesn't regard the folly.

"These are of those who rebel against the light.
  They don't know its ways,
  nor stay in its paths.
The murderer rises with the light.
  He kills the poor and needy.
  In the night he is like a thief.
The eye also of the adulterer waits for the twilight,
  saying, 'No eye will see me.'

He disguises his face.
In the dark they dig through houses.
They shut themselves up in the daytime.
They don't know the light.
For the morning is to all of them like thick darkness,
for they know the terrors of the thick darkness.

"They are foam on the surface of the waters.
Their portion is cursed in the earth.
They don't turn into the way of the vineyards.
Drought and heat consume the snow waters,
so does Sheol those who have sinned.
The womb will forget him.
The worm will feed sweetly on him.
He will be no more remembered.
Unrighteousness will be broken as a tree.
He devours the barren who don't bear.
He shows no kindness to the widow.
Yet God preserves the mighty by his power.
He rises up who has no assurance of life.
God gives them security, and they rest in it.
His eyes are on their ways.
They are exalted; yet a little while, and they are gone.
Yes, they are brought low, they are taken out of the way as all
others,
and are cut off as the tops of the ears of grain.
If it isn't so now, who will prove me a liar,
and make my speech worth nothing?"

....

Then Bildad the Shuhite answered,
"Dominion and fear are with him.
He makes peace in his high places.
Can his armies be counted?
On whom does his light not arise?
How then can man be just with God?
Or how can he who is born of a woman be clean?
Behold, even the moon has no brightness,
and the stars are not pure in his sight;

How much less man, who is a worm,
the son of man, who is a worm!"

....

Then Job answered,
"How have you helped him who is without power!
How have you saved the arm that has no strength!
How have you counseled him who has no wisdom,
and plentifully declared sound knowledge!
To whom have you uttered words?
Whose spirit came out of you?

"The departed spirits tremble,
those beneath the waters and all that live in them.
Sheol is naked before God,
and Abaddon has no covering.
He stretches out the north over empty space,
and hangs the earth on nothing.
He binds up the waters in his thick clouds,
and the cloud is not burst under them.
He encloses the face of his throne,
and spreads his cloud on it.
He has described a boundary on the surface of the waters,
and to the confines of light and darkness.
The pillars of heaven tremble
and are astonished at his rebuke.
He stirs up the sea with his power,
and by his understanding he strikes through Rahab.
By his Spirit the heavens are garnished.
His hand has pierced the swift serpent.
Behold, these are but the outskirts of his ways.
How small a whisper do we hear of him!
But the thunder of his power who can understand?"

....

Job again took up his parable, and said,
"As God lives, who has taken away my right,
the Almighty, who has made my soul bitter
(for the length of my life is still in me,
and the spirit of God is in my nostrils);

surely my lips will not speak unrighteousness,
    neither will my tongue utter deceit.
Far be it from me that I should justify you.
    Until I die I will not put away my integrity from me.
I hold fast to my righteousness, and will not let it go.
    My heart will not reproach me so long as I live.

"Let my enemy be as the wicked.
    Let him who rises up against me be as the unrighteous.

For what is the hope of the godless, when he is cut off, when God
takes away his life?
    Will God hear his cry when trouble comes on him?
Will he delight himself in the Almighty,
    and call on God at all times?
I will teach you about the hand of God.
    I will not conceal that which is with the Almighty.
Behold, all of you have seen it yourselves;
    why then have you become altogether vain?

"This is the portion of a wicked man with God,
    the heritage of oppressors, which they receive from the Al-
    mighty.
If his children are multiplied, it is for the sword.
    His offspring will not be satisfied with bread.
Those who remain of him will be buried in death.
    His widows will make no lamentation.
Though he heap up silver as the dust,
    and prepare clothing as the clay;
he may prepare it, but the just will put it on,
    and the innocent will divide the silver.
He builds his house as the moth,
    as a booth which the watchman makes.
He lies down rich, but he will not do so again.
    He opens his eyes, and he is not.
Terrors overtake him like waters.
    A storm steals him away in the night.
The east wind carries him away, and he departs.
    It sweeps him out of his place.
For it hurls at him, and does not spare,

as he flees away from his hand.
Men will clap their hands at him,
    and will hiss him out of his place.

....

"Surely there is a mine for silver,
    and a place for gold which they refine.
Iron is taken out of the earth,
    and copper is smelted out of the ore.
Man sets an end to darkness,
    and searches out, to the furthest bound,
    the stones of obscurity and of thick darkness.
He breaks open a shaft away from where people live.
    They are forgotten by the foot.
    They hang far from men, they swing back and forth.
As for the earth, out of it comes bread;
    Underneath it is turned up as it were by fire.
Sapphires come from its rocks.
    It has dust of gold.
That path no bird of prey knows,
    neither has the falcon's eye seen it.
The proud animals have not trodden it,
    nor has the fierce lion passed by there.
He puts his hand on the flinty rock,
    and he overturns the mountains by the roots.
He cuts out channels among the rocks.
    His eye sees every precious thing.
He binds the streams that they don't trickle.
    The thing that is hidden he brings out to light.

"But where will wisdom be found?
    Where is the place of understanding?
Man doesn't know its price;
    Neither is it found in the land of the living.
The deep says, 'It isn't in me.'
    The sea says, 'It isn't with me.'
It can't be gotten for gold,
    neither will silver be weighed for its price.

It can't be valued with the gold of Ophir,
*   with the precious onyx, or the sapphire.*
Gold and glass can't equal it,
*   neither will it be exchanged for jewels of fine gold.*
No mention will be made of coral or of crystal.
*   Yes, the price of wisdom is above rubies.*
The topaz of Ethiopia will not equal it,
*   nor will it be valued with pure gold.*
Where then does wisdom come from?
*   Where is the place of understanding?*
Seeing it is hidden from the eyes of all living,
*   and kept close from the birds of the sky.*
Destruction and Death say,
*   'We have heard a rumor of it with our ears.'*

"God understands its way,
*   and he knows its place.*
For he looks to the ends of the earth,
*   and sees under the whole sky.*
He establishes the force of the wind.
*   Yes, he measures out the waters by measure.*
When he made a decree for the rain,
*   and a way for the lightning of the thunder,*
then he saw it, and declared it.
*   He established it, yes, and searched it out.*
To man he said,
*   'Behold, the fear of the Lord, that is wisdom.*
*   To depart from evil is understanding.'"*

....

Job again took up his parable, and said,
*   "Oh that I were as in the months of old,*
*   as in the days when God watched over me;*
*   when his lamp shone on my head,*
*   and by his light I walked through darkness,*
*   as I was in my prime,*
*   when the friendship of God was in my tent,*
*   when the Almighty was yet with me,*
*   and my children were around me,*

when my steps were washed with butter,
     and the rock poured out streams of oil for me,
when I went out to the city gate,
     when I prepared my seat in the street.
The young men saw me and hid themselves.
     The aged rose up and stood.
The princes refrained from talking,
     and laid their hand on their mouth.
The voice of the nobles was hushed,
     and their tongue stuck to the roof of their mouth.
For when the ear heard me, then it blessed me;
     and when the eye saw me, it commended me:
Because I delivered the poor who cried,
     and the fatherless also, who had no one to help him,
the blessing of him who was ready to perish came on me,
     and I caused the widow's heart to sing for joy.
I put on righteousness, and it clothed me.
     My justice was as a robe and a diadem.
I was eyes to the blind,
     and feet to the lame.
I was a father to the needy.
     I researched the cause of him who I didn't know.
I broke the jaws of the unrighteous
     and plucked the prey out of his teeth.
Then I said, 'I will die in my own house,
     I will count my days as the sand.
My root is spread out to the waters.
     The dew lies all night on my branch.
My glory is fresh in me.
     My bow is renewed in my hand.'

"Men listened to me, waited,
     and kept silence for my counsel.
After my words they didn't speak again.
     My speech fell on them.
They waited for me as for the rain.
     Their mouths drank as with the spring rain.
I smiled on them when they had no confidence.
     They didn't reject the light of my face.
I chose out their way, and sat as chief.

I lived as a king in the army,
as one who comforts the mourners.

....

"But now those who are younger than I have me in derision,
whose fathers I considered unworthy to put with my sheep
dogs.
Of what use is the strength of their hands to me,
men in whom ripe age has perished?
They are gaunt from lack and famine.
They gnaw the dry ground, in the gloom of waste and desola-
tion.
They pluck salt herbs by the bushes.
The roots of the broom tree are their food.
They are driven out from among men.
They cry after them as after a thief;
So that they dwell in frightful valleys,
and in holes of the earth and of the rocks.
They bray among the bushes.
They are gathered together under the nettles .
They are children of fools, yes, children of wicked men.
They were flogged out of the land.

"Now I have become their song.
Yes, I am a byword to them.
They abhor me, they stand aloof from me,
and don't hesitate to spit in my face.
For he has untied his cord, and afflicted me;
and they have thrown off restraint before me.
On my right hand rise the rabble.
They thrust aside my feet,
They cast up against me their ways of destruction.
They mar my path.
They promote my destruction
without anyone's help.
As through a wide breach they come.
They roll themselves in amid the ruin.
Terrors have turned on me.

They chase my honor as the wind.
My welfare has passed away as a cloud.

"Now my soul is poured out within me.
Days of affliction have taken hold of me.
In the night season my bones are pierced in me,
and the pains that gnaw me take no rest.
My garment is disfigured by great force.
It binds me about as the collar of my tunic.
He has cast me into the mire.
I have become like dust and ashes.
I cry to you, and you do not answer me.
I stand up, and you gaze at me.
You have turned to be cruel to me.
With the might of your hand you persecute me.
You lift me up to the wind, and drive me with it.
You dissolve me in the storm.
For I know that you will bring me to death,
To the house appointed for all living.

"However doesn't one stretch out a hand in his fall?
Or in his calamity therefore cry for help?
Didn't I weep for him who was in trouble?
Wasn't my soul grieved for the needy?
When I looked for good, then evil came.
When I waited for light, darkness came.
My heart is troubled, and doesn't rest.
Days of affliction have come on me.
I go mourning without the sun.
I stand up in the assembly, and cry for help.
I am a brother to jackals,
and a companion to ostriches.
My skin grows black and peels from me.
My bones are burned with heat.
Therefore my harp has turned to mourning,
and my pipe into the voice of those who weep.

"I made a covenant with my eyes,
    how then should I look lustfully at a young woman?
For what is the portion from God above,
    and the heritage from the Almighty on high?
Is it not calamity to the unrighteous,
    and disaster to the workers of iniquity?
Doesn't he see my ways,
    and count all my steps?

"If I have walked with falsehood,
    and my foot has hurried to deceit
(let me be weighed in an even balance,
    that God may know my integrity);
if my step has turned out of the way,
    if my heart walked after my eyes,
    if any defilement has stuck to my hands,
then let me sow, and let another eat.
    Yes, let the produce of my field be rooted out.

"If my heart has been enticed to a woman,
    and I have laid wait at my neighbor's door,
then let my wife grind for another,
    and let others sleep with her.
For that would be a heinous crime.
    Yes, it would be an iniquity to be punished by the judges;
for it is a fire that consumes to destruction,
    and would root out all my increase.
"If I have despised the cause of my male servant
    or of my female servant,
    when they contended with me,
what then will I do when God rises up?
    When he visits, what will I answer him?
Didn't he who made me in the womb make him?
    Didn't one fashion us in the womb?
"If I have withheld the poor from their desire,
    or have caused the eyes of the widow to fail,
or have eaten my morsel alone,
    and the fatherless has not eaten of it
(no, from my youth he grew up with me as with a father,
    I have guided her from my mother's womb);

if I have seen any perish for want of clothing,
*   or that the needy had no covering;*
if his heart hasn't blessed me,
*   if he hasn't been warmed with my sheep's fleece;*
if I have lifted up my hand against the fatherless,
*   because I saw my help in the gate,*
then let my shoulder fall from the shoulder blade,
*   and my arm be broken from the bone.*
For calamity from God is a terror to me.
*   Because of his majesty, I can do nothing.*
"If I have made gold my hope,
*   and have said to the fine gold, 'You are my confidence;'*
If I have rejoiced because my wealth was great,
*   and because my hand had gotten much;*
if I have seen the sun when it shined,
*   or the moon moving in splendor,*
and my heart has been secretly enticed,
*   and my hand threw a kiss from my mouth,*
this also would be an iniquity to be punished by the judges;
*   for I should have denied the God who is above.*
"If I have rejoiced at the destruction of him who hated me,
*   or lifted up myself when evil found him*
(yes, I have not allowed my mouth to sin
*   by asking his life with a curse);*
if the men of my tent have not said,
*   'Who can find one who has not been filled with his meat?'*
(the foreigner has not camped in the street,
*   but I have opened my doors to the traveler);*
if like Adam I have covered my transgressions,
*   by hiding my iniquity in my heart,*
because I feared the great multitude,
*   and the contempt of families terrified me,*
*   so that I kept silence, and didn't go out of the door—*
oh that I had one to hear me!
*   Behold, here is my signature! Let the Almighty answer me!*
*   Let the accuser write my indictment!*
Surely I would carry it on my shoulder;
*   and I would bind it to me as a crown.*
I would declare to him the number of my steps.
*   as a prince would I go near to him.*

If my land cries out against me,
*   and its furrows weep together;*
if I have eaten its fruits without money,
*   or have caused its owners to lose their life,*
let briers grow instead of wheat,
*   and stinkweed instead of barley."*

The words of Job are ended.

....

So these three men ceased to answer Job, because he was righteous in his own eyes. Then the wrath of Elihu the son of Barachel, the Buzite, of the family of Ram, was kindled against Job. His wrath was kindled because he justified himself rather than God. Also his wrath was kindled against his three friends, because they had found no answer, and yet had condemned Job. Now Elihu had waited to speak to Job, because they were elder than he. When Elihu saw that there was no answer in the mouth of these three men, his wrath was kindled.

Elihu the son of Barachel the Buzite answered,
*   "I am young, and you are very old;*
*   Therefore I held back, and didn't dare show you my opinion.*
*   I said, 'Days should speak,*
*   and multitude of years should teach wisdom.'*
*   But there is a spirit in man,*
*   and the Spirit of the Almighty gives them understanding.*
*   It is not the great who are wise,*
*   nor the aged who understand justice.*
*   Therefore I said, 'Listen to me;*
*   I also will show my opinion.'*

*   "Behold, I waited for your words,*
*   and I listened for your reasoning,*
*   while you searched out what to say.*
*   Yes, I gave you my full attention,*
*   but there was no one who convinced Job,*
*   or who answered his words, among you.*
*   Beware lest you say, 'We have found wisdom.*
*   God may refute him, not man;'*

for he has not directed his words against me;
neither will I answer him with your speeches.

"*They are amazed. They answer no more.*
They don't have a word to say.
Shall I wait, because they don't speak,
because they stand still, and answer no more?
I also will answer my part,
and I also will show my opinion.
For I am full of words.
The spirit within me constrains me.
Behold, my breast is as wine which has no vent;
like new wineskins it is ready to burst.
I will speak, that I may be refreshed.
I will open my lips and answer.
Please don't let me respect any man's person,
neither will I give flattering titles to any man.
For I don't know how to give flattering titles,
or else my Maker would soon take me away.

....

"*However, Job, please hear my speech,*
and listen to all my words.
See now, I have opened my mouth.
My tongue has spoken in my mouth.
My words will utter the uprightness of my heart.
That which my lips know they will speak sincerely.
The Spirit of God has made me,
and the breath of the Almighty gives me life.
If you can, answer me.
Set your words in order before me, and stand up.
Behold, I am toward God even as you are.
I am also formed out of the clay.
Behold, my terror will not make you afraid,
neither will my pressure be heavy on you.

"*Surely you have spoken in my hearing,*
I have heard the voice of your words, saying,

'I am clean, without disobedience.
*   I am innocent, neither is there iniquity in me.*
Behold, he finds occasions against me.
*   He counts me for his enemy.*
He puts my feet in the stocks.
*   He marks all my paths.'*

"Behold, I will answer you. In this you are not just,
*   for God is greater than man.*

Why do you strive against him,
*   because he doesn't give account of any of his matters?*
For God speaks once,
*   yes twice, though man pays no attention.*
In a dream, in a vision of the night,
*   when deep sleep falls on men,*
*   in slumbering on the bed;*
Then he opens the ears of men,
*   and seals their instruction,*
that he may withdraw man from his purpose,
*   and hide pride from man.*
He keeps back his soul from the pit,
*   and his life from perishing by the sword.*

He is chastened also with pain on his bed,
*   with continual strife in his bones,*
so that his life abhors bread,
*   and his soul dainty food.*
His flesh is so consumed away that it can't be seen.
*   His bones that were not seen stick out.*
Yes, his soul draws near to the pit,
*   and his life to the destroyers.*

"If there is beside him an angel,
*   an interpreter, one among a thousand,*
*   to show to man what is right for him;*
then God is gracious to him, and says,
*   'Deliver him from going down to the pit,*
*   I have found a ransom.'*
His flesh will be fresher than a child's.

He returns to the days of his youth.
He prays to God, and he is favorable to him,
  so that he sees his face with joy.
  He restores to man his righteousness.
He sings before men, and says,
  'I have sinned, and perverted that which was right,
  and it didn't profit me.
He has redeemed my soul from going into the pit.
  My life will see the light.'

"Behold, God does all these things,
  twice, yes three times, with a man,
to bring back his soul from the pit,
  that he may be enlightened with the light of the living.
Mark well, Job, and listen to me.
  Hold your peace, and I will speak.
If you have anything to say, answer me.
  Speak, for I desire to justify you.
If not, listen to me.
  Hold your peace, and I will teach you wisdom."

....

Moreover Elihu answered,
  "Hear my words, you wise men.
  Give ear to me, you who have knowledge.
For the ear tries words,
  as the palate tastes food.
Let us choose for us that which is right.
  Let us know among ourselves what is good.
For Job has said, 'I am righteous,
  God has taken away my right:
Notwithstanding my right I am considered a liar.
  My wound is incurable, though I am without disobedience.'
What man is like Job,
  who drinks scorn like water,
Who goes in company with the workers of iniquity,
  and walks with wicked men?
For he has said, 'It profits a man nothing
  that he should delight himself with God.'

"Therefore listen to me, you men of understanding:
  far be it from God, that he should do wickedness,
  from the Almighty, that he should commit iniquity.
For the work of a man he will render to him,
  and cause every man to find according to his ways.
Yes surely, God will not do wickedly,
  neither will the Almighty pervert justice.
Who put him in charge of the earth?
  Or who has appointed him over the whole world?
If he set his heart on himself,
  if he gathered to himself his spirit and his breath,
all flesh would perish together,
  and man would turn again to dust.

"If now you have understanding, hear this.
  Listen to the voice of my words.
Should even one who hates justice govern?
  Will you condemn him who is righteous and mighty?—
Who says to a king, 'Vile!'
  or to nobles, 'Wicked!'?
He doesn't respect the persons of princes,
  nor respect the rich more than the poor;
  for they all are the work of his hands.
In a moment they die, even at midnight.
  The people are shaken and pass away.
  The mighty are taken away without a hand.

"For his eyes are on the ways of a man.
  He sees all his goings.
There is no darkness, nor thick gloom,
  where the workers of iniquity may hide themselves.
For he doesn't need to consider a man further,
  that he should go before God in judgment.
He breaks mighty men in pieces in ways past finding out,
  and sets others in their place.
Therefore he takes knowledge of their works.
  He overturns them in the night, so that they are destroyed.
He strikes them as wicked men
  in the open sight of others;

because they turned away from following him,
and wouldn't pay attention to any of his ways,
so that they caused the cry of the poor to come to him.
He heard the cry of the afflicted.
When he gives quietness, who then can condemn?
When he hides his face, who then can see him?
He is over a nation or a man alike,
that the godless man may not reign,
that there be no one to ensnare the people.

"For has any said to God,
'I am guilty, but I will not offend any more.
Teach me that which I don't see.
If I have done iniquity, I will do it no more'?
Shall his recompense be as you desire, that you refuse it?
For you must choose, and not I.
Therefore speak what you know.
Men of understanding will tell me,
yes, every wise man who hears me:
'Job speaks without knowledge.
His words are without wisdom.'
I wish that Job were tried to the end,
because of his answering like wicked men.
For he adds rebellion to his sin.
He claps his hands among us,
and multiplies his words against God."

Moreover Elihu answered,
"Do you think this to be your right,
or do you say, 'My righteousness is more than God's,'
that you ask, 'What advantage will it be to you?
What profit will I have, more than if I had sinned?'
I will answer you,
and your companions with you.
Look to the skies, and see.
See the skies, which are higher than you.
If you have sinned, what effect do you have against him?
If your transgressions are multiplied, what do you do to him?

If you are righteous, what do you give him?
Or what does he receive from your hand?
Your wickedness may hurt a man as you are,
and your righteousness may profit a son of man.

"By reason of the multitude of oppressions they cry out.
They cry for help by reason of the arm of the mighty.
But no one says, 'Where is God my Maker,
who gives songs in the night,
who teaches us more than the animals of the earth,
and makes us wiser than the birds of the sky?'
There they cry, but no one answers,
because of the pride of evil men.
Surely God will not hear an empty cry,
neither will the Almighty regard it.
How much less when you say you don't see him.
The cause is before him, and you wait for him!
But now, because he has not visited in his anger,
neither does he greatly regard arrogance.
Therefore Job opens his mouth with empty talk,
and he multiplies words without knowledge."

....

Elihu also continued, and said,
"Bear with me a little, and I will show you;
for I still have something to say on God's behalf.
I will get my knowledge from afar,
and will ascribe righteousness to my Maker.
For truly my words are not false.
One who is perfect in knowledge is with you.

"Behold, God is mighty, and doesn't despise anyone.
He is mighty in strength of understanding.
He doesn't preserve the life of the wicked,
but gives justice to the afflicted.
He doesn't withdraw his eyes from the righteous,
but with kings on the throne,
he sets them forever, and they are exalted.
If they are bound in fetters,

and are taken in the cords of afflictions,
then he shows them their work,
    and their transgressions, that they have behaved themselves
    proudly.
He also opens their ears to instruction,
    and commands that they return from iniquity.
If they listen and serve him,
    they will spend their days in prosperity,
    and their years in pleasures.
But if they don't listen, they will perish by the sword;
    they will die without knowledge.

"But those who are godless in heart lay up anger.
    They don't cry for help when he binds them.
They die in youth.
    Their life perishes among the unclean.
He delivers the afflicted by their affliction,
    and opens their ear in oppression.
Yes, he would have allured you out of distress,
    into a wide place, where there is no restriction.
    That which is set on your table would be full of fatness.

"But you are full of the judgment of the wicked.
    Judgment and justice take hold of you.
Don't let riches entice you to wrath,
    neither let the great size of a bribe turn you aside.
Would your wealth sustain you in distress,
    or all the might of your strength?
Don't desire the night,
    when people are cut off in their place.
Take heed, don't regard iniquity;
    for you have chosen this rather than affliction.
Behold, God is exalted in his power.
    Who is a teacher like him?
Who has prescribed his way for him?
    Or who can say, 'You have committed unrighteousness?'

"Remember that you magnify his work,
    about which men have sung.
All men have looked on it.

Man sees it afar off.
Behold, God is great, and we don't know him.
The number of his years is unsearchable.
For he draws up the drops of water,
which distill in rain from his vapor,
which the skies pour down
and which drop on man abundantly.
Yes, can any understand the spreading of the clouds,
and the thunderings of his pavilion?
Behold, he spreads his light around him.
He covers the bottom of the sea.
For by these he judges the people.
He gives food in abundance.
He covers his hands with the lightning,
and commands it to strike the mark.
Its noise tells about him,
and the livestock also concerning the storm that comes up.

....

"Yes, at this my heart trembles,
and is moved out of its place.
Hear, oh, hear the noise of his voice,
the sound that goes out of his mouth.
He sends it out under the whole sky,
and his lightning to the ends of the earth.
After it a voice roars.
He thunders with the voice of his majesty.
He doesn't hold back anything when his voice is heard.
God thunders marvelously with his voice.
He does great things, which we can't comprehend.
For he says to the snow, 'Fall on the earth,'
likewise to the shower of rain,
and to the showers of his mighty rain.
He seals up the hand of every man,
that all men whom he has made may know it.
Then the animals take cover,
and remain in their dens.
Out of its room comes the storm,
and cold out of the north.

By the breath of God, ice is given,
*   and the width of the waters is frozen.*
Yes, he loads the thick cloud with moisture.
*   He spreads abroad the cloud of his lightning.*
It is turned around by his guidance,
*   that they may do whatever he commands them*
*   on the surface of the habitable world,*
Whether it is for correction, or for his land,
*   or for loving kindness, that he causes it to come.*

"Listen to this, Job.
*   Stand still, and consider the wondrous works of God.*
Do you know how God controls them,
*   and causes the lightning of his cloud to shine?*
Do you know the workings of the clouds,
*   the wondrous works of him who is perfect in knowledge?*
You whose clothing is warm,
*   when the earth is still by reason of the south wind?*
Can you, with him, spread out the sky,
*   which is strong as a cast metal mirror?*
Teach us what we will tell him,
*   for we can't make our case by reason of darkness.*
Will it be told him that I would speak?
*   Or should a man wish that he were swallowed up?*

Now men don't see the light which is bright in the skies,
*   but the wind passes, and clears them.*
Out of the north comes golden splendor.
*   With God is awesome majesty.*
We can't reach the Almighty.
*   He is exalted in power.*
*   In justice and great righteousness, he will not oppress.*
Therefore men revere him.
*   He doesn't regard any who are wise of heart."*

Then yhwh answered Job out of the whirlwind,
"Who is this who darkens counsel
*   by words without knowledge?*

Brace yourself like a man,
*   for I will question you, then you answer me!*

"Where were you when I laid the foundations of the earth?
*   Declare, if you have understanding.*
Who determined its measures, if you know?
*   Or who stretched the line on it?*
What were its foundations fastened on?
*   Or who laid its cornerstone,*
when the morning stars sang together,
*   and all the sons of God shouted for joy?*

"Or who shut up the sea with doors,
*   when it broke out of the womb,*
when I made clouds its garment,
*   and wrapped it in thick darkness,*
marked out for it my bound,
*   set bars and doors,*
and said, 'You may come here, but no further.
*   Your proud waves shall be stopped here?'*

"Have you commanded the morning in your days,
*   and caused the dawn to know its place,*
that it might take hold of the ends of the earth,
*   and shake the wicked out of it?*
It is changed as clay under the seal,
*   and presented as a garment.*
From the wicked, their light is withheld.
*   The high arm is broken.*

"Have you entered into the springs of the sea?
*   Or have you walked in the recesses of the deep?*
Have the gates of death been revealed to you?
*   Or have you seen the gates of the shadow of death?*
Have you comprehended the earth in its width?
*   Declare, if you know it all.*

"What is the way to the dwelling of light?
*   As for darkness, where is its place,*
that you should take it to its bound,

that you should discern the paths to its house?
Surely you know, for you were born then,
and the number of your days is great!
Have you entered the treasuries of the snow,
or have you seen the treasures of the hail,
which I have reserved against the time of trouble,
against the day of battle and war?
By what way is the lightning distributed,
or the east wind scattered on the earth?

Who has cut a channel for the flood water,
or the path for the thunder storm,
to cause it to rain on a land where there is no man,
on the wilderness, in which there is no man,
to satisfy the waste and desolate ground,
to cause the tender grass to grow?
Does the rain have a father?
Or who fathers the drops of dew?
Whose womb did the ice come out of?
Who has given birth to the gray frost of the sky?
The waters become hard like stone,
when the surface of the deep is frozen.

"Can you bind the cluster of the Pleiades,
or loosen the cords of Orion?
Can you lead the constellations out in their season?
Or can you guide the Bear with her cubs?
Do you know the laws of the heavens?
Can you establish its dominion over the earth?

"Can you lift up your voice to the clouds,
That abundance of waters may cover you?
Can you send out lightnings, that they may go?
Do they report to you, 'Here we are?'
Who has put wisdom in the inward parts?
Or who has given understanding to the mind?
Who can count the clouds by wisdom?
Or who can pour out the containers of the sky,
when the dust runs into a mass,
and the clods of earth stick together?

"Can you hunt the prey for the lioness,
  or satisfy the appetite of the young lions,
when they crouch in their dens,
  and lie in wait in the thicket?
Who provides for the raven his prey,
  when his young ones cry to God,
  and wander for lack of food?

....

"Do you know the time when the mountain goats give birth?
  Do you watch when the doe bears fawns?
Can you count the months that they fulfill?
  Or do you know the time when they give birth?
They bow themselves. They bear their young.
  They end their labor pains.
Their young ones become strong.
  They grow up in the open field.
  They go out, and don't return again.

"Who has set the wild donkey free?
  Or who has loosened the bonds of the swift donkey,
whose home I have made the wilderness,
  and the salt land his dwelling place?
He scorns the tumult of the city,
  neither does he hear the shouting of the driver.
The range of the mountains is his pasture,
  He searches after every green thing.

"Will the wild ox be content to serve you?
  Or will he stay by your feeding trough?
Can you hold the wild ox in the furrow with his harness?
  Or will he till the valleys after you?
Will you trust him, because his strength is great?
  Or will you leave to him your labor?
Will you confide in him, that he will bring home your seed,
  and gather the grain of your threshing floor?

"The wings of the ostrich wave proudly;

but are they the feathers and plumage of love?
For she leaves her eggs on the earth,
    warms them in the dust,
and forgets that the foot may crush them,
    or that the wild animal may trample them.
She deals harshly with her young ones, as if they were not hers.
    Though her labor is in vain, she is without fear,
because God has deprived her of wisdom,
    neither has he imparted to her understanding.
When she lifts up herself on high,
    she scorns the horse and his rider.

"Have you given the horse might?
    Have you clothed his neck with a quivering mane?
Have you made him to leap as a locust?
    The glory of his snorting is awesome.
He paws in the valley, and rejoices in his strength.
    He goes out to meet the armed men.
He mocks at fear, and is not dismayed,
    neither does he turn back from the sword.
The quiver rattles against him,
    the flashing spear and the javelin.
He eats up the ground with fierceness and rage,
    neither does he stand still at the sound of the trumpet.
As often as the trumpet sounds he snorts, 'Aha!'
    He smells the battle afar off,
    the thunder of the captains, and the shouting.

"Is it by your wisdom that the hawk soars,
    and stretches her wings toward the south?
Is it at your command that the eagle mounts up,
    and makes his nest on high?
On the cliff he dwells, and makes his home,
    on the point of the cliff, and the stronghold.
From there he spies out the prey.
    His eyes see it afar off.
His young ones also suck up blood.
    Where the slain are, there he is."

Moreover YHWH answered Job,
  "Shall he who argues contend with the Almighty?
    He who argues with God, let him answer it."

Then Job answered YHWH,
  "Behold, I am of small account. What will I answer you?
    I lay my hand on my mouth.
  I have spoken once, and I will not answer;
    Yes, twice, but I will proceed no further."

Then YHWH answered Job out of the whirlwind,
  "Now brace yourself like a man.
    I will question you, and you will answer me.
  Will you even annul my judgment?
    Will you condemn me, that you may be justified?
  Or do you have an arm like God?
    Can you thunder with a voice like him?

  "Now deck yourself with excellency and dignity.
    Array yourself with honor and majesty.
  Pour out the fury of your anger.
    Look at everyone who is proud, and bring him low.
  Look at everyone who is proud, and humble him.
    Crush the wicked in their place.
  Hide them in the dust together.
    Bind their faces in the hidden place.
  Then I will also admit to you
    that your own right hand can save you.

  "See now, behemoth, which I made as well as you.
    He eats grass as an ox.
  Look now, his strength is in his thighs.
    His force is in the muscles of his belly.
  He moves his tail like a cedar.
    The sinews of his thighs are knit together.
  His bones are like tubes of bronze.
    His limbs are like bars of iron.

  He is the chief of the ways of God.
    He who made him gives him his sword.

Surely the mountains produce food for him,
where all the animals of the field play.
He lies under the lotus trees,
in the covert of the reed, and the marsh.
The lotuses cover him with their shade.
The willows of the brook surround him.
Behold, if a river overflows, he doesn't tremble.
He is confident, though the Jordan swells even to his mouth.
Shall any take him when he is on the watch,
or pierce through his nose with a snare?

....

"Can you draw out Leviathan with a fish hook,
or press down his tongue with a cord?
Can you put a rope into his nose,
or pierce his jaw through with a hook?
Will he make many petitions to you,
or will he speak soft words to you?
Will he make a covenant with you,
that you should take him for a servant forever?
Will you play with him as with a bird?
Or will you bind him for your girls?
Will traders barter for him?
Will they part him among the merchants?
Can you fill his skin with barbed irons,
or his head with fish spears?
Lay your hand on him.
Remember the battle, and do so no more.
Behold, the hope of him is in vain.
Won't one be cast down even at the sight of him?

None is so fierce that he dare stir him up.
Who then is he who can stand before me?
Who has first given to me, that I should repay him?
Everything under the heavens is mine.

"I will not keep silence concerning his limbs,
nor his mighty strength, nor his goodly frame.

Who can strip off his outer garment?
   Who will come within his jaws?
Who can open the doors of his face?
   Around his teeth is terror.
Strong scales are his pride,
   shut up together with a close seal.

One is so near to another,
   that no air can come between them.
They are joined to one another.
   They stick together, so that they can't be pulled apart.
His sneezing flashes out light.
   His eyes are like the eyelids of the morning.
Out of his mouth go burning torches.
   Sparks of fire leap out.
Out of his nostrils a smoke goes,
   as of a boiling pot over a fire of reeds.
His breath kindles coals.
   A flame goes out of his mouth.
There is strength in his neck.
   Terror dances before him.
The flakes of his flesh are joined together.
   They are firm on him.
   They can't be moved.
His heart is as firm as a stone,
   yes, firm as the lower millstone.
When he raises himself up, the mighty are afraid.
   They retreat before his thrashing.
If one attacks him with the sword, it can't prevail;
   nor the spear, the dart, nor the pointed shaft.
He counts iron as straw;
   and bronze as rotten wood.
The arrow can't make him flee.
   Sling stones are like chaff to him.
Clubs are counted as stubble.
   He laughs at the rushing of the javelin.
His undersides are like sharp potsherds,
   leaving a trail in the mud like a threshing sledge.
He makes the deep to boil like a pot.
   He makes the sea like a pot of ointment.

He makes a path shine after him.
    One would think the deep had white hair.
On earth there is not his equal,
    that is made without fear.
He sees everything that is high.
    He is king over all the sons of pride."

....

Then Job answered YHWH,
    "I know that you can do all things,
        and that no purpose of yours can be restrained.
    You asked, 'Who is this who hides counsel without knowledge?'
        therefore I have uttered that which I didn't understand,
        things too wonderful for me, which I didn't know.
    You said, 'Listen, now, and I will speak;
        I will question you, and you will answer me.'
    I had heard of you by the hearing of the ear,
        but now my eye sees you.
    Therefore I abhor myself,
        and repent in dust and ashes."

It was so, that after YHWH had spoken these words to Job, YHWH said to Eliphaz the Temanite, "My wrath is kindled against you, and against your two friends; for you have not spoken of me the thing that is right, as my servant Job has. Now therefore, take to yourselves seven bulls and seven rams, and go to my servant Job, and offer up for yourselves a burnt offering; and my servant Job shall pray for you, for I will accept him, that I not deal with you according to your folly. For you have not spoken of me the thing that is right, as my servant Job has."

So Eliphaz the Temanite and Bildad the Shuhite and Zophar the Naamathite went, and did what YHWH commanded them, and YHWH accepted Job.

YHWH turned the captivity of Job, when he prayed for his friends. YHWH gave Job twice as much as he had before. Then came there to him all his brothers, and all his sisters, and all those who had been of his acquaintance before, and ate bread with him in his house. They comforted him, and consoled him concerning all the evil that YHWH had brought on him. Everyone also gave him a piece of money, and everyone a ring of gold.

So YHWH blessed the latter end of Job more than his beginning. He had fourteen thousand sheep, six thousand camels, one thousand yoke of oxen, and a thousand female donkeys. He had also seven sons and three daughters. He called the name of the first, Jemimah; and the name of the second, Keziah; and the name of the third, Keren Happuch. In all the land were no women found so beautiful as the daughters of Job. Their father gave them an inheritance among their brothers. After this Job lived one hundred forty years, and saw his sons, and his sons' sons, to four generations. So Job died, being old and full of days.

THE

PSALMS

3 HR 56 MIN

BOOK 1

Blessed is the man who doesn't walk in the counsel of the wicked,
nor stand on the path of sinners,
nor sit in the seat of scoffers;
but his delight is in YHWH's law.
On his law he meditates day and night.
He will be like a tree planted by the streams of water,
that produces its fruit in its season,
whose leaf also does not wither.
Whatever he does shall prosper.
The wicked are not so,
but are like the chaff which the wind drives away.
Therefore the wicked shall not stand in the judgment,
nor sinners in the congregation of the righteous.
For YHWH knows the way of the righteous,
but the way of the wicked shall perish.

....

Why do the nations rage,
and the peoples plot a vain thing?
The kings of the earth take a stand,
and the rulers take counsel together,
against YHWH, and against his Anointed, saying,
"Let's break their bonds apart,
and cast their cords from us."
He who sits in the heavens will laugh.
The Lord will have them in derision.
Then he will speak to them in his anger,
and terrify them in his wrath:
"Yet I have set my King on my holy hill of Zion."
I will tell of the decree:
YHWH said to me, "You are my son.
Today I have become your father.
Ask of me, and I will give the nations for your inheritance,
the uttermost parts of the earth for your possession.
You shall break them with a rod of iron.
You shall dash them in pieces like a potter's vessel."
Now therefore be wise, you kings.
Be instructed, you judges of the earth.
Serve YHWH with fear,

and rejoice with trembling.
Give sincere homage to the Son, lest he be angry, and you perish on the way,
>   *for his wrath will soon be kindled.*
>   *Blessed are all those who take refuge in him.*

....

A Psalm by David, when he fled from Absalom his son. YHWH, *how my adversaries have increased!*
>   *Many are those who rise up against me.*
Many there are who say of my soul,
>   *"There is no help for him in God." Selah.*
But you, YHWH, *are a shield around me,*
>   *my glory, and the one who lifts up my head.*
I cry to YHWH *with my voice,*
>   *and he answers me out of his holy hill. Selah.*
I laid myself down and slept.
>   *I awakened; for* YHWH *sustains me.*
I will not be afraid of tens of thousands of people
>   *who have set themselves against me on every side.*
Arise, YHWH*!*
>   *Save me, my God!*
For you have struck all of my enemies on the cheek bone.
>   *You have broken the teeth of the wicked.*
Salvation belongs to YHWH.
>   *May your blessing be on your people. Selah.*

....

For the Chief Musician; on stringed instruments. A Psalm by David. Answer me when I call, God of my righteousness.
>   *Give me relief from my distress.*
>   *Have mercy on me, and hear my prayer.*
You sons of men, how long shall my glory be turned into dishonor?
>   *Will you love vanity and seek after falsehood? Selah.*
But know that YHWH *has set apart for himself him who is godly:*
>   YHWH *will hear when I call to him.*
Stand in awe, and don't sin.
>   *Search your own heart on your bed, and be still. Selah.*
Offer the sacrifices of righteousness.
>   *Put your trust in* YHWH.

Many say, "Who will show us any good?"
    YHWH, let the light of your face shine on us.
You have put gladness in my heart,
    more than when their grain and their new wine are increased.
In peace I will both lay myself down and sleep,
    for you, YHWH alone, make me live in safety.

....

For the Chief Musician, with the flutes. A Psalm by David. Give
ear to my words, YHWH.
    Consider my meditation.
Listen to the voice of my cry, my King and my God;
    for I pray to you.
YHWH, in the morning you will hear my voice.
    In the morning I will lay my requests before you, and will
    watch expectantly.
For you are not a God who has pleasure in wickedness.
    Evil can't live with you.
The arrogant will not stand in your sight.
    You hate all workers of iniquity.
You will destroy those who speak lies.
    YHWH abhors the bloodthirsty and deceitful man.
But as for me, in the abundance of your loving kindness I will
come into your house.
    I will bow toward your holy temple in reverence of you.
Lead me, YHWH, in your righteousness because of my enemies.
    Make your way straight before my face.
For there is no faithfulness in their mouth.
    Their heart is destruction.
    Their throat is an open tomb.
    They flatter with their tongue.
Hold them guilty, God.
    Let them fall by their own counsels.
Thrust them out in the multitude of their transgressions,
    for they have rebelled against you.
But let all those who take refuge in you rejoice.
    Let them always shout for joy, because you defend them.
Let them also who love your name be joyful in you.
    For you will bless the righteous.
YHWH, you will surround him with favor as with a shield.

....

For the Chief Musician; on stringed instruments, upon the eight-
stringed lyre. A Psalm by David. YHWH, *don't rebuke me in your*
anger,
    neither discipline me in your wrath.
Have mercy on me, YHWH, *for I am faint.*
    YHWH, *heal me, for my bones are troubled.*
My soul is also in great anguish.
    But you, YHWH—*how long?*
Return, YHWH. *Deliver my soul,*
    and save me for your loving kindness' sake.
For in death there is no memory of you.
    In Sheol, who shall give you thanks?
I am weary with my groaning.
    Every night I flood my bed.
    I drench my couch with my tears.
My eye wastes away because of grief.
    It grows old because of all my adversaries.
Depart from me, all you workers of iniquity,
    for YHWH *has heard the voice of my weeping.*
YHWH *has heard my supplication.*
    YHWH *accepts my prayer.*
May all my enemies be ashamed and dismayed.
    They shall turn back, they shall be disgraced suddenly.

....

A meditation by David, which he sang to YHWH, *concerning the*
words of Cush, the Benjamite. YHWH, *my God, I take refuge in*
you.
    Save me from all those who pursue me, and deliver me,
lest they tear apart my soul like a lion,
    ripping it in pieces, while there is no one to deliver.
YHWH, *my God, if I have done this,*
    if there is iniquity in my hands,
if I have rewarded evil to him who was at peace with me
    (yes, I have delivered him who without cause was my adver-
    sary),
    let the enemy pursue my soul, and overtake it;
yes, let him tread my life down to the earth,

and lay my glory in the dust. Selah.
Arise, YHWH, in your anger.
  Lift up yourself against the rage of my adversaries.
Awake for me. You have commanded judgment.
  Let the congregation of the peoples surround you.
  Rule over them on high.
YHWH administers judgment to the peoples.
  Judge me, YHWH, according to my righteousness,
  and to my integrity that is in me.
Oh let the wickedness of the wicked come to an end,
  but establish the righteous;
  their minds and hearts are searched by the righteous God.
My shield is with God,
  who saves the upright in heart.
God is a righteous judge,
  yes, a God who has indignation every day.
If a man doesn't repent, he will sharpen his sword;
  he has bent and strung his bow.
He has also prepared for himself the instruments of death.
  He makes ready his flaming arrows.
Behold, he travails with iniquity.
  Yes, he has conceived mischief,
  and brought out falsehood.
He has dug a hole,
  and has fallen into the pit which he made.
The trouble he causes shall return to his own head.
  His violence shall come down on the crown of his own head.
I will give thanks to YHWH according to his righteousness,
  and will sing praise to the name of YHWH Most High.

....

For the Chief Musician; on an instrument of Gath. A Psalm by
David. YHWH, our Lord, how majestic is your name in all the
earth!
  You have set your glory above the heavens!
From the lips of babes and infants you have established strength,
  because of your adversaries, that you might silence the enemy
  and the avenger.
When I consider your heavens, the work of your fingers,
  the moon and the stars, which you have ordained;

what is man, that you think of him?
What is the son of man, that you care for him?
For you have made him a little lower than the angels,
and crowned him with glory and honor.
You make him ruler over the works of your hands.
You have put all things under his feet:
All sheep and cattle,
yes, and the animals of the field,
the birds of the sky, the fish of the sea,
and whatever passes through the paths of the seas.
YHWH, our Lord,
how majestic is your name in all the earth!

....

For the Chief Musician. Set to "The Death of the Son." A Psalm
by David. I will give thanks to YHWH with my whole heart.
I will tell of all your marvelous works.
I will be glad and rejoice in you.
I will sing praise to your name, O Most High.
When my enemies turn back,
they stumble and perish in your presence.
For you have maintained my just cause.
You sit on the throne judging righteously.
You have rebuked the nations.
You have destroyed the wicked.
You have blotted out their name forever and ever.
The enemy is overtaken by endless ruin.
The very memory of the cities which you have overthrown has
perished.
But YHWH reigns forever.
He has prepared his throne for judgment.
He will judge the world in righteousness.
He will administer judgment to the peoples in uprightness.
YHWH will also be a high tower for the oppressed;
a high tower in times of trouble.
Those who know your name will put their trust in you,
for you, YHWH, have not forsaken those who seek you.
Sing praises to YHWH, who dwells in Zion,
and declare among the people what he has done.
For he who avenges blood remembers them.

He doesn't forget the cry of the afflicted.
Have mercy on me, YHWH.
　See my affliction by those who hate me,
and lift me up from the gates of death,
　that I may show all of your praise.
　I will rejoice in your salvation in the gates of the daughter of
　Zion.
The nations have sunk down in the pit that they made.
　In the net which they hid, their own foot is taken.
YHWH has made himself known.
　He has executed judgment.
　The wicked is snared by the work of his own hands. Meditation. Selah.
The wicked shall be turned back to Sheol,
　even all the nations that forget God.
For the needy shall not always be forgotten,
　nor the hope of the poor perish forever.
Arise, YHWH! Don't let man prevail.
　Let the nations be judged in your sight.
Put them in fear, YHWH.
　Let the nations know that they are only men. Selah.

....

Why do you stand far off, YHWH?
　Why do you hide yourself in times of trouble?
In arrogance, the wicked hunt down the weak.
　They are caught in the schemes that they devise.
For the wicked boasts of his heart's cravings.
　He blesses the greedy and condemns YHWH.
The wicked, in the pride of his face,
　has no room in his thoughts for God.
His ways are prosperous at all times.
　He is arrogant, and your laws are far from his sight.
As for all his adversaries, he sneers at them.
　He says in his heart, "I shall not be shaken.
　For generations I shall have no trouble."
His mouth is full of cursing, deceit, and oppression.
　Under his tongue is mischief and iniquity.
He lies in wait near the villages.
　From ambushes, he murders the innocent.

His eyes are secretly set against the helpless.
He lurks in secret as a lion in his ambush.
    He lies in wait to catch the helpless.
    He catches the helpless when he draws him in his net.
The helpless are crushed.
    They collapse.
    They fall under his strength.
He says in his heart, "God has forgotten.
    He hides his face.
    He will never see it."

Arise, YHWH!
    God, lift up your hand!
    Don't forget the helpless.
Why does the wicked person condemn God,
    and say in his heart, "God won't call me into account?"
But you do see trouble and grief.
    You consider it to take it into your hand.
    You help the victim and the fatherless.
Break the arm of the wicked.
    As for the evil man, seek out his wickedness until you find
    none.
YHWH is King forever and ever!
    The nations will perish out of his land.
YHWH, you have heard the desire of the humble.
    You will prepare their heart.
    You will cause your ear to hear,
    to judge the fatherless and the oppressed,
    that man who is of the earth may terrify no more.

....

For the Chief Musician. By David. In YHWH, I take refuge.
    How can you say to my soul, "Flee as a bird to your moun-
    tain"?
For, behold, the wicked bend their bows.
    They set their arrows on the strings,
    that they may shoot in darkness at the upright in heart.
If the foundations are destroyed,
    what can the righteous do?
YHWH is in his holy temple.

YHWH is on his throne in heaven.
His eyes observe.
    His eyes examine the children of men.
YHWH examines the righteous,
    but his soul hates the wicked and him who loves violence.
On the wicked he will rain blazing coals;
    fire, sulfur, and scorching wind shall be the portion of their
    cup.
For YHWH is righteous.
    He loves righteousness.
    The upright shall see his face.

....

For the Chief Musician; upon an eight-stringed lyre. A Psalm of
David. Help, YHWH; for the godly man ceases.
    For the faithful fail from among the children of men.
Everyone lies to his neighbor.
    They speak with flattering lips, and with a double heart.
May YHWH cut off all flattering lips,
    and the tongue that boasts,
who have said, "With our tongue we will prevail.
    Our lips are our own.
    Who is lord over us?"
"Because of the oppression of the weak and because of the groan-
ing of the needy,
    I will now arise," says YHWH;
"I will set him in safety from those who malign him."
YHWH's words are flawless words,
    as silver refined in a clay furnace, purified seven times.
You will keep them, YHWH.
    You will preserve them from this generation forever.
The wicked walk on every side,
    when what is vile is exalted among the sons of men.

....

For the Chief Musician. A Psalm by David. How long, YHWH?
    Will you forget me forever?
    How long will you hide your face from me?
How long shall I take counsel in my soul,
    having sorrow in my heart every day?

How long shall my enemy triumph over me?
Behold, and answer me, YHWH, my God.
  Give light to my eyes, lest I sleep in death;
  lest my enemy say, "I have prevailed against him;"
  lest my adversaries rejoice when I fall.

But I trust in your loving kindness.
  My heart rejoices in your salvation.
I will sing to YHWH,
  because he has been good to me.

....

For the Chief Musician. By David. The fool has said in his heart,
"There is no God."
  They are corrupt.
  They have done abominable deeds.
  There is no one who does good.
YHWH looked down from heaven on the children of men,
  to see if there were any who understood,
  who sought after God.
They have all gone aside.
  They have together become corrupt.
  There is no one who does good, no, not one.
Have all the workers of iniquity no knowledge,
  who eat up my people as they eat bread,
  and don't call on YHWH?
There they were in great fear,
  for God is in the generation of the righteous.
You frustrate the plan of the poor,
  because YHWH is his refuge.
Oh that the salvation of Israel would come out of Zion!
  When YHWH restores the fortunes of his people,
  then Jacob shall rejoice, and Israel shall be glad.

....

A Psalm by David. YHWH, who shall dwell in your sanctuary?
  Who shall live on your holy hill?
He who walks blamelessly and does what is right,
  and speaks truth in his heart;
he who doesn't slander with his tongue,

nor does evil to his friend,
  nor casts slurs against his fellow man;
in whose eyes a vile man is despised,
  but who honors those who fear YHWH;
  he who keeps an oath even when it hurts, and doesn't change;
he who doesn't lend out his money for usury,
  nor take a bribe against the innocent.

He who does these things shall never be shaken.

....

A Poem by David. Preserve me, God, for I take refuge in you.
My soul, you have said to YHWH, "You are my Lord.
  Apart from you I have no good thing."
As for the saints who are in the earth,
  they are the excellent ones in whom is all my delight.

Their sorrows shall be multiplied who give gifts to another god.
  Their drink offerings of blood I will not offer,
  nor take their names on my lips.
YHWH assigned my portion and my cup.
  You made my lot secure.

The lines have fallen to me in pleasant places.
  Yes, I have a good inheritance.
I will bless YHWH, who has given me counsel.
  Yes, my heart instructs me in the night seasons.
I have set YHWH always before me.
  Because he is at my right hand, I shall not be moved.
Therefore my heart is glad, and my tongue rejoices.
  My body shall also dwell in safety.
For you will not leave my soul in Sheol,
  neither will you allow your holy one to see corruption.
You will show me the path of life.
  In your presence is fullness of joy.
In your right hand there are pleasures forever more.

....

A Prayer by David. Hear, YHWH, my righteous plea;
  Give ear to my prayer, that doesn't go out of deceitful lips.

Let my sentence come out of your presence.
   Let your eyes look on equity.
You have proved my heart.
   You have visited me in the night.
   You have tried me, and found nothing.
   I have resolved that my mouth shall not disobey.
As for the deeds of men, by the word of your lips,
   I have kept myself from the ways of the violent.
My steps have held fast to your paths.
   My feet have not slipped.
I have called on you, for you will answer me, God.
   Turn your ear to me.
   Hear my speech.
Show your marvelous loving kindness,
   you who save those who take refuge by your right hand from
      their enemies.
Keep me as the apple of your eye.
   Hide me under the shadow of your wings,
from the wicked who oppress me,
   my deadly enemies, who surround me.
They close up their callous hearts.
   With their mouth they speak proudly.
They have now surrounded us in our steps.
   They set their eyes to cast us down to the earth.
He is like a lion that is greedy of his prey,
   as it were a young lion lurking in secret places.
Arise, YHWH, confront him.
   Cast him down.
Deliver my soul from the wicked by your sword;
   from men by your hand, YHWH,
   from men of the world, whose portion is in this life.
You fill the belly of your cherished ones.
   Your sons have plenty,
   and they store up wealth for their children.
As for me, I shall see your face in righteousness.
   I shall be satisfied, when I awake, with seeing your form.

....

For the Chief Musician. By David the servant of YHWH, who
spoke to YHWH the words of this song in the day that YHWH deliv-

ered him from the hand of all his enemies, and from the hand of
Saul. He said, I love you, YHWH, my strength.
YHWH is my rock, my fortress, and my deliverer;
    my God, my rock, in whom I take refuge;
    my shield, and the horn of my salvation, my high tower.
I call on YHWH, who is worthy to be praised;
    and I am saved from my enemies.
The cords of death surrounded me.
    The floods of ungodliness made me afraid.
The cords of Sheol were around me.
    The snares of death came on me.
In my distress I called on YHWH,
    and cried to my God.
He heard my voice out of his temple.
    My cry before him came into his ears.
Then the earth shook and trembled.
    The foundations also of the mountains quaked and were
    shaken,
    because he was angry.
Smoke went out of his nostrils.
    Consuming fire came out of his mouth.
    Coals were kindled by it.
He bowed the heavens also, and came down.
    Thick darkness was under his feet.
He rode on a cherub, and flew.
    Yes, he soared on the wings of the wind.
He made darkness his hiding place, his pavilion around him,
    darkness of waters, thick clouds of the skies.
At the brightness before him his thick clouds passed,
    hailstones and coals of fire.
YHWH also thundered in the sky.
    The Most High uttered his voice:
    hailstones and coals of fire.
He sent out his arrows, and scattered them;
    Yes, great lightning bolts, and routed them.
Then the channels of waters appeared.
    The foundations of the world were laid bare at your rebuke,
    YHWH,
    at the blast of the breath of your nostrils.
He sent from on high.

He took me.
He drew me out of many waters.
He delivered me from my strong enemy,
from those who hated me; for they were too mighty for me.
They came on me in the day of my calamity,
but YHWH was my support.
He brought me out also into a large place.
He delivered me, because he delighted in me.
YHWH has rewarded me according to my righteousness.
According to the cleanness of my hands, he has recompensed me.
For I have kept the ways of YHWH,
and have not wickedly departed from my God.
For all his ordinances were before me.
I didn't put away his statutes from me.
I was also blameless with him.
I kept myself from my iniquity.
Therefore YHWH has rewarded me according to my righteousness,
according to the cleanness of my hands in his eyesight.
With the merciful you will show yourself merciful.
With the perfect man, you will show yourself perfect.
With the pure, you will show yourself pure.
With the crooked you will show yourself shrewd.
For you will save the afflicted people,
but the arrogant eyes you will bring down.
For you will light my lamp, YHWH.
My God will light up my darkness.
For by you, I advance through a troop.
By my God, I leap over a wall.
As for God, his way is perfect.
YHWH's word is tried.
He is a shield to all those who take refuge in him.
For who is God, except YHWH?
Who is a rock, besides our God,
the God who arms me with strength, and makes my way perfect?
He makes my feet like deer's feet,
and sets me on my high places.
He teaches my hands to war,
so that my arms bend a bow of bronze.

You have also given me the shield of your salvation.
Your right hand sustains me.
Your gentleness has made me great.
You have enlarged my steps under me,
My feet have not slipped.
I will pursue my enemies, and overtake them.
I won't turn away until they are consumed.
I will strike them through, so that they will not be able to rise.
They shall fall under my feet.
For you have armed me with strength to the battle.
You have subdued under me those who rose up against me.
You have also made my enemies turn their backs to me,
that I might cut off those who hate me.
They cried, but there was no one to save;
even to YHWH, but he didn't answer them.
Then I beat them small as the dust before the wind.
I cast them out as the mire of the streets.
You have delivered me from the strivings of the people.
You have made me the head of the nations.
A people whom I have not known shall serve me.
As soon as they hear of me they shall obey me.
The foreigners shall submit themselves to me.
The foreigners shall fade away,
and shall come trembling out of their strongholds.
YHWH lives! Blessed be my rock.
Exalted be the God of my salvation,
even the God who executes vengeance for me,
and subdues peoples under me.
He rescues me from my enemies.
Yes, you lift me up above those who rise up against me.
You deliver me from the violent man.
Therefore I will give thanks to you, YHWH, among the nations,
and will sing praises to your name.
He gives great deliverance to his king,
and shows loving kindness to his anointed,
to David and to his offspring, forever more.

....

For the Chief Musician. A Psalm by David. The heavens declare
the glory of God.

The expanse shows his handiwork.
Day after day they pour out speech,
  and night after night they display knowledge.
There is no speech nor language,
  where their voice is not heard.
Their voice has gone out through all the earth,
  their words to the end of the world.
In them he has set a tent for the sun,
  which is as a bridegroom coming out of his room,
  like a strong man rejoicing to run his course.
His going out is from the end of the heavens,
  his circuit to its ends.
  There is nothing hidden from its heat.

YHWH's law is perfect, restoring the soul.
  YHWH's covenant is sure, making wise the simple.
YHWH's precepts are right, rejoicing the heart.
  YHWH's commandment is pure, enlightening the eyes.
The fear of YHWH is clean, enduring forever.
  YHWH's ordinances are true, and righteous altogether.
They are more to be desired than gold, yes, than much fine gold,
  sweeter also than honey and the extract of the honeycomb.
Moreover your servant is warned by them.
  In keeping them there is great reward.
Who can discern his errors?
  Forgive me from hidden errors.

Keep back your servant also from presumptuous sins.
  Let them not have dominion over me.
Then I will be upright.
  I will be blameless and innocent of great transgression.
Let the words of my mouth and the meditation of my heart
  be acceptable in your sight,
  YHWH, my rock, and my redeemer.

....

For the Chief Musician. A Psalm by David. May YHWH answer
you in the day of trouble.
  May the name of the God of Jacob set you up on high,
  send you help from the sanctuary,

grant you support from Zion,
remember all your offerings,
and accept your burned sacrifice. Selah.
May he grant you your heart's desire,
and fulfill all your counsel.
We will triumph in your salvation.
In the name of our God, we will set up our banners.
May YHWH grant all your requests.
Now I know that YHWH saves his anointed.
He will answer him from his holy heaven,
with the saving strength of his right hand.
Some trust in chariots, and some in horses,
but we trust in the name of YHWH our God.
They are bowed down and fallen,
but we rise up, and stand upright.
Save, YHWH!
Let the King answer us when we call!

....

For the Chief Musician. A Psalm by David. The king rejoices in
your strength, YHWH!
How greatly he rejoices in your salvation!
You have given him his heart's desire,
and have not withheld the request of his lips. Selah.
For you meet him with the blessings of goodness.
You set a crown of fine gold on his head.
He asked life of you and you gave it to him,
even length of days forever and ever.
His glory is great in your salvation.
You lay honor and majesty on him.
For you make him most blessed forever.
You make him glad with joy in your presence.
For the king trusts in YHWH.
Through the loving kindness of the Most High, he shall not be
moved.
Your hand will find out all of your enemies.
Your right hand will find out those who hate you.
You will make them as a fiery furnace in the time of your anger.
YHWH will swallow them up in his wrath.
The fire shall devour them.

You will destroy their descendants from the earth,
  their posterity from among the children of men.
For they intended evil against you.
  They plotted evil against you which cannot succeed.
For you will make them turn their back,
  when you aim drawn bows at their face.
Be exalted, YHWH, in your strength,
  so we will sing and praise your power.

....

For the Chief Musician; set to "The Doe of the Morning." A
Psalm by David. My God, my God, why have you forsaken me?
  Why are you so far from helping me, and from the words of
  my groaning?
My God, I cry in the daytime, but you don't answer;
  in the night season, and am not silent.
But you are holy,
  you who inhabit the praises of Israel.
Our fathers trusted in you.
  They trusted, and you delivered them.
They cried to you, and were delivered.
  They trusted in you, and were not disappointed.
But I am a worm, and no man;
  a reproach of men, and despised by the people.
All those who see me mock me.
  They insult me with their lips. They shake their heads, saying,
  "He trusts in YHWH.
  Let him deliver him.
  Let him rescue him, since he delights in him."
But you brought me out of the womb.
  You made me trust while at my mother's breasts.
I was thrown on you from my mother's womb.
  You are my God since my mother bore me.
Don't be far from me, for trouble is near.
  For there is no one to help.
Many bulls have surrounded me.
  Strong bulls of Bashan have encircled me.
They open their mouths wide against me,
  lions tearing prey and roaring.
I am poured out like water.

All my bones are out of joint.
My heart is like wax.
> *It is melted within me.*
My strength is dried up like a potsherd.
> *My tongue sticks to the roof of my mouth.*
You have brought me into the dust of death.
For dogs have surrounded me.
> *A company of evildoers have enclosed me.*
> *They have pierced my hands and feet.*
I can count all of my bones.
They look and stare at me.
They divide my garments among them.
> *They cast lots for my clothing.*

But don't be far off, YHWH.
> *You are my help. Hurry to help me!*
Deliver my soul from the sword,
> *my precious life from the power of the dog.*
Save me from the lion's mouth!
> *Yes, you have rescued me from the horns of the wild oxen.*

I will declare your name to my brothers.
> *Among the assembly, I will praise you.*
You who fear YHWH, praise him!
> *All you descendants of Jacob, glorify him!*
> *Stand in awe of him, all you descendants of Israel!*
For he has not despised nor abhorred the affliction of the afflicted,
> *Neither has he hidden his face from him;*
> *but when he cried to him, he heard.*

My praise of you comes in the great assembly.
> *I will pay my vows before those who fear him.*
The humble shall eat and be satisfied.
> *They shall praise YHWH who seek after him.*
> *Let your hearts live forever.*
All the ends of the earth shall remember and turn to YHWH.
> *All the relatives of the nations shall worship before you.*
For the kingdom is YHWH's.
> *He is the ruler over the nations.*
All the rich ones of the earth shall eat and worship.

All those who go down to the dust shall bow before him,
  even he who can't keep his soul alive.
Posterity shall serve him.
    Future generations shall be told about the Lord.
They shall come and shall declare his righteousness to a people that shall be born,
    for he has done it.

....

A Psalm by David. YHWH *is my shepherd:*
  I shall lack nothing.
He makes me lie down in green pastures.
    He leads me beside still waters.
He restores my soul.
    He guides me in the paths of righteousness for his name's sake.
Even though I walk through the valley of the shadow of death,
    I will fear no evil, for you are with me.
Your rod and your staff,
    they comfort me.
You prepare a table before me
    in the presence of my enemies.
You anoint my head with oil.
    My cup runs over.
Surely goodness and loving kindness shall follow me all the days of my life,
    and I will dwell in YHWH*'s house forever.*

....

A Psalm by David. The earth is YHWH*'s, with its fullness;*
    the world, and those who dwell in it.
For he has founded it on the seas,
    and established it on the floods.

Who may ascend to YHWH*'s hill?*
    Who may stand in his holy place?
He who has clean hands and a pure heart;
    who has not lifted up his soul to falsehood,
    and has not sworn deceitfully.
He shall receive a blessing from YHWH*,*
    righteousness from the God of his salvation.

This is the generation of those who seek Him,
   who seek your face—even Jacob. Selah.

Lift up your heads, you gates!
   Be lifted up, you everlasting doors,
   and the King of glory will come in.
Who is the King of glory?
   YHWH strong and mighty,
   YHWH mighty in battle.
Lift up your heads, you gates;
   yes, lift them up, you everlasting doors,
   and the King of glory will come in.
Who is this King of glory?
   YHWH of Armies is the King of glory! Selah.

....

By David. To you, YHWH, I lift up my soul.
My God, I have trusted in you.
   Don't let me be shamed.
   Don't let my enemies triumph over me.
Yes, no one who waits for you will be shamed.
   They will be shamed who deal treacherously without cause.

Show me your ways, YHWH.
   Teach me your paths.
Guide me in your truth, and teach me,
   For you are the God of my salvation,
   I wait for you all day long.
YHWH, remember your tender mercies and your loving kindness,
   for they are from old times.
Don't remember the sins of my youth, nor my transgressions.
   Remember me according to your loving kindness,
   for your goodness' sake, YHWH.
Good and upright is YHWH,
   therefore he will instruct sinners in the way.
He will guide the humble in justice.
   He will teach the humble his way.
All the paths of YHWH are loving kindness and truth
   to such as keep his covenant and his testimonies.
For your name's sake, YHWH,

pardon my iniquity, for it is great.
What man is he who fears YHWH?
    He shall instruct him in the way that he shall choose.
His soul will dwell at ease.
    His offspring will inherit the land.
The friendship of YHWH is with those who fear him.
    He will show them his covenant.

My eyes are ever on YHWH,
    for he will pluck my feet out of the net.
Turn to me, and have mercy on me,
    for I am desolate and afflicted.
The troubles of my heart are enlarged.
    Oh bring me out of my distresses.
Consider my affliction and my travail.
    Forgive all my sins.
Consider my enemies, for they are many.
    They hate me with cruel hatred.
Oh keep my soul, and deliver me.
    Let me not be disappointed, for I take refuge in you.
Let integrity and uprightness preserve me,
    for I wait for you.
Redeem Israel, God,
    out of all his troubles.

....

By David. Judge me, YHWH, for I have walked in my integrity.
    I have trusted also in YHWH without wavering.
Examine me, YHWH, and prove me.
    Try my heart and my mind.
For your loving kindness is before my eyes.
    I have walked in your truth.
I have not sat with deceitful men,
    neither will I go in with hypocrites.
I hate the assembly of evildoers,
    and will not sit with the wicked.
I will wash my hands in innocence,
    so I will go about your altar, YHWH,
    that I may make the voice of thanksgiving to be heard
    and tell of all your wondrous deeds.

YHWH, I love the habitation of your house,
  the place where your glory dwells.
Don't gather my soul with sinners,
  nor my life with bloodthirsty men;
  in whose hands is wickedness,
  their right hand is full of bribes.

But as for me, I will walk in my integrity.
  Redeem me, and be merciful to me.
My foot stands in an even place.
  In the congregations I will bless YHWH.

....

By David. YHWH is my light and my salvation.
  Whom shall I fear?
YHWH is the strength of my life.
  Of whom shall I be afraid?
When evildoers came at me to eat up my flesh,
  even my adversaries and my foes, they stumbled and fell.
Though an army should encamp against me,
  my heart shall not fear.
Though war should rise against me,
  even then I will be confident.
One thing I have asked of YHWH, that I will seek after:
  that I may dwell in YHWH's house all the days of my life,
  to see YHWH's beauty,
  and to inquire in his temple.
For in the day of trouble, he will keep me secretly in his pavilion.
  In the secret place of his tabernacle, he will hide me.
  He will lift me up on a rock.
Now my head will be lifted up above my enemies around me.
I will offer sacrifices of joy in his tent.
  I will sing, yes, I will sing praises to YHWH.

Hear, YHWH, when I cry with my voice.
  Have mercy also on me, and answer me.
When you said, "Seek my face,"
  my heart said to you, "I will seek your face, YHWH."
Don't hide your face from me.
  Don't put your servant away in anger.

You have been my help.
　　Don't abandon me,
　　neither forsake me, God of my salvation.
When my father and my mother forsake me,
　　then YHWH *will take me up.*
Teach me your way, YHWH.
　　Lead me in a straight path, because of my enemies.
Don't deliver me over to the desire of my adversaries,
　　for false witnesses have risen up against me,
　　such as breathe out cruelty.
I am still confident of this:
　　I will see the goodness of YHWH *in the land of the living.*
Wait for YHWH.
　　Be strong, and let your heart take courage.
Yes, wait for YHWH.

....

By David. To you, YHWH, *I call.*
　　My rock, don't be deaf to me,
　　lest, if you are silent to me,
　　I would become like those who go down into the pit.
Hear the voice of my petitions, when I cry to you,
　　when I lift up my hands toward your Most Holy Place.
Don't draw me away with the wicked,
　　with the workers of iniquity who speak peace with their neigh-
　　bors,
　　but mischief is in their hearts.
Give them according to their work, and according to the wicked-
ness of their doings.
　　Give them according to the operation of their hands.
　　Bring back on them what they deserve.
Because they don't respect the works of YHWH,
　　nor the operation of his hands,
　　he will break them down and not build them up.

Blessed be YHWH,
　　because he has heard the voice of my petitions.
YHWH *is my strength and my shield.*
　　My heart has trusted in him, and I am helped.
Therefore my heart greatly rejoices.

With my song I will thank him.
YHWH *is their strength.*
   He is a stronghold of salvation to his anointed.
Save your people,
   and bless your inheritance.
Be their shepherd also,
   and bear them up forever.

      ....

A Psalm by David. Ascribe to YHWH, *you sons of the mighty,*
   ascribe to YHWH *glory and strength.*
Ascribe to YHWH *the glory due to his name.*
   Worship YHWH *in holy array.*

YHWH'*s voice is on the waters.*
   The God of glory thunders, even YHWH *on many waters.*
YHWH'*s voice is powerful.*
   YHWH'*s voice is full of majesty.*
YHWH'*s voice breaks the cedars.*
   Yes, YHWH *breaks in pieces the cedars of Lebanon.*
He makes them also to skip like a calf;
   Lebanon and Sirion like a young, wild ox.
YHWH'*s voice strikes with flashes of lightning.*
   YHWH'*s voice shakes the wilderness.*
   YHWH *shakes the wilderness of Kadesh.*
YHWH'*s voice makes the deer calve,*
   and strips the forests bare.
   In his temple everything says, "Glory!"

YHWH *sat enthroned at the Flood.*
   Yes, YHWH *sits as King forever.*
YHWH *will give strength to his people.*
   YHWH *will bless his people with peace.*

      ....

A Psalm. A Song for the Dedication of the Temple. By David. I
will extol you, YHWH, *for you have raised me up,*
   and have not made my foes to rejoice over me.
YHWH *my God, I cried to you,*
   and you have healed me.

YHWH, you have brought up my soul from Sheol.
   You have kept me alive, that I should not go down to the pit.
Sing praise to YHWH, you saints of his.
   Give thanks to his holy name.
For his anger is but for a moment.
   His favor is for a lifetime.
Weeping may stay for the night,
   but joy comes in the morning.
As for me, I said in my prosperity,
   "I shall never be moved."
You, YHWH, when you favored me, made my mountain stand strong;
   but when you hid your face, I was troubled.
I cried to you, YHWH.
   I made supplication to the Lord:
"What profit is there in my destruction, if I go down to the pit?
   Shall the dust praise you?
   Shall it declare your truth?
Hear, YHWH, and have mercy on me.
   YHWH, be my helper."
You have turned my mourning into dancing for me.
   You have removed my sackcloth, and clothed me with gladness,
   to the end that my heart may sing praise to you, and not be silent.
YHWH my God, I will give thanks to you forever!

....

For the Chief Musician. A Psalm by David. In you, YHWH, I take refuge.
   Let me never be disappointed.
   Deliver me in your righteousness.
Bow down your ear to me.
   Deliver me speedily.
Be to me a strong rock,
   a house of defense to save me.
For you are my rock and my fortress,
   therefore for your name's sake lead me and guide me.
Pluck me out of the net that they have laid secretly for me,
   for you are my stronghold.
Into your hand I commend my spirit.

You redeem me, YHWH, God of truth.
I hate those who regard lying vanities,
but I trust in YHWH.
I will be glad and rejoice in your loving kindness,
for you have seen my affliction.
You have known my soul in adversities.
You have not shut me up into the hand of the enemy.
You have set my feet in a large place.
Have mercy on me, YHWH, for I am in distress.
My eye, my soul, and my body waste away with grief.
For my life is spent with sorrow,
my years with sighing.
My strength fails because of my iniquity.
My bones are wasted away.
Because of all my adversaries I have become utterly contemptible
to my neighbors,
a horror to my acquaintances.
Those who saw me on the street fled from me.
I am forgotten from their hearts like a dead man.
I am like broken pottery.
For I have heard the slander of many, terror on every side,
while they conspire together against me,
they plot to take away my life.
But I trust in you, YHWH.
I said, "You are my God."
My times are in your hand.
Deliver me from the hand of my enemies, and from those who
persecute me.
Make your face to shine on your servant.
Save me in your loving kindness.
Let me not be disappointed, YHWH, for I have called on you.
Let the wicked be disappointed.
Let them be silent in Sheol.
Let the lying lips be mute,
which speak against the righteous insolently, with pride and
contempt.
Oh how great is your goodness,
which you have laid up for those who fear you,
which you have worked for those who take refuge in you,
before the sons of men!

In the shelter of your presence you will hide them from the plotting of man.

> *You will keep them secretly in a dwelling away from the strife of tongues.*

Praise be to YHWH,

> *for he has shown me his marvelous loving kindness in a strong city.*

As for me, I said in my haste, "I am cut off from before your eyes."

> *Nevertheless you heard the voice of my petitions when I cried to you.*

Oh love YHWH, all you his saints!

> *YHWH preserves the faithful,*

and fully recompenses him who behaves arrogantly.

Be strong, and let your heart take courage,

> *all you who hope in YHWH.*

....

By David. A contemplative psalm. Blessed is he whose disobedience is forgiven,

> *whose sin is covered.*

Blessed is the man to whom YHWH doesn't impute iniquity,

> *in whose spirit there is no deceit.*

When I kept silence, my bones wasted away through my groaning all day long.

For day and night your hand was heavy on me.

> *My strength was sapped in the heat of summer. Selah.*

I acknowledged my sin to you.

> *I didn't hide my iniquity.*

I said, I will confess my transgressions to YHWH,

> *and you forgave the iniquity of my sin. Selah.*

For this, let everyone who is godly pray to you in a time when you may be found.

> *Surely when the great waters overflow, they shall not reach to him.*

You are my hiding place.

> *You will preserve me from trouble.*

> *You will surround me with songs of deliverance. Selah.*

I will instruct you and teach you in the way which you shall go.

> *I will counsel you with my eye on you.*

Don't be like the horse, or like the mule, which have no under-

standing,

who are controlled by bit and bridle, or else they will not come near to you.

Many sorrows come to the wicked,

but loving kindness shall surround him who trusts in YHWH.

Be glad in YHWH, and rejoice, you righteous!

Shout for joy, all you who are upright in heart!

....

Rejoice in YHWH, you righteous!

Praise is fitting for the upright.

Give thanks to YHWH with the lyre.

Sing praises to him with the harp of ten strings.

Sing to him a new song.

Play skillfully with a shout of joy!

For YHWH's word is right.

All his work is done in faithfulness.

He loves righteousness and justice.

The earth is full of the loving kindness of YHWH.

By YHWH's word, the heavens were made:

all their army by the breath of his mouth.

He gathers the waters of the sea together as a heap.

He lays up the deeps in storehouses.

Let all the earth fear YHWH.

Let all the inhabitants of the world stand in awe of him.

For he spoke, and it was done.

He commanded, and it stood firm.

YHWH brings the counsel of the nations to nothing.

He makes the thoughts of the peoples to be of no effect.

The counsel of YHWH stands fast forever,

the thoughts of his heart to all generations.

Blessed is the nation whose God is YHWH,

the people whom he has chosen for his own inheritance.

YHWH looks from heaven.

He sees all the sons of men.

From the place of his habitation he looks out on all the inhabitants of the earth,

he who fashions all of their hearts;

and he considers all of their works.

There is no king saved by the multitude of an army.

A mighty man is not delivered by great strength.
A horse is a vain thing for safety,
   neither does he deliver any by his great power.
Behold, YHWH's eye is on those who fear him,
   on those who hope in his loving kindness,
   to deliver their soul from death,
   to keep them alive in famine.
Our soul has waited for YHWH.
   He is our help and our shield.
For our heart rejoices in him,
   because we have trusted in his holy name.
Let your loving kindness be on us, YHWH,
   since we have hoped in you.

....

By David; when he pretended to be insane before Abimelech, who
drove him away, and he departed. I will bless YHWH at all times.
   His praise will always be in my mouth.
My soul shall boast in YHWH.
   The humble shall hear of it and be glad.
Oh magnify YHWH with me.
   Let's exalt his name together.
I sought YHWH, and he answered me,
   and delivered me from all my fears.
They looked to him, and were radiant.
   Their faces shall never be covered with shame.
This poor man cried, and YHWH heard him,
   and saved him out of all his troubles.
YHWH's angel encamps around those who fear him,
   and delivers them.
Oh taste and see that YHWH is good.
   Blessed is the man who takes refuge in him.
Oh fear YHWH, you his saints,
   for there is no lack with those who fear him.
The young lions do lack, and suffer hunger,
   but those who seek YHWH shall not lack any good thing.

Come, you children, listen to me.
   I will teach you the fear of YHWH.
Who is someone who desires life,

and loves many days, that he may see good?
Keep your tongue from evil,
  and your lips from speaking lies.
Depart from evil, and do good.
  Seek peace, and pursue it.
YHWH's eyes are toward the righteous.
  His ears listen to their cry.
YHWH's face is against those who do evil,
  to cut off their memory from the earth.
The righteous cry, and YHWH hears,
  and delivers them out of all their troubles.
YHWH is near to those who have a broken heart,
  and saves those who have a crushed spirit.
Many are the afflictions of the righteous,
  but YHWH delivers him out of them all.
He protects all of his bones.
  Not one of them is broken.
Evil shall kill the wicked.
  Those who hate the righteous shall be condemned.
YHWH redeems the soul of his servants.
  None of those who take refuge in him shall be condemned.

....

By David. Contend, YHWH, with those who contend with me.
  Fight against those who fight against me.
Take hold of shield and buckler,
  and stand up for my help.
Brandish the spear and block those who pursue me.
  Tell my soul, "I am your salvation."
Let those who seek after my soul be disappointed and brought to
dishonor.
  Let those who plot my ruin be turned back and confounded.
Let them be as chaff before the wind,
  YHWH's angel driving them on.
Let their way be dark and slippery,
  YHWH's angel pursuing them.
For without cause they have hidden their net in a pit for me.
  Without cause they have dug a pit for my soul.
Let destruction come on him unawares.
  Let his net that he has hidden catch himself.

Let him fall into that destruction.

My soul shall be joyful in YHWH.
> *It shall rejoice in his salvation.*
All my bones shall say, "YHWH, who is like you,
>> *who delivers the poor from him who is too strong for him;*
>> *yes, the poor and the needy from him who robs him?"*
Unrighteous witnesses rise up.
> *They ask me about things that I don't know about.*
They reward me evil for good,
> *to the bereaving of my soul.*

But as for me, when they were sick, my clothing was sackcloth.
> *I afflicted my soul with fasting.*
> *My prayer returned into my own bosom.*
I behaved myself as though it had been my friend or my brother.
> *I bowed down mourning, as one who mourns his mother.*
But in my adversity, they rejoiced, and gathered themselves together.
> *The attackers gathered themselves together against me, and I didn't know it.*
> *They tore at me, and didn't cease.*
Like the profane mockers in feasts,
> *they gnashed their teeth at me.*
Lord, how long will you look on?
> *Rescue my soul from their destruction,*
> *my precious life from the lions.*
I will give you thanks in the great assembly.
> *I will praise you among many people.*
Don't let those who are my enemies wrongfully rejoice over me;
> *neither let those who hate me without a cause wink their eyes.*
For they don't speak peace,
> *but they devise deceitful words against those who are quiet in the land.*
Yes, they opened their mouth wide against me.
> *They said, "Aha! Aha! Our eye has seen it!"*
You have seen it, YHWH. Don't keep silent.
> *Lord, don't be far from me.*
Wake up! Rise up to defend me, my God!
> *My Lord, contend for me!*

Vindicate me, YHWH my God, according to your righteousness.
Don't let them gloat over me.
Don't let them say in their heart, "Aha! That's the way we want it!"
Don't let them say, "We have swallowed him up!"
Let them be disappointed and confounded together who rejoice at my calamity.
Let them be clothed with shame and dishonor who magnify themselves against me.

Let those who favor my righteous cause shout for joy and be glad.
Yes, let them say continually, "May YHWH be magnified, who has pleasure in the prosperity of his servant!"
My tongue shall talk about your righteousness and about your praise all day long.

....

For the Chief Musician. By David, the servant of YHWH. A revelation is within my heart about the disobedience of the wicked:
"There is no fear of God before his eyes."
For he flatters himself in his own eyes,
too much to detect and hate his sin.
The words of his mouth are iniquity and deceit.
He has ceased to be wise and to do good.
He plots iniquity on his bed.
He sets himself in a way that is not good.
He doesn't abhor evil.

Your loving kindness, YHWH, is in the heavens.
Your faithfulness reaches to the skies.
Your righteousness is like the mountains of God.
Your judgments are like a great deep.
YHWH, you preserve man and animal.
How precious is your loving kindness, God!
The children of men take refuge under the shadow of your wings.
They shall be abundantly satisfied with the abundance of your house.
You will make them drink of the river of your pleasures.
For with you is the spring of life.

In your light we will see light.
Oh continue your loving kindness to those who know you,
    your righteousness to the upright in heart.
Don't let the foot of pride come against me.
    Don't let the hand of the wicked drive me away.
There the workers of iniquity are fallen.
    They are thrust down, and shall not be able to rise.

....

By David. Don't fret because of evildoers,
    neither be envious against those who work unrighteousness.
For they shall soon be cut down like the grass,
    and wither like the green herb.
Trust in YHWH, and do good.
    Dwell in the land, and enjoy safe pasture.
Also delight yourself in YHWH,
    and he will give you the desires of your heart.
Commit your way to YHWH.
    Trust also in him, and he will do this:
he will make your righteousness shine out like light,
    and your justice as the noon day sun.
Rest in YHWH, and wait patiently for him.
    Don't fret because of him who prospers in his way,
    because of the man who makes wicked plots happen.
Cease from anger, and forsake wrath.
    Don't fret; it leads only to evildoing.
For evildoers shall be cut off,
    but those who wait for YHWH shall inherit the land.
For yet a little while, and the wicked will be no more.
    Yes, though you look for his place, he isn't there.
But the humble shall inherit the land,
    and shall delight themselves in the abundance of peace.
The wicked plots against the just,
    and gnashes at him with his teeth.
The Lord will laugh at him,
    for he sees that his day is coming.
The wicked have drawn out the sword, and have bent their bow,
    to cast down the poor and needy,
    to kill those who are upright on the path.
Their sword shall enter into their own heart.

Their bows shall be broken.
Better is a little that the righteous has,
  than the abundance of many wicked.
For the arms of the wicked shall be broken,
  but YHWH upholds the righteous.
YHWH knows the days of the perfect.
  Their inheritance shall be forever.
They shall not be disappointed in the time of evil.
  In the days of famine they shall be satisfied.

But the wicked shall perish.
  The enemies of YHWH shall be like the beauty of the fields.
  They will vanish—
  vanish like smoke.
The wicked borrow, and don't pay back,
  but the righteous give generously.
For such as are blessed by him shall inherit the land.
  Those who are cursed by him shall be cut off.
A man's steps are established by YHWH.
  He delights in his way.
Though he stumble, he shall not fall,
  for YHWH holds him up with his hand.
I have been young, and now am old,
  yet I have not seen the righteous forsaken,
  nor his children begging for bread.
All day long he deals graciously, and lends.
  His offspring is blessed.
Depart from evil, and do good.
  Live securely forever.
For YHWH loves justice,
  and doesn't forsake his saints.
  They are preserved forever,
  but the children of the wicked shall be cut off.
The righteous shall inherit the land,
  and live in it forever.

The mouth of the righteous talks of wisdom.
  His tongue speaks justice.
The law of his God is in his heart.
  None of his steps shall slide.

The wicked watch the righteous,
and seek to kill him.
YHWH will not leave him in his hand,
nor condemn him when he is judged.
Wait for YHWH, and keep his way,
and he will exalt you to inherit the land.
When the wicked are cut off, you shall see it.

I have seen the wicked in great power,
spreading himself like a green tree in its native soil.
But he passed away, and behold, he was not.
Yes, I sought him, but he could not be found.
Mark the perfect man, and see the upright,
for there is a future for the man of peace.
As for transgressors, they shall be destroyed together.
The future of the wicked shall be cut off.
But the salvation of the righteous is from YHWH.
He is their stronghold in the time of trouble.
YHWH helps them and rescues them.
He rescues them from the wicked and saves them,
because they have taken refuge in him.

....

A Psalm by David, for a memorial. YHWH, don't rebuke me in
your wrath,
neither chasten me in your hot displeasure.
For your arrows have pierced me,
your hand presses hard on me.
There is no soundness in my flesh because of your indignation,
neither is there any health in my bones because of my sin.
For my iniquities have gone over my head.
As a heavy burden, they are too heavy for me.
My wounds are loathsome and corrupt
because of my foolishness.
I am in pain and bowed down greatly.
I go mourning all day long.
For my waist is filled with burning.
There is no soundness in my flesh.
I am faint and severely bruised.
I have groaned by reason of the anguish of my heart.

Lord, all my desire is before you.
My groaning is not hidden from you.
My heart throbs.
My strength fails me.
As for the light of my eyes, it has also left me.
My lovers and my friends stand aloof from my plague.
My kinsmen stand far away.
They also who seek after my life lay snares.
Those who seek my hurt speak mischievous things,
and meditate deceits all day long.
But I, as a deaf man, don't hear.
I am as a mute man who doesn't open his mouth.
Yes, I am as a man who doesn't hear,
in whose mouth are no reproofs.
For I hope in you, YHWH.
You will answer, Lord my God.
For I said, "Don't let them gloat over me,
or exalt themselves over me when my foot slips."
For I am ready to fall.
My pain is continually before me.
For I will declare my iniquity.
I will be sorry for my sin.
But my enemies are vigorous and many.
Those who hate me without reason are numerous.
They who render evil for good are also adversaries to me,
because I follow what is good.
Don't forsake me, YHWH.
My God, don't be far from me.
Hurry to help me,
Lord, my salvation.

....

For the Chief Musician. For Jeduthun. A Psalm by David. I said,
"I will watch my ways, so that I don't sin with my tongue.
I will keep my mouth with a bridle while the wicked is before
me."
I was mute with silence.
I held my peace, even from good.
My sorrow was stirred.
My heart was hot within me.

While I meditated, the fire burned.
I spoke with my tongue:
   "YHWH, *show me my end,*
   what is the measure of my days.
   Let me know how frail I am.
Behold, you have made my days hand widths.
   My lifetime is as nothing before you.
Surely every man stands as a breath." Selah.
"Surely every man walks like a shadow.
   Surely they busy themselves in vain.
   He heaps up, and doesn't know who shall gather.
Now, Lord, what do I wait for?
   My hope is in you.
Deliver me from all my transgressions.
   Don't make me the reproach of the foolish.
I was mute.
   I didn't open my mouth,
   because you did it.
Remove your scourge away from me.
   I am overcome by the blow of your hand.
When you rebuke and correct man for iniquity,
   you consume his wealth like a moth.
Surely every man is but a breath." Selah.
"Hear my prayer, YHWH, *and give ear to my cry.*
   Don't be silent at my tears.
For I am a stranger with you,
   a foreigner, as all my fathers were.
Oh spare me, that I may recover strength,
   before I go away and exist no more."

....

For the Chief Musician. A Psalm by David. I waited patiently for
YHWH.
   He turned to me, and heard my cry.
He brought me up also out of a horrible pit,
   out of the miry clay.
He set my feet on a rock,
   and gave me a firm place to stand.
He has put a new song in my mouth, even praise to our God.
   Many shall see it, and fear, and shall trust in YHWH.

Blessed is the man who makes YHWH his trust,
and doesn't respect the proud, nor such as turn away to lies.
Many, YHWH, my God, are the wonderful works which you have done,
and your thoughts which are toward us.
They can't be declared back to you.
If I would declare and speak of them, they are more than can be counted.
Sacrifice and offering you didn't desire.
You have opened my ears.
You have not required burnt offering and sin offering.
Then I said, "Behold, I have come.
It is written about me in the book in the scroll.
I delight to do your will, my God.
Yes, your law is within my heart."
I have proclaimed glad news of righteousness in the great assembly.
Behold, I will not seal my lips, YHWH, you know.
I have not hidden your righteousness within my heart.
I have declared your faithfulness and your salvation.
I have not concealed your loving kindness and your truth from the great assembly.
Don't withhold your tender mercies from me, YHWH.
Let your loving kindness and your truth continually preserve me.
For innumerable evils have surrounded me.
My iniquities have overtaken me, so that I am not able to look up.
They are more than the hairs of my head.
My heart has failed me.
Be pleased, YHWH, to deliver me.
Hurry to help me, YHWH.
Let them be disappointed and confounded together who seek after my soul to destroy it.
Let them be turned backward and brought to dishonor who delight in my hurt.
Let them be desolate by reason of their shame that tell me, "Aha! Aha!"
Let all those who seek you rejoice and be glad in you.
Let such as love your salvation say continually, "Let YHWH be exalted!"

But I am poor and needy.
May the Lord think about me.
You are my help and my deliverer.
Don't delay, my God.

....

For the Chief Musician. A Psalm by David. Blessed is he who
considers the poor.
YHWH will deliver him in the day of evil.
YHWH will preserve him, and keep him alive.
He shall be blessed on the earth,
and he will not surrender him to the will of his enemies.
YHWH will sustain him on his sickbed,
and restore him from his bed of illness.
I said, "YHWH, have mercy on me!
Heal me, for I have sinned against you."
My enemies speak evil against me:
"When will he die, and his name perish?"
If he comes to see me, he speaks falsehood.
His heart gathers iniquity to itself.
When he goes abroad, he tells it.
All who hate me whisper together against me.
They imagine the worst for me.
"An evil disease", they say, "has afflicted him.
Now that he lies he shall rise up no more."
Yes, my own familiar friend, in whom I trusted,
who ate bread with me,
has lifted up his heel against me.

But you, YHWH, have mercy on me, and raise me up,
that I may repay them.
By this I know that you delight in me,
because my enemy doesn't triumph over me.
As for me, you uphold me in my integrity,
and set me in your presence forever.

Blessed be YHWH, the God of Israel,
from everlasting and to everlasting!
Amen and amen.

....

BOOK 2

For the Chief Musician. A contemplation by the sons of Korah. As
the deer pants for the water brooks,
    so my soul pants after you, God.
My soul thirsts for God, for the living God.
    When shall I come and appear before God?
My tears have been my food day and night,
    while they continually ask me, "Where is your God?"
These things I remember, and pour out my soul within me,
    how I used to go with the crowd, and led them to God's house,
    with the voice of joy and praise, a multitude keeping a holy
    day.
Why are you in despair, my soul?
    Why are you disturbed within me?
Hope in God!
    For I shall still praise him for the saving help of his presence.
My God, my soul is in despair within me.
    Therefore I remember you from the land of the Jordan,
    the heights of Hermon, from the hill Mizar.
Deep calls to deep at the noise of your waterfalls.
    All your waves and your billows have swept over me.

YHWH will command his loving kindness in the daytime.
    In the night his song shall be with me:
    a prayer to the God of my life.
I will ask God, my rock, "Why have you forgotten me?
    Why do I go mourning because of the oppression of the ene-
    my?"
As with a sword in my bones, my adversaries reproach me,
    while they continually ask me, "Where is your God?"
Why are you in despair, my soul?
    Why are you disturbed within me?
Hope in God! For I shall still praise him,
    the saving help of my countenance, and my God.

....

Vindicate me, God, and plead my cause against an ungodly
nation.
    Oh, deliver me from deceitful and wicked men.
For you are the God of my strength. Why have you rejected me?

Why do I go mourning because of the oppression of the enemy?
Oh, send out your light and your truth.
> Let them lead me.
> Let them bring me to your holy hill,
> to your tents.
Then I will go to the altar of God,
> to God, my exceeding joy.
I will praise you on the harp, God, my God.
Why are you in despair, my soul?
> Why are you disturbed within me?
Hope in God!
> For I shall still praise him:
> my Savior, my helper, and my God.

....

For the Chief Musician. By the sons of Korah. A contemplative
psalm. We have heard with our ears, God;
> our fathers have told us what work you did in their days,
> in the days of old.
You drove out the nations with your hand,
> but you planted them.
You afflicted the peoples,
> but you spread them abroad.
For they didn't get the land in possession by their own sword,
> neither did their own arm save them;
but your right hand, your arm, and the light of your face,
> because you were favorable to them.
You are my King, God.
> Command victories for Jacob!
Through you, will we push down our adversaries.
> Through your name, we will tread down those who rise up
> against us.
For I will not trust in my bow,
> neither shall my sword save me.
But you have saved us from our adversaries,
> and have shamed those who hate us.
In God we have made our boast all day long,
> we will give thanks to your name forever. Selah.

But now you rejected us, and brought us to dishonor,

and don't go out with our armies.
You make us turn back from the adversary.
    Those who hate us take plunder for themselves.
You have made us like sheep for food,
    and have scattered us among the nations.
You sell your people for nothing,
    and have gained nothing from their sale.
You make us a reproach to our neighbors,
    a scoffing and a derision to those who are around us.
You make us a byword among the nations,
    a shaking of the head among the peoples.
All day long my dishonor is before me,
    and shame covers my face,
    at the taunt of one who reproaches and verbally abuses,
    because of the enemy and the avenger.
All this has come on us,
    yet we haven't forgotten you.
    We haven't been false to your covenant.
Our heart has not turned back,
    neither have our steps strayed from your path,
    though you have crushed us in the haunt of jackals,
    and covered us with the shadow of death.
If we have forgotten the name of our God,
    or spread out our hands to a strange god,
    won't God search this out?
    For he knows the secrets of the heart.
Yes, for your sake we are killed all day long.
    We are regarded as sheep for the slaughter.
Wake up!
    Why do you sleep, Lord?
Arise!
    Don't reject us forever.
Why do you hide your face,
    and forget our affliction and our oppression?
For our soul is bowed down to the dust.
    Our body clings to the earth.
Rise up to help us.
    Redeem us for your loving kindness' sake.

....

For the Chief Musician. Set to "The Lilies." A contemplation by the sons of Korah. A wedding song. My heart overflows with a noble theme.

> *I recite my verses for the king.*
> *My tongue is like the pen of a skillful writer.*

You are the most excellent of the sons of men.

> *Grace has anointed your lips,*
> *therefore God has blessed you forever.*

Strap your sword on your thigh, mighty one:

> *your splendor and your majesty.*

In your majesty ride on victoriously on behalf of truth, humility, and righteousness.

> *Let your right hand display awesome deeds.*

Your arrows are sharp.

> *The nations fall under you, with arrows in the heart of the king's enemies.*

Your throne, God, is forever and ever.

> *A scepter of equity is the scepter of your kingdom.*

You have loved righteousness, and hated wickedness.

> *Therefore God, your God, has anointed you with the oil of gladness above your fellows.*

All your garments smell like myrrh, aloes, and cassia.

> *Out of ivory palaces stringed instruments have made you glad.*

Kings' daughters are among your honorable women.

> *At your right hand the queen stands in gold of Ophir.*

Listen, daughter, consider, and turn your ear.

> *Forget your own people, and also your father's house.*
> *So the king will desire your beauty,*
> *honor him, for he is your lord.*

The daughter of Tyre comes with a gift.

> *The rich among the people entreat your favor.*

The princess inside is all glorious.

> *Her clothing is interwoven with gold.*

She shall be led to the king in embroidered work.

> *The virgins, her companions who follow her, shall be brought to you.*

With gladness and rejoicing they shall be led.

> *They shall enter into the king's palace.*

Your sons will take the place of your fathers.

> *You shall make them princes in all the earth.*

I will make your name to be remembered in all generations.
Therefore the peoples shall give you thanks forever and ever.

....

For the Chief Musician. By the sons of Korah. According to Alam-
oth. God is our refuge and strength,
a very present help in trouble.
Therefore we won't be afraid, though the earth changes,
though the mountains are shaken into the heart of the seas;
though its waters roar and are troubled,
though the mountains tremble with their swelling. Selah.

There is a river, the streams of which make the city of God glad,
the holy place of the tents of the Most High.
God is within her. She shall not be moved.
God will help her at dawn.
The nations raged. The kingdoms were moved.
He lifted his voice and the earth melted.
YHWH of Armies is with us.
The God of Jacob is our refuge. Selah.

Come, see YHWH's works,
what desolations he has made in the earth.
He makes wars cease to the end of the earth.
He breaks the bow, and shatters the spear.
He burns the chariots in the fire.
"Be still, and know that I am God.
I will be exalted among the nations.
I will be exalted in the earth."
YHWH of Armies is with us.
The God of Jacob is our refuge. Selah.

....

For the Chief Musician. A Psalm by the sons of Korah. Oh clap
your hands, all you nations.
Shout to God with the voice of triumph!
For YHWH Most High is awesome.
He is a great King over all the earth.
He subdues nations under us,

and peoples under our feet.
He chooses our inheritance for us,
  the glory of Jacob whom he loved. Selah.
God has gone up with a shout,
  YHWH with the sound of a trumpet.
Sing praises to God! Sing praises!
  Sing praises to our King! Sing praises!
For God is the King of all the earth.
  Sing praises with understanding.
God reigns over the nations.
  God sits on his holy throne.
The princes of the peoples are gathered together,
the people of the God of Abraham.
  For the shields of the earth belong to God.
  He is greatly exalted!

....

A Song. A Psalm by the sons of Korah. Great is YHWH, and greatly
to be praised,
  in the city of our God, in his holy mountain.
Beautiful in elevation, the joy of the whole earth,
  is Mount Zion, on the north sides,
  the city of the great King.
God has shown himself in her citadels as a refuge.
For, behold, the kings assembled themselves,
  they passed by together.
They saw it, then they were amazed.
  They were dismayed.
  They hurried away.
Trembling took hold of them there,
  pain, as of a woman in travail.
With the east wind, you break the ships of Tarshish.
As we have heard, so we have seen,
  in the city of YHWH of Armies, in the city of our God.
God will establish it forever. Selah.
We have thought about your loving kindness, God,
  in the middle of your temple.
As is your name, God,
  so is your praise to the ends of the earth.
  Your right hand is full of righteousness.

Let Mount Zion be glad!
Let the daughters of Judah rejoice because of your judgments.
Walk about Zion, and go around her.
Number its towers.
Notice her bulwarks.
Consider her palaces,
that you may tell it to the next generation.
For this God is our God forever and ever.
He will be our guide even to death.

....

For the Chief Musician. A Psalm by the sons of Korah. Hear this,
all you peoples.
Listen, all you inhabitants of the world,
both low and high,
rich and poor together.
My mouth will speak words of wisdom.
My heart will utter understanding.
I will incline my ear to a proverb.
I will solve my riddle on the harp.
Why should I fear in the days of evil,
when iniquity at my heels surrounds me?
Those who trust in their wealth,
and boast in the multitude of their riches—
none of them can by any means redeem his brother,
nor give God a ransom for him.
For the redemption of their life is costly,
no payment is ever enough,
that he should live on forever,
that he should not see corruption.
For he sees that wise men die;
likewise the fool and the senseless perish,
and leave their wealth to others.
Their inward thought is that their houses will endure forever,
and their dwelling places to all generations.
They name their lands after themselves.
But man, despite his riches, doesn't endure.
He is like the animals that perish.

This is the destiny of those who are foolish,

and of those who approve their sayings. Selah.
They are appointed as a flock for Sheol.
  Death shall be their shepherd.
The upright shall have dominion over them in the morning.
  Their beauty shall decay in Sheol,
  far from their mansion.
But God will redeem my soul from the power of Sheol,
  for he will receive me. Selah.
Don't be afraid when a man is made rich,
  when the glory of his house is increased;
for when he dies he will carry nothing away.
  His glory won't descend after him.
Though while he lived he blessed his soul—
  and men praise you when you do well for yourself—
he shall go to the generation of his fathers.
  They shall never see the light.
A man who has riches without understanding,
  is like the animals that perish.

....

A Psalm by Asaph. The Mighty One, God, YHWH, speaks,
  and calls the earth from sunrise to sunset.
Out of Zion, the perfection of beauty,
  God shines out.
Our God comes, and does not keep silent.
  A fire devours before him.
  It is very stormy around him.
He calls to the heavens above,
  to the earth, that he may judge his people:
"Gather my saints together to me,
  those who have made a covenant with me by sacrifice."
The heavens shall declare his righteousness,
  for God himself is judge. Selah.
"Hear, my people, and I will speak.
  Israel, I will testify against you.
I am God, your God.
I don't rebuke you for your sacrifices.
  Your burnt offerings are continually before me.
I have no need for a bull from your stall,
  nor male goats from your pens.

For every animal of the forest is mine,
and the livestock on a thousand hills.
I know all the birds of the mountains.
The wild animals of the field are mine.
If I were hungry, I would not tell you,
for the world is mine, and all that is in it.
Will I eat the meat of bulls,
or drink the blood of goats?
Offer to God the sacrifice of thanksgiving.
Pay your vows to the Most High.
Call on me in the day of trouble.
I will deliver you, and you will honor me."

But to the wicked God says,
"What right do you have to declare my statutes,
that you have taken my covenant on your lips,
since you hate instruction,
and throw my words behind you?
When you saw a thief, you consented with him,
and have participated with adulterers.

"You give your mouth to evil.
Your tongue frames deceit.
You sit and speak against your brother.
You slander your own mother's son.
You have done these things, and I kept silent.
You thought that I was just like you.
I will rebuke you, and accuse you in front of your eyes.

"Now consider this, you who forget God,
lest I tear you into pieces, and there be no one to deliver.
Whoever offers the sacrifice of thanksgiving glorifies me,
and prepares his way so that I will show God's salvation to
him."

....

For the Chief Musician. A Psalm by David, when Nathan the
prophet came to him, after he had gone in to Bathsheba. Have
mercy on me, God, according to your loving kindness.
According to the multitude of your tender mercies, blot out my

transgressions.
Wash me thoroughly from my iniquity.
    Cleanse me from my sin.
For I know my transgressions.
    My sin is constantly before me.
Against you, and you only, I have sinned,
    and done that which is evil in your sight,
so you may be proved right when you speak,
    and justified when you judge.
Behold, I was born in iniquity.
    My mother conceived me in sin.
Behold, you desire truth in the inward parts.
    You teach me wisdom in the inmost place.
Purify me with hyssop, and I will be clean.
    Wash me, and I will be whiter than snow.
Let me hear joy and gladness,
    that the bones which you have broken may rejoice.
Hide your face from my sins,
    and blot out all of my iniquities.
Create in me a clean heart, O God.
    Renew a right spirit within me.
Don't throw me from your presence,
    and don't take your Holy Spirit from me.
Restore to me the joy of your salvation.
    Uphold me with a willing spirit.
Then I will teach transgressors your ways.
    Sinners will be converted to you.
Deliver me from the guilt of bloodshed, O God, the God of my
salvation.
    My tongue will sing aloud of your righteousness.
Lord, open my lips.
    My mouth will declare your praise.
For you don't delight in sacrifice, or else I would give it.
    You have no pleasure in burnt offering.
The sacrifices of God are a broken spirit.
    O God, you will not despise a broken and contrite heart.

Do well in your good pleasure to Zion.
    Build the walls of Jerusalem.
Then you will delight in the sacrifices of righteousness,

in burnt offerings and in whole burnt offerings.
Then they will offer bulls on your altar.

....

For the Chief Musician. A contemplation by David, when Doeg
the Edomite came and told Saul, "David has come to Ahimelech's
house." Why do you boast of mischief, mighty man?
God's loving kindness endures continually.
Your tongue plots destruction,
like a sharp razor, working deceitfully.
You love evil more than good,
lying rather than speaking the truth. Selah.
You love all devouring words,
you deceitful tongue.
God will likewise destroy you forever.
He will take you up, and pluck you out of your tent,
and root you out of the land of the living. Selah.
The righteous also will see it, and fear,
and laugh at him, saying,
"Behold, this is the man who didn't make God his strength,
but trusted in the abundance of his riches,
and strengthened himself in his wickedness."
But as for me, I am like a green olive tree in God's house.
I trust in God's loving kindness forever and ever.
I will give you thanks forever, because you have done it.
I will hope in your name, for it is good,
in the presence of your saints.

....

For the Chief Musician. To the tune of "Mahalath." A contempla-
tion by David. The fool has said in his heart, "There is no God."
They are corrupt, and have done abominable iniquity.
There is no one who does good.
God looks down from heaven on the children of men,
to see if there are any who understood,
who seek after God.
Every one of them has gone back.
They have become filthy together.
There is no one who does good, no, not one.
Have the workers of iniquity no knowledge,

who eat up my people as they eat bread,
and don't call on God?
There they were in great fear, where no fear was,
for God has scattered the bones of him who encamps against
you.
You have put them to shame,
because God has rejected them.
Oh that the salvation of Israel would come out of Zion!
When God brings back his people from captivity,
then Jacob shall rejoice,
and Israel shall be glad.

....

For the Chief Musician. On stringed instruments. A contempla-
tion by David, when the Ziphites came and said to Saul, "Isn't
David hiding himself among us?" Save me, God, by your name.
Vindicate me in your might.
Hear my prayer, God.
Listen to the words of my mouth.
For strangers have risen up against me.
Violent men have sought after my soul.
They haven't set God before them. Selah.
Behold, God is my helper.
The Lord is the one who sustains my soul.
He will repay the evil to my enemies.
Destroy them in your truth.
With a free will offering, I will sacrifice to you.
I will give thanks to your name, YHWH, for it is good.
For he has delivered me out of all trouble.
My eye has seen triumph over my enemies.

....

For the Chief Musician. On stringed instruments. A contempla-
tion by David. Listen to my prayer, God.
Don't hide yourself from my supplication.
Attend to me, and answer me.
I am restless in my complaint,
and moan because of the voice of the enemy,
because of the oppression of the wicked.
For they bring suffering on me.

In anger they hold a grudge against me.
My heart is severely pained within me.
    The terrors of death have fallen on me.
Fearfulness and trembling have come on me.
    Horror has overwhelmed me.
I said, "Oh that I had wings like a dove!
    Then I would fly away, and be at rest.
Behold, then I would wander far off.
    I would lodge in the wilderness." Selah.
"I would hurry to a shelter from the stormy wind and storm."
Confuse them, Lord, and confound their language,
    for I have seen violence and strife in the city.
Day and night they prowl around on its walls.
    Malice and abuse are also within her.
Destructive forces are within her.
    Threats and lies don't depart from her streets.
For it was not an enemy who insulted me,
    then I could have endured it.
Neither was it he who hated me who raised himself up against
me,
    then I would have hidden myself from him.
But it was you, a man like me,
    my companion, and my familiar friend.
We took sweet fellowship together.
    We walked in God's house with company.
Let death come suddenly on them.
    Let them go down alive into Sheol.
    For wickedness is among them, in their dwelling.
As for me, I will call on God.
    YHWH will save me.
Evening, morning, and at noon, I will cry out in distress.
    He will hear my voice.
He has redeemed my soul in peace from the battle that was
against me,
    although there are many who oppose me.
God, who is enthroned forever,
    will hear and answer them. Selah.

They never change,
    who don't fear God.

He raises his hands against his friends.
*   He has violated his covenant.*
His mouth was smooth as butter,
*   but his heart was war.*
His words were softer than oil,
*   yet they were drawn swords.*

Cast your burden on YHWH and he will sustain you.
*   He will never allow the righteous to be moved.*
But you, God, will bring them down into the pit of destruction.
*   Bloodthirsty and deceitful men shall not live out half their*
*   days,*
*   but I will trust in you.*

....

For the Chief Musician. To the tune of "Silent Dove in Distant
Lands." A poem by David, when the Philistines seized him in
Gath. Be merciful to me, God, for man wants to swallow me up.
*   All day long, he attacks and oppresses me.*
My enemies want to swallow me up all day long,
*   for they are many who fight proudly against me.*
When I am afraid,
*   I will put my trust in you.*
In God, I praise his word.
*   In God, I put my trust.*
I will not be afraid.
*   What can flesh do to me?*
All day long they twist my words.
*   All their thoughts are against me for evil.*
They conspire and lurk,
*   watching my steps.*
*   They are eager to take my life.*
Shall they escape by iniquity?
*   In anger cast down the peoples, God.*
You count my wanderings.
*   You put my tears into your container.*
*   Aren't they in your book?*
Then my enemies shall turn back in the day that I call.
*   I know this: that God is for me.*
In God, I will praise his word.

In YHWH, I will praise his word.
I have put my trust in God.
I will not be afraid.
What can man do to me?
Your vows are on me, God.
I will give thank offerings to you.
For you have delivered my soul from death,
and prevented my feet from falling,
that I may walk before God in the light of the living.

....

For the Chief Musician. To the tune of "Do Not Destroy." A poem
by David, when he fled from Saul, in the cave. Be merciful to me,
God, be merciful to me,
for my soul takes refuge in you.
Yes, in the shadow of your wings, I will take refuge,
until disaster has passed.
I cry out to God Most High,
to God who accomplishes my requests for me.
He will send from heaven, and save me,
he rebukes the one who is pursuing me. Selah.
God will send out his loving kindness and his truth.
My soul is among lions.
I lie among those who are set on fire,
even the sons of men, whose teeth are spears and arrows,
and their tongue a sharp sword.
Be exalted, God, above the heavens!
Let your glory be above all the earth!

They have prepared a net for my steps.
My soul is bowed down.
They dig a pit before me.
They fall into the middle of it themselves. Selah.
My heart is steadfast, God.
My heart is steadfast.
I will sing, yes, I will sing praises.
Wake up, my glory! Wake up, lute and harp!
I will wake up the dawn.
I will give thanks to you, Lord, among the peoples.
I will sing praises to you among the nations.

For your great loving kindness reaches to the heavens,
and your truth to the skies.
Be exalted, God, above the heavens.
Let your glory be over all the earth.

....

For the Chief Musician. To the tune of "Do Not Destroy." A poem
by David. Do you indeed speak righteousness, silent ones?
Do you judge blamelessly, you sons of men?
No, in your heart you plot injustice.
You measure out the violence of your hands in the earth.
The wicked go astray from the womb.
They are wayward as soon as they are born, speaking lies.
Their poison is like the poison of a snake,
like a deaf cobra that stops its ear,
which doesn't listen to the voice of charmers,
no matter how skillful the charmer may be.
Break their teeth, God, in their mouth.
Break out the great teeth of the young lions, YHWH.
Let them vanish like water that flows away.
When they draw the bow, let their arrows be made blunt.
Let them be like a snail which melts and passes away,
like the stillborn child, who has not seen the sun.
Before your pots can feel the heat of the thorns,
he will sweep away the green and the burning alike.
The righteous shall rejoice when he sees the vengeance.
He shall wash his feet in the blood of the wicked,
so that men shall say, "Most certainly there is a reward for the
righteous.
Most certainly there is a God who judges the earth."

....

For the Chief Musician. To the tune of "Do Not Destroy." A poem
by David, when Saul sent, and they watched the house to kill
him. Deliver me from my enemies, my God.
Set me on high from those who rise up against me.
Deliver me from the workers of iniquity.
Save me from the bloodthirsty men.
For, behold, they lie in wait for my soul.
The mighty gather themselves together against me,

not for my disobedience, nor for my sin, YHWH.
I have done no wrong, yet they are ready to attack me.
   Rise up, behold, and help me!
You, YHWH God of Armies, the God of Israel,
   rouse yourself to punish the nations.
   Show no mercy to the wicked traitors. Selah.
They return at evening, howling like dogs,
   and prowl around the city.
Behold, they spew with their mouth.
   Swords are in their lips,
   "For", they say, "who hears us?"
But you, YHWH, laugh at them.
   You scoff at all the nations.
Oh, my Strength, I watch for you,
   for God is my high tower.
My God will go before me with his loving kindness.
   God will let me look at my enemies in triumph.
Don't kill them, or my people may forget.
   Scatter them by your power, and bring them down, Lord our
   shield.
For the sin of their mouth, and the words of their lips,
   let them be caught in their pride,
   for the curses and lies which they utter.
Consume them in wrath.
   Consume them, and they will be no more.
Let them know that God rules in Jacob,
   to the ends of the earth. Selah.
At evening let them return.
   Let them howl like a dog, and go around the city.
They shall wander up and down for food,
   and wait all night if they aren't satisfied.

But I will sing of your strength.
   Yes, I will sing aloud of your loving kindness in the morning.
For you have been my high tower,
   a refuge in the day of my distress.
To you, my strength, I will sing praises.
   For God is my high tower, the God of my mercy.

....

For the Chief Musician. To the tune of "The Lily of the Cove-
nant." A teaching poem by David, when he fought with Aram
Naharaim and with Aram Zobah, and Joab returned, and killed
twelve thousand of Edom in the Valley of Salt. God, you have
rejected us.
> *You have broken us down.*
You have been angry.
> *Restore us, again.*
You have made the land tremble.
> *You have torn it.*
Mend its fractures,
> *for it quakes.*
You have shown your people hard things.
> *You have made us drink the wine that makes us stagger.*
You have given a banner to those who fear you,
> *that it may be displayed because of the truth. Selah.*

So that your beloved may be delivered,
> *save with your right hand, and answer us.*
God has spoken from his sanctuary:
> *"I will triumph.*
> *I will divide Shechem,*
> *and measure out the valley of Succoth.*
Gilead is mine, and Manasseh is mine.
> *Ephraim also is the defense of my head.*
> *Judah is my scepter.*
Moab is my wash basin.
> *I will throw my sandal on Edom.*
> *I shout in triumph over Philistia."*

Who will bring me into the strong city?
> *Who has led me to Edom?*
Haven't you, God, rejected us?
> *You don't go out with our armies, God.*
Give us help against the adversary,
> *for the help of man is vain.*
Through God we will do valiantly,
> *for it is he who will tread down our adversaries.*

....

*For the Chief Musician. For a stringed instrument. By David.
Hear my cry, God.*

Listen to my prayer.

*From the end of the earth, I will call to you when my heart is
overwhelmed.*

Lead me to the rock that is higher than I.

*For you have been a refuge for me,
a strong tower from the enemy.*

I will dwell in your tent forever.

I will take refuge in the shelter of your wings. Selah.

For you, God, have heard my vows.

You have given me the heritage of those who fear your name.

You will prolong the king's life.

His years will be for generations.

He shall be enthroned in God's presence forever.

*Appoint your loving kindness and truth, that they may pre-
serve him.*

*So I will sing praise to your name forever,
that I may fulfill my vows daily.*

....

*For the Chief Musician. To Jeduthun. A Psalm by David. My
soul rests in God alone.*

My salvation is from him.

He alone is my rock, my salvation, and my fortress.

I will never be greatly shaken.

How long will you assault a man?

*Would all of you throw him down,
like a leaning wall, like a tottering fence?*

They fully intend to throw him down from his lofty place.

They delight in lies.

They bless with their mouth, but they curse inwardly. Selah.

*My soul, wait in silence for God alone,
for my expectation is from him.*

He alone is my rock and my salvation, my fortress.

I will not be shaken.

My salvation and my honor is with God.

The rock of my strength, and my refuge, is in God.

Trust in him at all times, you people.

Pour out your heart before him.

God is a refuge for us. Selah.
Surely men of low degree are just a breath,
and men of high degree are a lie.
In the balances they will go up.
They are together lighter than a breath.
Don't trust in oppression.
Don't become vain in robbery.
If riches increase,
don't set your heart on them.
God has spoken once;
twice I have heard this,
that power belongs to God.
Also to you, Lord, belongs loving kindness,
for you reward every man according to his work.

....

A Psalm by David, when he was in the desert of Judah. God, you
are my God.
I will earnestly seek you.
My soul thirsts for you.
My flesh longs for you,
in a dry and weary land, where there is no water.
So I have seen you in the sanctuary,
watching your power and your glory.
Because your loving kindness is better than life,
my lips shall praise you.
So I will bless you while I live.
I will lift up my hands in your name.
My soul shall be satisfied as with the richest food.
My mouth shall praise you with joyful lips,
when I remember you on my bed,
and think about you in the night watches.
For you have been my help.
I will rejoice in the shadow of your wings.
My soul stays close to you.
Your right hand holds me up.
But those who seek my soul to destroy it
shall go into the lower parts of the earth.
They shall be given over to the power of the sword.
They shall be jackal food.

But the king shall rejoice in God.
Everyone who swears by him will praise him,
for the mouth of those who speak lies shall be silenced.

....

For the Chief Musician. A Psalm by David. Hear my voice, God,
in my complaint.
Preserve my life from fear of the enemy.
Hide me from the conspiracy of the wicked,
from the noisy crowd of the ones doing evil;
who sharpen their tongue like a sword,
and aim their arrows, deadly words,
to shoot innocent men from ambushes.
They shoot at him suddenly and fearlessly.
They encourage themselves in evil plans.
They talk about laying snares secretly.
They say, "Who will see them?"
They plot injustice, saying, "We have made a perfect plan!"
Surely man's mind and heart are cunning.
But God will shoot at them.
They will be suddenly struck down with an arrow.
Their own tongues shall ruin them.
All who see them will shake their heads.
All mankind shall be afraid.
They shall declare the work of God,
and shall wisely ponder what he has done.
The righteous shall be glad in YHWH,
and shall take refuge in him.
All the upright in heart shall praise him!

....

For the Chief Musician. A Psalm by David. A song. Praise waits
for you, God, in Zion.
Vows shall be performed to you.
You who hear prayer,
all men will come to you.
Sins overwhelmed me,
but you atoned for our transgressions.
Blessed is the one whom you choose and cause to come near,
that he may live in your courts.

We will be filled with the goodness of your house,
your holy temple.
By awesome deeds of righteousness, you answer us,
God of our salvation.
You who are the hope of all the ends of the earth,
of those who are far away on the sea.
By your power, you form the mountains,
having armed yourself with strength.
You still the roaring of the seas,
the roaring of their waves,
and the turmoil of the nations.
They also who dwell in faraway places are afraid at your wonders.
You call the morning's dawn and the evening with songs of joy.
You visit the earth, and water it.
You greatly enrich it.
The river of God is full of water.
You provide them grain, for so you have ordained it.
You drench its furrows.
You level its ridges.
You soften it with showers.
You bless it with a crop.
You crown the year with your bounty.
Your carts overflow with abundance.
The wilderness grasslands overflow.
The hills are clothed with gladness.
The pastures are covered with flocks.
The valleys also are clothed with grain.
They shout for joy!
They also sing.

....

For the Chief Musician. A song. A Psalm. Make a joyful shout to
God, all the earth!
Sing to the glory of his name!
Offer glory and praise!
Tell God, "How awesome are your deeds!
Through the greatness of your power, your enemies submit
themselves to you.
All the earth will worship you,
and will sing to you;

they will sing to your name." Selah.
Come, and see God's deeds—
   awesome work on behalf of the children of men.
He turned the sea into dry land.
   They went through the river on foot.
   There, we rejoiced in him.
He rules by his might forever.
   His eyes watch the nations.
   Don't let the rebellious rise up against him. Selah.
Praise our God, you peoples!
   Make the sound of his praise heard,
who preserves our life among the living,
   and doesn't allow our feet to be moved.
For you, God, have tested us.
   You have refined us, as silver is refined.
You brought us into prison.
   You laid a burden on our backs.
You allowed men to ride over our heads.
   We went through fire and through water,
   but you brought us to the place of abundance.
I will come into your temple with burnt offerings.
   I will pay my vows to you, which my lips promised,
   and my mouth spoke, when I was in distress.
I will offer to you burnt offerings of fat animals,
   with the offering of rams,
   I will offer bulls with goats. Selah.
Come and hear, all you who fear God.
   I will declare what he has done for my soul.
I cried to him with my mouth.
   He was extolled with my tongue.
If I cherished sin in my heart,
   the Lord wouldn't have listened.
But most certainly, God has listened.
   He has heard the voice of my prayer.
Blessed be God, who has not turned away my prayer,
   nor his loving kindness from me.

....

*For the Chief Musician. With stringed instruments. A Psalm. A
song. May God be merciful to us, bless us,*

and cause his face to shine on us. Selah.
That your way may be known on earth,
 and your salvation among all nations,
let the peoples praise you, God.
 Let all the peoples praise you.
Oh let the nations be glad and sing for joy,
 for you will judge the peoples with equity,
 and govern the nations on earth. Selah.
Let the peoples praise you, God.
 Let all the peoples praise you.
The earth has yielded its increase.
 God, even our own God, will bless us.
God will bless us.
 All the ends of the earth shall fear him.

....

For the Chief Musician. A Psalm by David. A song. Let God
arise!
 Let his enemies be scattered!
 Let them who hate him also flee before him.
As smoke is driven away,
 so drive them away.
As wax melts before the fire,
 so let the wicked perish at the presence of God.
But let the righteous be glad.
 Let them rejoice before God.
 Yes, let them rejoice with gladness.
Sing to God! Sing praises to his name!
 Extol him who rides on the clouds:
to Yah, his name!
 Rejoice before him!
A father of the fatherless, and a defender of the widows,
 is God in his holy habitation.
God sets the lonely in families.
He brings out the prisoners with singing,
 but the rebellious dwell in a sun-scorched land.

God, when you went out before your people,
 when you marched through the wilderness... Selah.
The earth trembled.

The sky also poured down rain at the presence of the God of
Sinai—
   at the presence of God, the God of Israel.
You, God, sent a plentiful rain.
   You confirmed your inheritance when it was weary.
Your congregation lived therein.
   You, God, prepared your goodness for the poor.
The Lord announced the word.
   The ones who proclaim it are a great company.
"Kings of armies flee! They flee!"
   She who waits at home divides the plunder,
   while you sleep among the camp fires,
   the wings of a dove sheathed with silver,
   her feathers with shining gold.
When the Almighty scattered kings in her,
   it snowed on Zalmon.
The mountains of Bashan are majestic mountains.
   The mountains of Bashan are rugged.
Why do you look in envy, you rugged mountains,
   at the mountain where God chooses to reign?
   Yes, YHWH will dwell there forever.
The chariots of God are tens of thousands and thousands of thou-
sands.
   The Lord is among them, from Sinai, into the sanctuary.
You have ascended on high.
   You have led away captives.
You have received gifts among people,
   yes, among the rebellious also, that Yah God might dwell there.

Blessed be the Lord, who daily bears our burdens,
   even the God who is our salvation. Selah.
God is to us a God of deliverance.
   To YHWH, the Lord, belongs escape from death.
But God will strike through the head of his enemies,
   the hairy scalp of such a one as still continues in his guiltiness.
The Lord said, "I will bring you again from Bashan,
   I will bring you again from the depths of the sea,
that you may crush them, dipping your foot in blood,
   that the tongues of your dogs may have their portion from your
   enemies."

They have seen your processions, God,
  even the processions of my God, my King, into the sanctuary.
The singers went before, the minstrels followed after,
  among the ladies playing with tambourines,
"Bless God in the congregations,
  even the Lord in the assembly of Israel!"
There is little Benjamin, their ruler,
  the princes of Judah, their council,
  the princes of Zebulun, and the princes of Naphtali.

Your God has commanded your strength.
  Strengthen, God, that which you have done for us.
Because of your temple at Jerusalem,
  kings shall bring presents to you.
Rebuke the wild animal of the reeds,
  the multitude of the bulls, with the calves of the peoples.
Being humbled, may it bring bars of silver.
  Scatter the nations that delight in war.
Princes shall come out of Egypt.
  Ethiopia shall hurry to stretch out her hands to God.
Sing to God, you kingdoms of the earth!
  Sing praises to the Lord! Selah.
To him who rides on the heaven of heavens, which are of old;
  behold, he utters his voice, a mighty voice.
Ascribe strength to God!
  His excellency is over Israel,
  his strength is in the skies.
You are awesome, God, in your sanctuaries.
  The God of Israel gives strength and power to his people.
  Praise be to God!

....

*For the Chief Musician. To the tune of "Lilies." By David. Save
me, God,*
  for the waters have come up to my neck!
I sink in deep mire, where there is no foothold.
  I have come into deep waters, where the floods overflow me.
I am weary with my crying.
  My throat is dry.
  My eyes fail looking for my God.

Those who hate me without a cause are more than the hairs of my head.

Those who want to cut me off, being my enemies wrongfully, are mighty.

I have to restore what I didn't take away.

God, you know my foolishness.

My sins aren't hidden from you.

Don't let those who wait for you be shamed through me, Lord YHWH of Armies.

Don't let those who seek you be brought to dishonor through me, God of Israel.

Because for your sake, I have borne reproach.

Shame has covered my face.

I have become a stranger to my brothers, an alien to my mother's children.

For the zeal of your house consumes me.

The reproaches of those who reproach you have fallen on me.

When I wept and I fasted, that was to my reproach.

When I made sackcloth my clothing, I became a byword to them.

Those who sit in the gate talk about me.

I am the song of the drunkards.

But as for me, my prayer is to you, YHWH, in an acceptable time.

God, in the abundance of your loving kindness, answer me in the truth of your salvation.

Deliver me out of the mire, and don't let me sink.

Let me be delivered from those who hate me, and out of the deep waters.

Don't let the flood waters overwhelm me, neither let the deep swallow me up.

Don't let the pit shut its mouth on me.

Answer me, YHWH, for your loving kindness is good.

According to the multitude of your tender mercies, turn to me.

Don't hide your face from your servant, for I am in distress.

Answer me speedily!

Draw near to my soul and redeem it.

Ransom me because of my enemies.

You know my reproach, my shame, and my dishonor.

My adversaries are all before you.
Reproach has broken my heart, and I am full of heaviness.
 I looked for some to take pity, but there was none;
 for comforters, but I found none.
They also gave me poison for my food.
 In my thirst, they gave me vinegar to drink.
Let their table before them become a snare.
 May it become a retribution and a trap.
Let their eyes be darkened, so that they can't see.
 Let their backs be continually bent.
Pour out your indignation on them.
 Let the fierceness of your anger overtake them.
Let their habitation be desolate.
 Let no one dwell in their tents.
For they persecute him whom you have wounded.
 They tell of the sorrow of those whom you have hurt.
Charge them with crime upon crime.
 Don't let them come into your righteousness.
Let them be blotted out of the book of life,
 and not be written with the righteous.
But I am in pain and distress.
 Let your salvation, God, protect me.
I will praise the name of God with a song,
 and will magnify him with thanksgiving.
It will please YHWH better than an ox,
 or a bull that has horns and hoofs.
The humble have seen it, and are glad.
 You who seek after God, let your heart live.
For YHWH hears the needy,
 and doesn't despise his captive people.
Let heaven and earth praise him;
 the seas, and everything that moves therein!
For God will save Zion, and build the cities of Judah.
 They shall settle there, and own it.
The children also of his servants shall inherit it.
 Those who love his name shall dwell therein.

....

For the Chief Musician. By David. A reminder. Hurry, God, to
deliver me.

Come quickly to help me, YHWH.
Let them be disappointed and confounded who seek my soul.
    Let those who desire my ruin be turned back in disgrace.
Let them be turned because of their shame
    who say, "Aha! Aha!"
Let all those who seek you rejoice and be glad in you.
    Let those who love your salvation continually say,
    "Let God be exalted!"
But I am poor and needy.
    Come to me quickly, God.
You are my help and my deliverer.
    YHWH, don't delay.

....

In you, YHWH, I take refuge.
    Never let me be disappointed.
Deliver me in your righteousness, and rescue me.
    Turn your ear to me, and save me.
Be to me a rock of refuge to which I may always go.
    Give the command to save me,
    for you are my rock and my fortress.
Rescue me, my God, from the hand of the wicked,
    from the hand of the unrighteous and cruel man.
For you are my hope, Lord YHWH,
    my confidence from my youth.
I have relied on you from the womb.
    You are he who took me out of my mother's womb.
    I will always praise you.
I am a marvel to many,
    but you are my strong refuge.
My mouth shall be filled with your praise,
    with your honor all day long.
Don't reject me in my old age.
    Don't forsake me when my strength fails.
For my enemies talk about me.
    Those who watch for my soul conspire together,
    saying, "God has forsaken him.
    Pursue and take him, for no one will rescue him."
God, don't be far from me.

My God, hurry to help me.
Let my accusers be disappointed and consumed.
 Let them be covered with disgrace and scorn who want to
 harm me.
But I will always hope,
 and will add to all of your praise.
My mouth will tell about your righteousness,
 and of your salvation all day,
 though I don't know its full measure.
I will come with the mighty acts of the Lord YHWH.
 I will make mention of your righteousness, even of yours alone.
God, you have taught me from my youth.
 Until now, I have declared your wondrous works.
Yes, even when I am old and gray-haired, God, don't forsake me,
 until I have declared your strength to the next generation,
 your might to everyone who is to come.
Your righteousness also, God, reaches to the heavens;
 you have done great things.
 God, who is like you?
You, who have shown us many and bitter troubles,
 you will let me live.
 You will bring us up again from the depths of the earth.
Increase my honor
 and comfort me again.
I will also praise you with the harp for your faithfulness, my God.
 I sing praises to you with the lyre, Holy One of Israel.
My lips shall shout for joy!
 My soul, which you have redeemed, sings praises to you!
My tongue will also talk about your righteousness all day long,
 for they are disappointed, and they are confounded,
 who want to harm me.

By Solomon. God, give the king your justice;
 your righteousness to the royal son.
He will judge your people with righteousness,
 and your poor with justice.
The mountains shall bring prosperity to the people.
 The hills bring the fruit of righteousness.
He will judge the poor of the people.

He will save the children of the needy,
and will break the oppressor in pieces.
They shall fear you while the sun endures;
and as long as the moon, throughout all generations.
He will come down like rain on the mown grass,
as showers that water the earth.
In his days, the righteous shall flourish,
and abundance of peace, until the moon is no more.
He shall have dominion also from sea to sea,
from the River to the ends of the earth.
Those who dwell in the wilderness shall bow before him.
His enemies shall lick the dust.
The kings of Tarshish and of the islands will bring tribute.
The kings of Sheba and Seba shall offer gifts.
Yes, all kings shall fall down before him.
All nations shall serve him.
For he will deliver the needy when he cries;
the poor, who has no helper.
He will have pity on the poor and needy.
He will save the souls of the needy.
He will redeem their soul from oppression and violence.
Their blood will be precious in his sight.
They shall live, and to him shall be given of the gold of Sheba.
Men shall pray for him continually.
They shall bless him all day long.
Abundance of grain shall be throughout the land.
Its fruit sways like Lebanon.
Let it flourish, thriving like the grass of the field.
His name endures forever.
His name continues as long as the sun.
Men shall be blessed by him.
All nations will call him blessed.

Praise be to YHWH God, the God of Israel,
who alone does marvelous deeds.
Blessed be his glorious name forever!
Let the whole earth be filled with his glory!
Amen and amen.

This ends the prayers by David, the son of Jesse.

....

BOOK 3

A Psalm by Asaph. Surely God is good to Israel,
to those who are pure in heart.
But as for me, my feet were almost gone.
My steps had nearly slipped.
For I was envious of the arrogant,
when I saw the prosperity of the wicked.
For there are no struggles in their death,
but their strength is firm.
They are free from burdens of men,
neither are they plagued like other men.
Therefore pride is like a chain around their neck.
Violence covers them like a garment.
Their eyes bulge with fat.
Their minds pass the limits of conceit.
They scoff and speak with malice.
In arrogance, they threaten oppression.
They have set their mouth in the heavens.
Their tongue walks through the earth.
Therefore their people return to them,
and they drink up waters of abundance.
They say, "How does God know?
Is there knowledge in the Most High?"
Behold, these are the wicked.
Being always at ease, they increase in riches.
Surely I have cleansed my heart in vain,
and washed my hands in innocence,
For all day long I have been plagued,
and punished every morning.
If I had said, "I will speak thus";
behold, I would have betrayed the generation of your children.
When I tried to understand this,
it was too painful for me,
until I entered God's sanctuary,
and considered their latter end.
Surely you set them in slippery places.
You throw them down to destruction.
How they are suddenly destroyed!

They are completely swept away with terrors.
As a dream when one wakes up,
    so, Lord, when you awake, you will despise their fantasies.
For my soul was grieved.
    I was embittered in my heart.
I was so senseless and ignorant.
    I was a brute beast before you.
Nevertheless, I am continually with you.
    You have held my right hand.
You will guide me with your counsel,
    and afterward receive me to glory.
Whom do I have in heaven?
    There is no one on earth whom I desire besides you.
My flesh and my heart fails,
    but God is the strength of my heart and my portion forever.
For, behold, those who are far from you shall perish.
    You have destroyed all those who are unfaithful to you.
But it is good for me to come close to God.
    I have made the Lord YHWH my refuge,
    that I may tell of all your works.

....

A contemplation by Asaph. God, why have you rejected us forever?
    Why does your anger smolder against the sheep of your pasture?
Remember your congregation, which you purchased of old,
    which you have redeemed to be the tribe of your inheritance:
    Mount Zion, in which you have lived.
Lift up your feet to the perpetual ruins,
    all the evil that the enemy has done in the sanctuary.
Your adversaries have roared in the middle of your assembly.
    They have set up their standards as signs.
They behaved like men wielding axes,
    cutting through a thicket of trees.
Now they break all its carved work down with hatchet and hammers.
    They have burned your sanctuary to the ground.
    They have profaned the dwelling place of your Name.
They said in their heart, "We will crush them completely."
    They have burned up all the places in the land where God was

worshiped.
We see no miraculous signs.
  There is no longer any prophet,
  neither is there among us anyone who knows how long.
How long, God, shall the adversary reproach?
  Shall the enemy blaspheme your name forever?
Why do you draw back your hand, even your right hand?
  Take it from your chest and consume them!

Yet God is my King of old,
  working salvation throughout the earth.
You divided the sea by your strength.
  You broke the heads of the sea monsters in the waters.
You broke the heads of Leviathan in pieces.
  You gave him as food to people and desert creatures.
You opened up spring and stream.
  You dried up mighty rivers.
The day is yours, the night is also yours.
  You have prepared the light and the sun.
You have set all the boundaries of the earth.
  You have made summer and winter.

Remember this, that the enemy has mocked you, YHWH.
  Foolish people have blasphemed your name.
Don't deliver the soul of your dove to wild beasts.
  Don't forget the life of your poor forever.
Honor your covenant,
  for haunts of violence fill the dark places of the earth.
Don't let the oppressed return ashamed.
  Let the poor and needy praise your name.
Arise, God! Plead your own cause.
  Remember how the foolish man mocks you all day.
Don't forget the voice of your adversaries.
  The tumult of those who rise up against you ascends continually.

....

*For the Chief Musician. To the tune of "Do Not Destroy." A
Psalm by Asaph. A song. We give thanks to you, God.*

We give thanks, for your Name is near.
Men tell about your wondrous works.

When I choose the appointed time,
    I will judge blamelessly.
The earth and all its inhabitants quake.
    I firmly hold its pillars. Selah.
I said to the arrogant, "Don't boast!"
    I said to the wicked, "Don't lift up the horn.
Don't lift up your horn on high.
    Don't speak with a stiff neck."
For neither from the east, nor from the west,
    nor yet from the south, comes exaltation.
But God is the judge.
    He puts down one, and lifts up another.
For in YHWH's hand there is a cup,
    full of foaming wine mixed with spices.
He pours it out.
    Indeed the wicked of the earth drink and drink it to its very
    dregs.

But I will declare this forever:
    I will sing praises to the God of Jacob.
I will cut off all the horns of the wicked,
    but the horns of the righteous shall be lifted up.

....

For the Chief Musician. On stringed instruments. A Psalm by
Asaph. A song. In Judah, God is known.
    His name is great in Israel.
His tabernacle is also in Salem;
    His dwelling place in Zion.
There he broke the flaming arrows of the bow,
    the shield, and the sword, and the weapons of war. Selah.
Glorious are you, and excellent,
    more than mountains of game.
Valiant men lie plundered,
    they have slept their last sleep.
    None of the men of war can lift their hands.

At your rebuke, God of Jacob,
both chariot and horse are cast into a dead sleep.
You, even you, are to be feared.
Who can stand in your sight when you are angry?
You pronounced judgment from heaven.
The earth feared, and was silent,
when God arose to judgment,
to save all the afflicted ones of the earth. Selah.
Surely the wrath of man praises you.
The survivors of your wrath are restrained.
Make vows to YHWH your God, and fulfill them!
Let all of his neighbors bring presents to him who is to be
feared.
He will cut off the spirit of princes.
He is feared by the kings of the earth.

For the Chief Musician. To Jeduthun. A Psalm by Asaph. My cry
goes to God!
Indeed, I cry to God for help,
and for him to listen to me.
In the day of my trouble I sought the Lord.
My hand was stretched out in the night, and didn't get tired.
My soul refused to be comforted.
I remember God, and I groan.
I complain, and my spirit is overwhelmed. Selah.

You hold my eyelids open.
I am so troubled that I can't speak.
I have considered the days of old,
the years of ancient times.
I remember my song in the night.
I consider in my own heart;
my spirit diligently inquires:
"Will the Lord reject us forever?
Will he be favorable no more?
Has his loving kindness vanished forever?
Does his promise fail for generations?
Has God forgotten to be gracious?

Has he, in anger, withheld his compassion?" Selah.
Then I thought, "I will appeal to this:
   the years of the right hand of the Most High."
I will remember Yah's deeds;
   for I will remember your wonders of old.
I will also meditate on all your work,
   and consider your doings.
Your way, God, is in the sanctuary.
   What god is great like God?
You are the God who does wonders.
   You have made your strength known among the peoples.
You have redeemed your people with your arm,
   the sons of Jacob and Joseph. Selah.
The waters saw you, God.
   The waters saw you, and they writhed.
   The depths also convulsed.
The clouds poured out water.
   The skies resounded with thunder.
   Your arrows also flashed around.
The voice of your thunder was in the whirlwind.
   The lightnings lit up the world.
   The earth trembled and shook.
Your way was through the sea;
   your paths through the great waters.
   Your footsteps were not known.
You led your people like a flock,
   by the hand of Moses and Aaron.

....

A contemplation by Asaph. Hear my teaching, my people.
   Turn your ears to the words of my mouth.
I will open my mouth in a parable.
   I will utter dark sayings of old,
Which we have heard and known,
   and our fathers have told us.
We will not hide them from their children,
   telling to the generation to come the praises of YHWH,
   his strength, and his wondrous deeds that he has done.
For he established a covenant in Jacob,

and appointed a teaching in Israel,
which he commanded our fathers,
that they should make them known to their children;
that the generation to come might know, even the children who
should be born;
who should arise and tell their children,
that they might set their hope in God,
and not forget God's deeds,
but keep his commandments,
and might not be as their fathers,
a stubborn and rebellious generation,
a generation that didn't make their hearts loyal,
whose spirit was not steadfast with God.
The children of Ephraim, being armed and carrying bows,
turned back in the day of battle.
They didn't keep God's covenant,
and refused to walk in his law.
They forgot his doings,
his wondrous deeds that he had shown them.
He did marvelous things in the sight of their fathers,
in the land of Egypt, in the field of Zoan.
He split the sea, and caused them to pass through.
He made the waters stand as a heap.
In the daytime he also led them with a cloud,
and all night with a light of fire.
He split rocks in the wilderness,
and gave them drink abundantly as out of the depths.
He brought streams also out of the rock,
and caused waters to run down like rivers.
Yet they still went on to sin against him,
to rebel against the Most High in the desert.
They tempted God in their heart
by asking food according to their desire.
Yes, they spoke against God.
They said, "Can God prepare a table in the wilderness?
Behold, he struck the rock, so that waters gushed out,
and streams overflowed.
Can he give bread also?
Will he provide meat for his people?"
Therefore YHWH *heard, and was angry.*

A fire was kindled against Jacob,
  anger also went up against Israel,
because they didn't believe in God,
  and didn't trust in his salvation.
Yet he commanded the skies above,
  and opened the doors of heaven.
He rained down manna on them to eat,
  and gave them food from the sky.
Man ate the bread of angels.
  He sent them food to the full.
He caused the east wind to blow in the sky.
  By his power he guided the south wind.
He also rained meat on them as the dust,
  winged birds as the sand of the seas.
He let them fall in the middle of their camp,
  around their habitations.
So they ate, and were well filled.
  He gave them their own desire.
They didn't turn from their cravings.
  Their food was yet in their mouths,
  when the anger of God went up against them,
  killed some of their fattest,
  and struck down the young men of Israel.
For all this they still sinned,
  and didn't believe in his wondrous works.
Therefore he consumed their days in vanity,
  and their years in terror.
When he killed them, then they inquired after him.
  They returned and sought God earnestly.
They remembered that God was their rock,
  the Most High God, their redeemer.
But they flattered him with their mouth,
  and lied to him with their tongue.
For their heart was not right with him,
  neither were they faithful in his covenant.
But he, being merciful, forgave iniquity, and didn't destroy them.
  Yes, many times he turned his anger away,
  and didn't stir up all his wrath.
He remembered that they were but flesh,
  a wind that passes away, and doesn't come again.

How often they rebelled against him in the wilderness,
  and grieved him in the desert!
They turned again and tempted God,
  and provoked the Holy One of Israel.
They didn't remember his hand,
  nor the day when he redeemed them from the adversary;
how he set his signs in Egypt,
  his wonders in the field of Zoan,
he turned their rivers into blood,
  and their streams, so that they could not drink.
He sent among them swarms of flies, which devoured them;
  and frogs, which destroyed them.
He gave also their increase to the caterpillar,
  and their labor to the locust.
He destroyed their vines with hail,
  their sycamore fig trees with frost.
He gave over their livestock also to the hail,
  and their flocks to hot thunderbolts.
He threw on them the fierceness of his anger,
  wrath, indignation, and trouble,
  and a band of angels of evil.
He made a path for his anger.
  He didn't spare their soul from death,
  but gave their life over to the pestilence,
and struck all the firstborn in Egypt,
  the chief of their strength in the tents of Ham.
But he led out his own people like sheep,
  and guided them in the wilderness like a flock.
He led them safely, so that they weren't afraid,
  but the sea overwhelmed their enemies.
He brought them to the border of his sanctuary,
  to this mountain, which his right hand had taken.
He also drove out the nations before them,
  allotted them for an inheritance by line,
  and made the tribes of Israel to dwell in their tents.
Yet they tempted and rebelled against the Most High God,
  and didn't keep his testimonies,
but turned back, and dealt treacherously like their fathers.
  They were twisted like a deceitful bow.
For they provoked him to anger with their high places,

and moved him to jealousy with their engraved images.
When God heard this, he was angry,
    and greatly abhorred Israel,
so that he abandoned the tent of Shiloh,
    the tent which he placed among men,
and delivered his strength into captivity,
    his glory into the adversary's hand.
He also gave his people over to the sword,
    and was angry with his inheritance.
Fire devoured their young men.
    Their virgins had no wedding song.
Their priests fell by the sword,
    and their widows couldn't weep.
Then the Lord awakened as one out of sleep,
    like a mighty man who shouts by reason of wine.
He struck his adversaries backward.
    He put them to a perpetual reproach.
Moreover he rejected the tent of Joseph,
    and didn't choose the tribe of Ephraim,
But chose the tribe of Judah,
    Mount Zion which he loved.
He built his sanctuary like the heights,
    like the earth which he has established forever.
He also chose David his servant,
    and took him from the sheepfolds;
from following the ewes that have their young,
    he brought him to be the shepherd of Jacob, his people,
    and Israel, his inheritance.
So he was their shepherd according to the integrity of his heart,
    and guided them by the skillfulness of his hands.

....

A Psalm by Asaph. God, the nations have come into your inheritance.
    They have defiled your holy temple.
    They have laid Jerusalem in heaps.
They have given the dead bodies of your servants to be food for the birds of the sky,
    the flesh of your saints to the animals of the earth.

They have shed their blood like water around Jerusalem.
    There was no one to bury them.
We have become a reproach to our neighbors,
    a scoffing and derision to those who are around us.
How long, YHWH?
      Will you be angry forever?
      Will your jealousy burn like fire?
Pour out your wrath on the nations that don't know you,
    on the kingdoms that don't call on your name;
for they have devoured Jacob,
    and destroyed his homeland.
Don't hold the iniquities of our forefathers against us.
    Let your tender mercies speedily meet us,
    for we are in desperate need.
Help us, God of our salvation, for the glory of your name.
    Deliver us, and forgive our sins, for your name's sake.
Why should the nations say, "Where is their God?"
    Let it be known among the nations, before our eyes,
    that vengeance for your servants' blood is being poured out.
Let the sighing of the prisoner come before you.
    According to the greatness of your power, preserve those who
    are sentenced to death.
Pay back to our neighbors seven times into their bosom
    their reproach with which they have reproached you, Lord.
So we, your people and sheep of your pasture,
    will give you thanks forever.
    We will praise you forever, to all generations.

For the Chief Musician. To the tune of "The Lilies of the Covenant." A Psalm by Asaph. Hear us, Shepherd of Israel,
    you who lead Joseph like a flock,
    you who sit above the cherubim, shine out.
Before Ephraim and Benjamin and Manasseh, stir up your might!
    Come to save us!
Turn us again, God.
    Cause your face to shine,
    and we will be saved.

YHWH *God of Armies,*
how long will you be angry against the prayer of your people?
You have fed them with the bread of tears,
and given them tears to drink in large measure.
You make us a source of contention to our neighbors.
Our enemies laugh among themselves.
Turn us again, God of Armies.
Cause your face to shine,
and we will be saved.

You brought a vine out of Egypt.
You drove out the nations, and planted it.
You cleared the ground for it.
It took deep root, and filled the land.
The mountains were covered with its shadow.
Its boughs were like God's cedars.
It sent out its branches to the sea,
its shoots to the River.
Why have you broken down its walls,
so that all those who pass by the way pluck it?
The boar out of the wood ravages it.
The wild animals of the field feed on it.
Turn again, we beg you, God of Armies.
Look down from heaven, and see, and visit this vine,
the stock which your right hand planted,
the branch that you made strong for yourself.
It's burned with fire.
It's cut down.
They perish at your rebuke.
Let your hand be on the man of your right hand,
on the son of man whom you made strong for yourself.
So we will not turn away from you.
Revive us, and we will call on your name.
Turn us again, YHWH *God of Armies.*
Cause your face to shine, and we will be saved.

....

For the Chief Musician. On an instrument of Gath. By Asaph.
Sing aloud to God, our strength!
Make a joyful shout to the God of Jacob!

Raise a song, and bring here the tambourine,
the pleasant lyre with the harp.
Blow the trumpet at the New Moon,
at the full moon, on our feast day.
For it is a statute for Israel,
an ordinance of the God of Jacob.
He appointed it in Joseph for a covenant,
when he went out over the land of Egypt,
I heard a language that I didn't know.
"I removed his shoulder from the burden.
His hands were freed from the basket.
You called in trouble, and I delivered you.
I answered you in the secret place of thunder.
I tested you at the waters of Meribah." Selah.

"Hear, my people, and I will testify to you,
Israel, if you would listen to me!
There shall be no strange god in you,
neither shall you worship any foreign god.
I am YHWH, your God,
who brought you up out of the land of Egypt.
Open your mouth wide, and I will fill it.
But my people didn't listen to my voice.
Israel desired none of me.
So I let them go after the stubbornness of their hearts,
that they might walk in their own counsels.
Oh that my people would listen to me,
that Israel would walk in my ways!
I would soon subdue their enemies,
and turn my hand against their adversaries.
The haters of YHWH would cringe before him,
and their punishment would last forever.
But he would have also fed them with the finest of the wheat.
I will satisfy you with honey out of the rock."

....

A Psalm by Asaph. God presides in the great assembly.
He judges among the gods.
"How long will you judge unjustly,
and show partiality to the wicked?" Selah.

"Defend the weak, the poor, and the fatherless.
  Maintain the rights of the poor and oppressed.
Rescue the weak and needy.
  Deliver them out of the hand of the wicked."
They don't know, neither do they understand.
  They walk back and forth in darkness.
  All the foundations of the earth are shaken.
I said, "You are gods,
  all of you are sons of the Most High.
Nevertheless you shall die like men,
  and fall like one of the rulers."
Arise, God, judge the earth,
  for you inherit all of the nations.

....

A song. A Psalm by Asaph. God, don't keep silent.
  Don't keep silent,
  and don't be still, God.
For, behold, your enemies are stirred up.
  Those who hate you have lifted up their heads.
They conspire with cunning against your people.
  They plot against your cherished ones.
"Come," they say, "let's destroy them as a nation,
  that the name of Israel may be remembered no more."
For they have conspired together with one mind.
  They form an alliance against you.
The tents of Edom and the Ishmaelites;
  Moab, and the Hagrites;
Gebal, Ammon, and Amalek;
  Philistia with the inhabitants of Tyre;
Assyria also is joined with them.
  They have helped the children of Lot. Selah.
Do to them as you did to Midian,
  as to Sisera, as to Jabin, at the river Kishon;
who perished at Endor,
  who became as dung for the earth.
Make their nobles like Oreb and Zeeb,
  yes, all their princes like Zebah and Zalmunna,
  who said, "Let's take possession of God's pasture lands."

My God, make them like tumbleweed,
*   like chaff before the wind.*
As the fire that burns the forest,
*   as the flame that sets the mountains on fire,*
*   so pursue them with your tempest,*
*   and terrify them with your storm.*
Fill their faces with confusion,
*   that they may seek your name, YHWH.*
Let them be disappointed and dismayed forever.
*   Yes, let them be confounded and perish;*
that they may know that you alone, whose name is YHWH,
*   are the Most High over all the earth.*

....

For the Chief Musician. On an instrument of Gath. A Psalm by
the sons of Korah. How lovely are your dwellings,
*   YHWH of Armies!*
My soul longs, and even faints for the courts of YHWH.
*   My heart and my flesh cry out for the living God.*
Yes, the sparrow has found a home,
*   and the swallow a nest for herself, where she may have her*
*   young,*
*   near your altars, YHWH of Armies, my King, and my God.*
Blessed are those who dwell in your house.
*   They are always praising you. Selah.*
Blessed are those whose strength is in you,
*   who have set their hearts on a pilgrimage.*
Passing through the valley of Weeping, they make it a place of
springs.
*   Yes, the autumn rain covers it with blessings.*
They go from strength to strength.
*   Every one of them appears before God in Zion.*
YHWH, God of Armies, hear my prayer.
*   Listen, God of Jacob. Selah.*
Behold, God our shield,
*   look at the face of your anointed.*
For a day in your courts is better than a thousand.
*   I would rather be a doorkeeper in the house of my God,*
*   than to dwell in the tents of wickedness.*
For YHWH God is a sun and a shield.

YHWH will give grace and glory.
He withholds no good thing from those who walk blamelessly.
YHWH of Armies,
blessed is the man who trusts in you.

....

For the Chief Musician. A Psalm by the sons of Korah. YHWH, you
have been favorable to your land.
You have restored the fortunes of Jacob.
You have forgiven the iniquity of your people.
You have covered all their sin. Selah.
You have taken away all your wrath.
You have turned from the fierceness of your anger.
Turn us, God of our salvation,
and cause your indignation toward us to cease.
Will you be angry with us forever?
Will you draw out your anger to all generations?
Won't you revive us again,
that your people may rejoice in you?
Show us your loving kindness, YHWH.
Grant us your salvation.
I will hear what God, YHWH, will speak,
for he will speak peace to his people, his saints;
but let them not turn again to folly.
Surely his salvation is near those who fear him,
that glory may dwell in our land.
Mercy and truth meet together.
Righteousness and peace have kissed each other.
Truth springs out of the earth.
Righteousness has looked down from heaven.
Yes, YHWH will give that which is good.
Our land will yield its increase.
Righteousness goes before him,
And prepares the way for his steps.

....

A Prayer by David. Hear, YHWH, and answer me,
for I am poor and needy.
Preserve my soul, for I am godly.
You, my God, save your servant who trusts in you.

Be merciful to me, Lord,
  for I call to you all day long.
Bring joy to the soul of your servant,
  for to you, Lord, do I lift up my soul.
For you, Lord, are good, and ready to forgive,
  abundant in loving kindness to all those who call on you.
Hear, YHWH, my prayer.
  Listen to the voice of my petitions.
In the day of my trouble I will call on you,
  for you will answer me.
There is no one like you among the gods, Lord,
  nor any deeds like your deeds.
All nations you have made will come and worship before you,
Lord.
  They shall glorify your name.
For you are great, and do wondrous things.
  You are God alone.
Teach me your way, YHWH.
  I will walk in your truth.
  Make my heart undivided to fear your name.
I will praise you, Lord my God, with my whole heart.
  I will glorify your name forever more.
For your loving kindness is great toward me.
  You have delivered my soul from the lowest Sheol.
God, the proud have risen up against me.
  A company of violent men have sought after my soul,
  and they don't hold regard for you before them.
But you, Lord, are a merciful and gracious God,
  slow to anger, and abundant in loving kindness and truth.
Turn to me, and have mercy on me!
  Give your strength to your servant.
  Save the son of your servant.
Show me a sign of your goodness,
  that those who hate me may see it, and be shamed,
  because you, YHWH, have helped me, and comforted me.

....

A Psalm by the sons of Korah; a Song. His foundation is in the
holy mountains.
  YHWH loves the gates of Zion more than all the dwellings of

Jacob.
Glorious things are spoken about you, city of God. Selah.
I will record Rahab and Babylon among those who acknowledge me.

Behold, Philistia, Tyre, and also Ethiopia:
"This one was born there."
Yes, of Zion it will be said, "This one and that one was born in her;"

the Most High himself will establish her.
YHWH *will count, when he writes up the peoples,*
"This one was born there." Selah.
Those who sing as well as those who dance say,
"All my springs are in you."

....

A Song. A Psalm by the sons of Korah. For the Chief Musician. To the tune of "The Suffering of Affliction." A contemplation by Heman, the Ezrahite. YHWH, *the God of my salvation,*
I have cried day and night before you.
Let my prayer enter into your presence.
Turn your ear to my cry.
For my soul is full of troubles.
My life draws near to Sheol.
I am counted among those who go down into the pit.
I am like a man who has no help,
set apart among the dead,
like the slain who lie in the grave,
whom you remember no more.
They are cut off from your hand.
You have laid me in the lowest pit,
in the darkest depths.
Your wrath lies heavily on me.
You have afflicted me with all your waves. Selah.
You have taken my friends from me.
You have made me an abomination to them.
I am confined, and I can't escape.
My eyes are dim from grief.
I have called on you daily, YHWH.
I have spread out my hands to you.
Do you show wonders to the dead?

Do the departed spirits rise up and praise you? Selah.
Is your loving kindness declared in the grave?
*   Or your faithfulness in Destruction?*
Are your wonders made known in the dark?
*   Or your righteousness in the land of forgetfulness?*
But to you, YHWH, I have cried.
*   In the morning, my prayer comes before you.*
YHWH, why do you reject my soul?
*   Why do you hide your face from me?*
I am afflicted and ready to die from my youth up.
*   While I suffer your terrors, I am distracted.*
Your fierce wrath has gone over me.
*   Your terrors have cut me off.*
They came around me like water all day long.
*   They completely engulfed me.*
You have put lover and friend far from me,
*   and my friends into darkness.*

....

A contemplation by Ethan, the Ezrahite. I will sing of the loving
kindness of YHWH forever.
*   With my mouth, I will make known your faithfulness to all*
*   generations.*
I indeed declare, "Love stands firm forever.
*   You established the heavens.*
*   Your faithfulness is in them."*

"I have made a covenant with my chosen one,
*   I have sworn to David, my servant,*
'I will establish your offspring forever,
*   and build up your throne to all generations.'" Selah.*
The heavens will praise your wonders, YHWH,
*   your faithfulness also in the assembly of the holy ones.*
For who in the skies can be compared to YHWH?
*   Who among the sons of the heavenly beings is like YHWH,*
a very awesome God in the council of the holy ones,
*   to be feared above all those who are around him?*
YHWH, God of Armies, who is a mighty one, like you?
*   Yah, your faithfulness is around you.*
You rule the pride of the sea.

When its waves rise up, you calm them.
You have broken Rahab in pieces, like one of the slain.
    You have scattered your enemies with your mighty arm.
The heavens are yours.
    The earth also is yours,
    the world and its fullness.
    You have founded them.
You have created the north and the south.
    Tabor and Hermon rejoice in your name.
You have a mighty arm.
    Your hand is strong, and your right hand is exalted.
Righteousness and justice are the foundation of your throne.
    Loving kindness and truth go before your face.
Blessed are the people who learn to acclaim you.
    They walk in the light of your presence, YHWH.
In your name they rejoice all day.
    In your righteousness, they are exalted.
For you are the glory of their strength.
    In your favor, our horn will be exalted.
For our shield belongs to YHWH,
    our king to the Holy One of Israel.

Then you spoke in vision to your saints,
    and said, "I have given strength to the warrior.
    I have exalted a young man from the people.
I have found David, my servant.
    I have anointed him with my holy oil,
with whom my hand shall be established.
    My arm will also strengthen him.
No enemy will tax him.
    No wicked man will oppress him.
I will beat down his adversaries before him,
    and strike those who hate him.
But my faithfulness and my loving kindness will be with him.
    In my name, his horn will be exalted.
I will set his hand also on the sea,
    and his right hand on the rivers.
He will call to me, 'You are my Father,
    my God, and the rock of my salvation!'
I will also appoint him my firstborn,

the highest of the kings of the earth.
I will keep my loving kindness for him forever more.
　　My covenant will stand firm with him.
I will also make his offspring endure forever,
　　and his throne as the days of heaven.
If his children forsake my law,
　　and don't walk in my ordinances;
if they break my statutes,
　　and don't keep my commandments;
then I will punish their sin with the rod,
　　and their iniquity with stripes.
But I will not completely take my loving kindness from him,
　　nor allow my faithfulness to fail.
I will not break my covenant,
　　nor alter what my lips have uttered.
Once I have sworn by my holiness,
　　I will not lie to David.
His offspring will endure forever,
　　his throne like the sun before me.
It will be established forever like the moon,
　　the faithful witness in the sky." Selah.

But you have rejected and spurned.
　　You have been angry with your anointed.
You have renounced the covenant of your servant.
　　You have defiled his crown in the dust.
You have broken down all his hedges.
　　You have brought his strongholds to ruin.
All who pass by the way rob him.
He has become a reproach to his neighbors.
You have exalted the right hand of his adversaries.
　　You have made all of his enemies rejoice.
Yes, you turn back the edge of his sword,
　　and haven't supported him in battle.
You have ended his splendor,
　　and thrown his throne down to the ground.
You have shortened the days of his youth.
　　You have covered him with shame. Selah.
How long, YHWH?
　　Will you hide yourself forever?

Will your wrath burn like fire?
Remember how short my time is,
> *for what vanity you have created all the children of men!*
What man is he who shall live and not see death,
> *who shall deliver his soul from the power of Sheol? Selah.*
Lord, where are your former loving kindnesses,
> *which you swore to David in your faithfulness?*
Remember, Lord, the reproach of your servants,
> *how I bear in my heart the taunts of all the mighty peoples,*
With which your enemies have mocked, YHWH,
> *with which they have mocked the footsteps of your anointed one.*

Blessed be YHWH forever more.
Amen, and Amen.

....

BOOK 4

A Prayer by Moses, the man of God. Lord, you have been our dwelling place for all generations.
> *Before the mountains were born,*
> *before you had formed the earth and the world,*
> *even from everlasting to everlasting, you are God.*
You turn man to destruction, saying,
> *"Return, you children of men."*
For a thousand years in your sight are just like yesterday when it is past,
> *like a watch in the night.*
You sweep them away as they sleep.
> *In the morning they sprout like new grass.*
In the morning it sprouts and springs up.
> *By evening, it is withered and dry.*
For we are consumed in your anger.
> *We are troubled in your wrath.*
You have set our iniquities before you,
> *our secret sins in the light of your presence.*
For all our days have passed away in your wrath.
> *We bring our years to an end as a sigh.*
The days of our years are seventy,
> *or even by reason of strength eighty years;*

yet their pride is but labor and sorrow,
  for it passes quickly, and we fly away.
Who knows the power of your anger,
  your wrath according to the fear that is due to you?
So teach us to count our days,
  that we may gain a heart of wisdom.
Relent, YHWH!
    How long?
    Have compassion on your servants!
Satisfy us in the morning with your loving kindness,
  that we may rejoice and be glad all our days.
Make us glad for as many days as you have afflicted us,
  for as many years as we have seen evil.
Let your work appear to your servants,
  your glory to their children.
Let the favor of the Lord our God be on us.
  Establish the work of our hands for us.
  Yes, establish the work of our hands.

....

He who dwells in the secret place of the Most High
  will rest in the shadow of the Almighty.
I will say of YHWH, "He is my refuge and my fortress;
  my God, in whom I trust."
For he will deliver you from the snare of the fowler,
  and from the deadly pestilence.
He will cover you with his feathers.
    Under his wings you will take refuge.
    His faithfulness is your shield and rampart.
You shall not be afraid of the terror by night,
  nor of the arrow that flies by day,
  nor of the pestilence that walks in darkness,
  nor of the destruction that wastes at noonday.
A thousand may fall at your side,
  and ten thousand at your right hand;
  but it will not come near you.
You will only look with your eyes,
  and see the recompense of the wicked.
Because you have made YHWH your refuge,
  and the Most High your dwelling place,

no evil shall happen to you,
　neither shall any plague come near your dwelling.
For he will put his angels in charge of you,
　to guard you in all your ways.
They will bear you up in their hands,
　so that you won't dash your foot against a stone.
You will tread on the lion and cobra.
　You will trample the young lion and the serpent underfoot.
"Because he has set his love on me, therefore I will deliver him.
　I will set him on high, because he has known my name.
He will call on me, and I will answer him.
　I will be with him in trouble.
　I will deliver him, and honor him.
I will satisfy him with long life,
　and show him my salvation."

....

A Psalm. A song for the Sabbath day. It is a good thing to give thanks to YHWH,
　to sing praises to your name, Most High,
to proclaim your loving kindness in the morning,
　and your faithfulness every night,
with the ten-stringed lute, with the harp,
　and with the melody of the lyre.
For you, YHWH, have made me glad through your work.
　I will triumph in the works of your hands.
How great are your works, YHWH!
　Your thoughts are very deep.
A senseless man doesn't know,
　neither does a fool understand this:
though the wicked spring up as the grass,
　and all the evildoers flourish,
　they will be destroyed forever.
But you, YHWH, are on high forever more.
For, behold, your enemies, YHWH,
　for, behold, your enemies shall perish.
　All the evildoers will be scattered.
But you have exalted my horn like that of the wild ox.
　I am anointed with fresh oil.
My eye has also seen my enemies.

*My ears have heard of the wicked enemies who rise up against
me.*
The righteous shall flourish like the palm tree.
He will grow like a cedar in Lebanon.
They are planted in YHWH's house.
They will flourish in our God's courts.
They will still produce fruit in old age.
They will be full of sap and green,
to show that YHWH is upright.
He is my rock,
and there is no unrighteousness in him.

....

YHWH reigns!
He is clothed with majesty!
YHWH is armed with strength.
The world also is established.
It can't be moved.
Your throne is established from long ago.
You are from everlasting.
The floods have lifted up, YHWH,
the floods have lifted up their voice.
The floods lift up their waves.
Above the voices of many waters,
the mighty breakers of the sea,
YHWH on high is mighty.
Your statutes stand firm.
Holiness adorns your house,
YHWH, forever more.

....

YHWH, you God to whom vengeance belongs,
you God to whom vengeance belongs, shine out.
Rise up, you judge of the earth.
Pay back the proud what they deserve.
YHWH, how long will the wicked,
how long will the wicked triumph?
They pour out arrogant words.
All the evildoers boast.
They break your people in pieces, YHWH,

and afflict your heritage.
They kill the widow and the alien,
and murder the fatherless.
They say, "Yah will not see,
neither will Jacob's God consider."
Consider, you senseless among the people;
you fools, when will you be wise?
He who implanted the ear, won't he hear?
He who formed the eye, won't he see?
He who disciplines the nations, won't he punish?
He who teaches man knows.
YHWH knows the thoughts of man,
that they are futile.
Blessed is the man whom you discipline, Yah,
and teach out of your law,
that you may give him rest from the days of adversity,
until the pit is dug for the wicked.
For YHWH won't reject his people,
neither will he forsake his inheritance.
For judgment will return to righteousness.
All the upright in heart shall follow it.
Who will rise up for me against the wicked?
Who will stand up for me against the evildoers?
Unless YHWH had been my help,
my soul would have soon lived in silence.
When I said, "My foot is slipping!"
Your loving kindness, YHWH, held me up.
In the multitude of my thoughts within me,
your comforts delight my soul.
Shall the throne of wickedness have fellowship with you,
which brings about mischief by statute?
They gather themselves together against the soul of the righteous,
and condemn the innocent blood.
But YHWH has been my high tower,
my God, the rock of my refuge.
He has brought on them their own iniquity,
and will cut them off in their own wickedness.
YHWH, our God, will cut them off.

Oh come, let's sing to YHWH.
  Let's shout aloud to the rock of our salvation!
Let's come before his presence with thanksgiving.
  Let's extol him with songs!
For YHWH *is a great God,*
  a great King above all gods.
In his hand are the deep places of the earth.
  The heights of the mountains are also his.
The sea is his, and he made it.
  His hands formed the dry land.
Oh come, let's worship and bow down.
  Let's kneel before YHWH, *our Maker,*
  for he is our God.
We are the people of his pasture,
  and the sheep in his care.
Today, oh that you would hear his voice!
  Don't harden your heart, as at Meribah,
  as in the day of Massah in the wilderness,
when your fathers tempted me,
  tested me, and saw my work.
Forty long years I was grieved with that generation,
  and said, "It is a people that errs in their heart.
  They have not known my ways."
Therefore I swore in my wrath,
  "They won't enter into my rest."

....

Sing to YHWH *a new song!*
  Sing to YHWH, *all the earth.*
Sing to YHWH!
  Bless his name!
  Proclaim his salvation from day to day!
Declare his glory among the nations,
  his marvelous works among all the peoples.
For YHWH *is great, and greatly to be praised!*
  He is to be feared above all gods.
For all the gods of the peoples are idols,
  but YHWH *made the heavens.*
Honor and majesty are before him.
  Strength and beauty are in his sanctuary.

Ascribe to YHWH, you families of nations,
  ascribe to YHWH glory and strength.
Ascribe to YHWH the glory due to his name.
  Bring an offering, and come into his courts.
Worship YHWH in holy array.
  Tremble before him, all the earth.
Say among the nations, "YHWH reigns."
  The world is also established.
  It can't be moved.
  He will judge the peoples with equity.
Let the heavens be glad, and let the earth rejoice.
  Let the sea roar, and its fullness!
  Let the field and all that is in it exult!
  Then all the trees of the woods shall sing for joy
  before YHWH; for he comes,
  for he comes to judge the earth.
He will judge the world with righteousness,
  the peoples with his truth.

....

YHWH reigns!
  Let the earth rejoice!
  Let the multitude of islands be glad!
Clouds and darkness are around him.
  Righteousness and justice are the foundation of his throne.
A fire goes before him,
  and burns up his adversaries on every side.
His lightning lights up the world.
  The earth sees, and trembles.
The mountains melt like wax at the presence of YHWH,
  at the presence of the Lord of the whole earth.
The heavens declare his righteousness.
  All the peoples have seen his glory.
Let all them be shamed who serve engraved images,
  who boast in their idols.
  Worship him, all you gods!
Zion heard and was glad.
  The daughters of Judah rejoiced
  because of your judgments, YHWH.
For you, YHWH, are most high above all the earth.

You are exalted far above all gods.
You who love YHWH, hate evil!
He preserves the souls of his saints.
He delivers them out of the hand of the wicked.
Light is sown for the righteous,
and gladness for the upright in heart.
Be glad in YHWH, you righteous people!
Give thanks to his holy Name.

....

A Psalm. Sing to YHWH a new song,
for he has done marvelous things!
His right hand and his holy arm have worked salvation for him.
YHWH has made known his salvation.
He has openly shown his righteousness in the sight of the nations.
He has remembered his loving kindness and his faithfulness toward the house of Israel.
All the ends of the earth have seen the salvation of our God.
Make a joyful noise to YHWH, all the earth!
Burst out and sing for joy, yes, sing praises!
Sing praises to YHWH with the harp,
with the harp and the voice of melody.
With trumpets and sound of the ram's horn,
make a joyful noise before the King, YHWH.
Let the sea roar with its fullness;
the world, and those who dwell therein.
Let the rivers clap their hands.
Let the mountains sing for joy together.
Let them sing before YHWH,
for he comes to judge the earth.
He will judge the world with righteousness,
and the peoples with equity.

....

YHWH reigns! Let the peoples tremble.
He sits enthroned among the cherubim.
Let the earth be moved.
YHWH is great in Zion.

He is high above all the peoples.
Let them praise your great and awesome name.
 He is Holy!

The King's strength also loves justice.
 You establish equity.
 You execute justice and righteousness in Jacob.
Exalt YHWH our God.
 Worship at his footstool.
 He is Holy!

Moses and Aaron were among his priests,
 Samuel was among those who call on his name.
 They called on YHWH, and he answered them.
He spoke to them in the pillar of cloud.
 They kept his testimonies,
 the statute that he gave them.
You answered them, YHWH our God.
 You are a God who forgave them,
 although you took vengeance for their doings.
Exalt YHWH, our God.
 Worship at his holy hill,
 for YHWH, our God, is holy!

....

A Psalm of thanksgiving. Shout for joy to YHWH, all you lands!
 Serve YHWH with gladness.
 Come before his presence with singing.
Know that YHWH, he is God.
 It is he who has made us, and we are his.
 We are his people, and the sheep of his pasture.
Enter into his gates with thanksgiving,
 and into his courts with praise.
 Give thanks to him, and bless his name.
For YHWH is good.
 His loving kindness endures forever,
 his faithfulness to all generations.

....

A Psalm by David. I will sing of loving kindness and justice.

To you, YHWH, I will sing praises.
I will be careful to live a blameless life.
When will you come to me?
I will walk within my house with a blameless heart.
I will set no vile thing before my eyes.
I hate the deeds of faithless men.
They will not cling to me.
A perverse heart will be far from me.
I will have nothing to do with evil.
I will silence whoever secretly slanders his neighbor.
I won't tolerate one who is arrogant and conceited.
My eyes will be on the faithful of the land,
that they may dwell with me.
He who walks in a perfect way,
he will serve me.
He who practices deceit won't dwell within my house.
He who speaks falsehood won't be established before my eyes.
Morning by morning, I will destroy all the wicked of the land,
to cut off all the workers of iniquity from YHWH's city.

....

A Prayer of the afflicted, when he is overwhelmed and pours out
his complaint before YHWH. Hear my prayer, YHWH!
Let my cry come to you.
Don't hide your face from me in the day of my distress.
Turn your ear to me.
Answer me quickly in the day when I call.
For my days consume away like smoke.
My bones are burned as a torch.
My heart is blighted like grass, and withered,
for I forget to eat my bread.
By reason of the voice of my groaning,
my bones stick to my skin.
I am like a pelican of the wilderness.
I have become as an owl of the waste places.
I watch, and have become like a sparrow that is alone on the
housetop.
My enemies reproach me all day.
Those who are mad at me use my name as a curse.
For I have eaten ashes like bread,

and mixed my drink with tears,
because of your indignation and your wrath;
for you have taken me up and thrown me away.
My days are like a long shadow.
I have withered like grass.

But you, YHWH, will remain forever;
your renown endures to all generations.
You will arise and have mercy on Zion;
for it is time to have pity on her.
Yes, the set time has come.
For your servants take pleasure in her stones,
and have pity on her dust.
So the nations will fear YHWH's name,
all the kings of the earth your glory.
For YHWH has built up Zion.
He has appeared in his glory.
He has responded to the prayer of the destitute,
and has not despised their prayer.
This will be written for the generation to come.
A people which will be created will praise Yah.
For he has looked down from the height of his sanctuary.
From heaven, YHWH saw the earth;
to hear the groans of the prisoner;
to free those who are condemned to death;
that men may declare YHWH's name in Zion,
and his praise in Jerusalem;
when the peoples are gathered together,
the kingdoms, to serve YHWH.

He weakened my strength along the course.
He shortened my days.
I said, "My God, don't take me away in the middle of my days.
Your years are throughout all generations.
Of old, you laid the foundation of the earth.
The heavens are the work of your hands.
They will perish, but you will endure.
Yes, all of them will wear out like a garment.
You will change them like a cloak, and they will be changed.
But you are the same.

Your years will have no end.
The children of your servants will continue.
Their offspring will be established before you."

....

By David. Praise YHWH, my soul!
All that is within me, praise his holy name!
Praise YHWH, my soul,
and don't forget all his benefits,
who forgives all your sins,
who heals all your diseases,
who redeems your life from destruction,
who crowns you with loving kindness and tender mercies,
who satisfies your desire with good things,
so that your youth is renewed like the eagle's.
YHWH executes righteous acts,
and justice for all who are oppressed.
He made known his ways to Moses,
his deeds to the children of Israel.
YHWH is merciful and gracious,
slow to anger, and abundant in loving kindness.
He will not always accuse;
neither will he stay angry forever.
He has not dealt with us according to our sins,
nor repaid us for our iniquities.
For as the heavens are high above the earth,
so great is his loving kindness toward those who fear him.
As far as the east is from the west,
so far has he removed our transgressions from us.
Like a father has compassion on his children,
so YHWH has compassion on those who fear him.
For he knows how we are made.
He remembers that we are dust.
As for man, his days are like grass.
As a flower of the field, so he flourishes.
For the wind passes over it, and it is gone.
Its place remembers it no more.
But YHWH's loving kindness is from everlasting to everlasting with
those who fear him,
his righteousness to children's children,

to those who keep his covenant,
to those who remember to obey his precepts.
YHWH has established his throne in the heavens.
His kingdom rules over all.
Praise YHWH, you angels of his,
who are mighty in strength, who fulfill his word,
obeying the voice of his word.
Praise YHWH, all you armies of his,
you servants of his, who do his pleasure.
Praise YHWH, all you works of his,
in all places of his dominion.
Praise YHWH, my soul!

....

Bless YHWH, my soul.
YHWH, my God, you are very great.
You are clothed with honor and majesty.
He covers himself with light as with a garment.
He stretches out the heavens like a curtain.
He lays the beams of his rooms in the waters.
He makes the clouds his chariot.
He walks on the wings of the wind.
He makes his messengers winds,
and his servants flames of fire.
He laid the foundations of the earth,
that it should not be moved forever.
You covered it with the deep as with a cloak.
The waters stood above the mountains.
At your rebuke they fled.
At the voice of your thunder they hurried away.
The mountains rose,
the valleys sank down,
to the place which you had assigned to them.
You have set a boundary that they may not pass over,
that they don't turn again to cover the earth.
He sends springs into the valleys.
They run among the mountains.
They give drink to every animal of the field.
The wild donkeys quench their thirst.
The birds of the sky nest by them.

They sing among the branches.
He waters the mountains from his rooms.
The earth is filled with the fruit of your works.
He causes the grass to grow for the livestock,
and plants for man to cultivate,
that he may produce food out of the earth:
wine that makes the heart of man glad,
oil to make his face to shine,
and bread that strengthens man's heart.
YHWH's trees are well watered,
the cedars of Lebanon, which he has planted;
where the birds make their nests.
The stork makes its home in the cypress trees.
The high mountains are for the wild goats.
The rocks are a refuge for the rock badgers.
He appointed the moon for seasons.
The sun knows when to set.
You make darkness, and it is night,
in which all the animals of the forest prowl.
The young lions roar after their prey,
and seek their food from God.
The sun rises, and they steal away,
and lie down in their dens.
Man goes out to his work,
to his labor until the evening.
YHWH, how many are your works!
In wisdom, you have made them all.
The earth is full of your riches.
There is the sea, great and wide,
in which are innumerable living things,
both small and large animals.
There the ships go,
and leviathan, whom you formed to play there.
These all wait for you,
that you may give them their food in due season.
You give to them; they gather.
You open your hand; they are satisfied with good.
You hide your face; they are troubled.
You take away their breath; they die and return to the dust.
You send out your Spirit and they are created.

You renew the face of the ground.
Let YHWH's glory endure forever.
Let YHWH rejoice in his works.
He looks at the earth, and it trembles.
He touches the mountains, and they smoke.
I will sing to YHWH as long as I live.
I will sing praise to my God while I have any being.
Let my meditation be sweet to him.
I will rejoice in YHWH.
Let sinners be consumed out of the earth.
Let the wicked be no more.
Bless YHWH, my soul.
Praise Yah!

....

Give thanks to YHWH! Call on his name!
Make his doings known among the peoples.
Sing to him, sing praises to him!
Tell of all his marvelous works.
Glory in his holy name.
Let the heart of those who seek YHWH rejoice.
Seek YHWH and his strength.
Seek his face forever more.
Remember his marvelous works that he has done:
his wonders, and the judgments of his mouth,
you offspring of Abraham, his servant,
you children of Jacob, his chosen ones.
He is YHWH, our God.
His judgments are in all the earth.
He has remembered his covenant forever,
the word which he commanded to a thousand generations,
the covenant which he made with Abraham,
his oath to Isaac,
and confirmed it to Jacob for a statute;
to Israel for an everlasting covenant,
saying, "To you I will give the land of Canaan,
the lot of your inheritance,"
when they were but a few men in number,
yes, very few, and foreigners in it.
They went about from nation to nation,

from one kingdom to another people.
He allowed no one to do them wrong.
Yes, he reproved kings for their sakes,
"Don't touch my anointed ones!
Do my prophets no harm!"
He called for a famine on the land.
He destroyed the food supplies.
He sent a man before them.
Joseph was sold for a slave.
They bruised his feet with shackles.
His neck was locked in irons,
until the time that his word happened,
and YHWH's word proved him true.
The king sent and freed him,
even the ruler of peoples, and let him go free.
He made him lord of his house,
and ruler of all of his possessions,
to discipline his princes at his pleasure,
and to teach his elders wisdom.
Israel also came into Egypt.
Jacob lived in the land of Ham.
He increased his people greatly,
and made them stronger than their adversaries.
He turned their heart to hate his people,
to conspire against his servants.
He sent Moses, his servant,
and Aaron, whom he had chosen.
They performed miracles among them,
and wonders in the land of Ham.
He sent darkness, and made it dark.
They didn't rebel against his words.
He turned their waters into blood,
and killed their fish.
Their land swarmed with frogs,
even in the rooms of their kings.
He spoke, and swarms of flies came,
and lice in all their borders.
He gave them hail for rain,
with lightning in their land.
He struck their vines and also their fig trees,

and shattered the trees of their country.
He spoke, and the locusts came
  with the grasshoppers, without number,
ate up every plant in their land,
  and ate up the fruit of their ground.
He struck also all the firstborn in their land,
  the first fruits of all their manhood.
He brought them out with silver and gold.
  There was not one feeble person among his tribes.
Egypt was glad when they departed,
  for the fear of them had fallen on them.
He spread a cloud for a covering,
  fire to give light in the night.
They asked, and he brought quails,
  and satisfied them with the bread of the sky.
He opened the rock, and waters gushed out.
  They ran as a river in the dry places.
For he remembered his holy word,
  and Abraham, his servant.
He brought his people out with joy,
  his chosen with singing.
He gave them the lands of the nations.
  They took the labor of the peoples in possession,
that they might keep his statutes,
  and observe his laws.
  Praise Yah!

....

Praise YHWH!
  Give thanks to YHWH, for he is good,
  for his loving kindness endures forever.
Who can utter the mighty acts of YHWH,
  or fully declare all his praise?
Blessed are those who keep justice.
  Blessed is one who does what is right at all times.
Remember me, YHWH, with the favor that you show to your
people.
  Visit me with your salvation,
that I may see the prosperity of your chosen,
  that I may rejoice in the gladness of your nation,

that I may glory with your inheritance.

We have sinned with our fathers.
  We have committed iniquity.
  We have done wickedly.
Our fathers didn't understand your wonders in Egypt.
  They didn't remember the multitude of your loving kindnesses,
  but were rebellious at the sea, even at the Red Sea.
Nevertheless he saved them for his name's sake,
  that he might make his mighty power known.
He rebuked the Red Sea also, and it was dried up;
  so he led them through the depths, as through a desert.
He saved them from the hand of him who hated them,
  and redeemed them from the hand of the enemy.
The waters covered their adversaries.
  There was not one of them left.
Then they believed his words.
  They sang his praise.

They soon forgot his works.
  They didn't wait for his counsel,
  but gave in to craving in the desert,
  and tested God in the wasteland.
He gave them their request,
  but sent leanness into their soul.
They envied Moses also in the camp,
  and Aaron, YHWH's saint.
The earth opened and swallowed up Dathan,
  and covered the company of Abiram.
A fire was kindled in their company.
  The flame burned up the wicked.
They made a calf in Horeb,
  and worshiped a molten image.
Thus they exchanged their glory
  for an image of a bull that eats grass.
They forgot God, their Savior,
  who had done great things in Egypt,
  wondrous works in the land of Ham,
  and awesome things by the Red Sea.
Therefore he said that he would destroy them,

had Moses, his chosen, not stood before him in the breach,
to turn away his wrath, so that he wouldn't destroy them.
Yes, they despised the pleasant land.
They didn't believe his word,
but murmured in their tents,
and didn't listen to YHWH's voice.
Therefore he swore to them
that he would overthrow them in the wilderness,
that he would overthrow their offspring among the nations,
and scatter them in the lands.
They joined themselves also to Baal Peor,
and ate the sacrifices of the dead.
Thus they provoked him to anger with their deeds.
The plague broke in on them.
Then Phinehas stood up and executed judgment,
so the plague was stopped.
That was credited to him for righteousness,
for all generations to come.
They angered him also at the waters of Meribah,
so that Moses was troubled for their sakes;
because they were rebellious against his spirit,
he spoke rashly with his lips.
They didn't destroy the peoples,
as YHWH commanded them,
but mixed themselves with the nations,
and learned their works.
They served their idols,
which became a snare to them.
Yes, they sacrificed their sons and their daughters to demons.
They shed innocent blood,
even the blood of their sons and of their daughters,
whom they sacrificed to the idols of Canaan.
The land was polluted with blood.
Thus they were defiled with their works,
and prostituted themselves in their deeds.
Therefore YHWH burned with anger against his people.
He abhorred his inheritance.
He gave them into the hand of the nations.
Those who hated them ruled over them.
Their enemies also oppressed them.

They were brought into subjection under their hand.
He rescued them many times,
>   but they were rebellious in their counsel,
>   and were brought low in their iniquity.
Nevertheless he regarded their distress,
>   when he heard their cry.
He remembered for them his covenant,
>   and repented according to the multitude of his loving kind-
>   nesses.
He made them also to be pitied
>   by all those who carried them captive.

Save us, YHWH, our God,
>   gather us from among the nations,
>   to give thanks to your holy name,
>   to triumph in your praise!

Blessed be YHWH, the God of Israel,
>   from everlasting even to everlasting!
Let all the people say, "Amen."
Praise Yah!

....

BOOK 5

Give thanks to YHWH, for he is good,
>   for his loving kindness endures forever.
Let the redeemed by YHWH say so,
>   whom he has redeemed from the hand of the adversary,
>   And gathered out of the lands,
>   from the east and from the west,
>   from the north and from the south.

They wandered in the wilderness in a desert way.
>   They found no city to live in.
Hungry and thirsty,
>   their soul fainted in them.
Then they cried to YHWH in their trouble,
>   and he delivered them out of their distresses,
he led them also by a straight way,
>   that they might go to a city to live in.

Let them praise YHWH *for his loving kindness,*
   for his wonderful deeds to the children of men!

For he satisfies the longing soul.
   He fills the hungry soul with good.

Some sat in darkness and in the shadow of death,
   being bound in affliction and iron,
   because they rebelled against the words of God,
   and condemned the counsel of the Most High.
Therefore he brought down their heart with labor.
   They fell down, and there was no one to help.
Then they cried to YHWH *in their trouble,*
   and he saved them out of their distresses.
He brought them out of darkness and the shadow of death,
   and broke away their chains.
Let them praise YHWH *for his loving kindness,*
   for his wonderful deeds to the children of men!

For he has broken the gates of bronze,
   and cut through bars of iron.

Fools are afflicted because of their disobedience,
   and because of their iniquities.
Their soul abhors all kinds of food.
   They draw near to the gates of death.
Then they cry to YHWH *in their trouble,*
   he saves them out of their distresses.
He sends his word, and heals them,
   and delivers them from their graves.
Let them praise YHWH *for his loving kindness,*
   for his wonderful deeds to the children of men!

Let them offer the sacrifices of thanksgiving,
   and declare his deeds with singing.

Those who go down to the sea in ships,
   who do business in great waters;
   These see YHWH's *deeds,*
   and his wonders in the deep.

For he commands, and raises the stormy wind,
    which lifts up its waves.
They mount up to the sky; they go down again to the depths.
    Their soul melts away because of trouble.
They reel back and forth, and stagger like a drunken man,
    and are at their wits' end.
Then they cry to YHWH in their trouble,
    and he brings them out of their distress.
He makes the storm a calm,
    so that its waves are still.
Then they are glad because it is calm,
    so he brings them to their desired haven.
Let them praise YHWH for his loving kindness,
    for his wonderful deeds for the children of men!

Let them exalt him also in the assembly of the people,
    and praise him in the seat of the elders.

He turns rivers into a desert,
    water springs into a thirsty ground,
    and a fruitful land into a salt waste,
    for the wickedness of those who dwell in it.
He turns a desert into a pool of water,
    and a dry land into water springs.
There he makes the hungry live,
    that they may prepare a city to live in,
    sow fields, plant vineyards,
    and reap the fruits of increase.
He blesses them also, so that they are multiplied greatly.
    He doesn't allow their livestock to decrease.
Again, they are diminished and bowed down
    through oppression, trouble, and sorrow.
He pours contempt on princes,
    and causes them to wander in a trackless waste.
Yet he lifts the needy out of their affliction,
    and increases their families like a flock.
The upright will see it, and be glad.
    All the wicked will shut their mouths.
Whoever is wise will pay attention to these things.
    They will consider the loving kindnesses of YHWH.

....

A Song. A Psalm by David. My heart is steadfast, God.
I will sing and I will make music with my soul.
Wake up, harp and lyre!
I will wake up the dawn.
I will give thanks to you, YHWH, among the nations.
I will sing praises to you among the peoples.
For your loving kindness is great above the heavens.
Your faithfulness reaches to the skies.
Be exalted, God, above the heavens!
Let your glory be over all the earth.
That your beloved may be delivered,
save with your right hand, and answer us.
God has spoken from his sanctuary: "In triumph,
I will divide Shechem, and measure out the valley of Succoth.
Gilead is mine. Manasseh is mine.
Ephraim also is my helmet.
Judah is my scepter.
Moab is my wash pot.
I will toss my sandal on Edom.
I will shout over Philistia."
Who will bring me into the fortified city?
Who has led me to Edom?
Haven't you rejected us, God?
You don't go out, God, with our armies.
Give us help against the enemy,
for the help of man is vain.
Through God, we will do valiantly.
For it is he who will tread down our enemies.

....

For the Chief Musician. A Psalm by David. God of my praise,
don't remain silent,
for they have opened the mouth of the wicked and the mouth
of deceit against me.
They have spoken to me with a lying tongue.
They have also surrounded me with words of hatred,
and fought against me without a cause.
In return for my love, they are my adversaries;

but I am in prayer.
They have rewarded me evil for good,
   and hatred for my love.
Set a wicked man over him.
   Let an adversary stand at his right hand.
When he is judged, let him come out guilty.
   Let his prayer be turned into sin.
Let his days be few.
   Let another take his office.
Let his children be fatherless,
   and his wife a widow.
Let his children be wandering beggars.
   Let them be sought from their ruins.
Let the creditor seize all that he has.
   Let strangers plunder the fruit of his labor.
Let there be no one to extend kindness to him,
   neither let there be anyone to have pity on his fatherless children.
Let his posterity be cut off.
   In the generation following let their name be blotted out.
Let the iniquity of his fathers be remembered by YHWH.
   Don't let the sin of his mother be blotted out.
Let them be before YHWH *continually,*
   that he may cut off their memory from the earth;
because he didn't remember to show kindness,
   but persecuted the poor and needy man,
   the broken in heart, to kill them.
Yes, he loved cursing, and it came to him.
   He didn't delight in blessing, and it was far from him.
He clothed himself also with cursing as with his garment.
   It came into his inward parts like water,
   like oil into his bones.
Let it be to him as the clothing with which he covers himself,
   for the belt that is always around him.
This is the reward of my adversaries from YHWH,
   of those who speak evil against my soul.

But deal with me, YHWH *the Lord, for your name's sake,*
   because your loving kindness is good, deliver me;
   for I am poor and needy.

My heart is wounded within me.
I fade away like an evening shadow.
   I am shaken off like a locust.
My knees are weak through fasting.
   My body is thin and lacks fat.
I have also become a reproach to them.
   When they see me, they shake their head.
Help me, YHWH, my God.
   Save me according to your loving kindness;
that they may know that this is your hand;
   that you, YHWH, have done it.
They may curse, but you bless.
   When they arise, they will be shamed,
   but your servant shall rejoice.
Let my adversaries be clothed with dishonor.
   Let them cover themselves with their own shame as with a
   robe.
I will give great thanks to YHWH with my mouth.
   Yes, I will praise him among the multitude.
For he will stand at the right hand of the needy,
   to save him from those who judge his soul.

....

A Psalm by David. YHWH says to my Lord, "Sit at my right hand,
   until I make your enemies your footstool for your feet."
YHWH will send out the rod of your strength out of Zion.
   Rule among your enemies.
Your people offer themselves willingly in the day of your power, in
holy array.
   Out of the womb of the morning, you have the dew of your
   youth.
YHWH has sworn, and will not change his mind:
   "You are a priest forever in the order of Melchizedek."
The Lord is at your right hand.
   He will crush kings in the day of his wrath.
He will judge among the nations.
   He will heap up dead bodies.
   He will crush the ruler of the whole earth.
He will drink of the brook on the way;
   therefore he will lift up his head.

....

Praise Yah!
I will give thanks to YHWH *with my whole heart,*
in the council of the upright, and in the congregation.
YHWH's *works are great,*
pondered by all those who delight in them.
His work is honor and majesty.
His righteousness endures forever.
He has caused his wonderful works to be remembered.
YHWH *is gracious and merciful.*
He has given food to those who fear him.
He always remembers his covenant.
He has shown his people the power of his works,
in giving them the heritage of the nations.
The works of his hands are truth and justice.
All his precepts are sure.
They are established forever and ever.
They are done in truth and uprightness.
He has sent redemption to his people.
He has ordained his covenant forever.
His name is holy and awesome!
The fear of YHWH *is the beginning of wisdom.*
All those who do his work have a good understanding.
His praise endures forever!

....

Praise Yah!
Blessed is the man who fears YHWH,
who delights greatly in his commandments.
His offspring will be mighty in the land.
The generation of the upright will be blessed.
Wealth and riches are in his house.
His righteousness endures forever.
Light dawns in the darkness for the upright,
gracious, merciful, and righteous.
It is well with the man who deals graciously and lends.
He will maintain his cause in judgment.
For he will never be shaken.
The righteous will be remembered forever.

He will not be afraid of evil news.
His heart is steadfast, trusting in YHWH.
His heart is established.
He will not be afraid in the end when he sees his adversaries.
He has dispersed, he has given to the poor.
His righteousness endures forever.
His horn will be exalted with honor.
The wicked will see it, and be grieved.
He shall gnash with his teeth, and melt away.
The desire of the wicked will perish.

....

Praise Yah!
Praise, you servants of YHWH,
praise YHWH's name.
Blessed be YHWH's name,
from this time forward and forever more.
From the rising of the sun to its going down,
YHWH's name is to be praised.
YHWH is high above all nations,
his glory above the heavens.
Who is like YHWH, our God,
who has his seat on high,
Who stoops down to see in heaven and in the earth?
He raises up the poor out of the dust.
Lifts up the needy from the ash heap,
that he may set him with princes,
even with the princes of his people.
He settles the barren woman in her home
as a joyful mother of children.
Praise Yah!

....

When Israel went out of Egypt,
the house of Jacob from a people of foreign language,
Judah became his sanctuary,
Israel his dominion.
The sea saw it, and fled.
The Jordan was driven back.
The mountains skipped like rams,

the little hills like lambs.
What was it, you sea, that you fled?
   You Jordan, that you turned back?
You mountains, that you skipped like rams;
   you little hills, like lambs?
Tremble, you earth, at the presence of the Lord,
   at the presence of the God of Jacob,
who turned the rock into a pool of water,
   the flint into a spring of waters.

....

Not to us, YHWH, *not to us,*
   but to your name give glory,
   for your loving kindness, and for your truth's sake.
Why should the nations say,
   "Where is their God, now?"
But our God is in the heavens.
   He does whatever he pleases.
Their idols are silver and gold,
   the work of men's hands.
They have mouths, but they don't speak.
   They have eyes, but they don't see.
They have ears, but they don't hear.
   They have noses, but they don't smell.
They have hands, but they don't feel.
   They have feet, but they don't walk,
   neither do they speak through their throat.
Those who make them will be like them;
   yes, everyone who trusts in them.
Israel, trust in YHWH!
   He is their help and their shield.
House of Aaron, trust in YHWH!
   He is their help and their shield.
You who fear YHWH, *trust in* YHWH!
   He is their help and their shield.
YHWH *remembers us. He will bless us.*
   He will bless the house of Israel.
   He will bless the house of Aaron.
He will bless those who fear YHWH,
   both small and great.

May YHWH increase you more and more,
    you and your children.
Blessed are you by YHWH,
    who made heaven and earth.
The heavens are YHWH's heavens,
    but he has given the earth to the children of men.
The dead don't praise Yah,
    neither any who go down into silence;
but we will bless Yah,
    from this time forward and forever more.
Praise Yah!

....

I love YHWH, because he listens to my voice,
    and my cries for mercy.
Because he has turned his ear to me,
    therefore I will call on him as long as I live.
The cords of death surrounded me,
    the pains of Sheol got a hold of me.
    I found trouble and sorrow.
Then I called on YHWH's name:
    "YHWH, I beg you, deliver my soul."
YHWH is Gracious and righteous.
    Yes, our God is merciful.
YHWH preserves the simple.
    I was brought low, and he saved me.
Return to your rest, my soul,
    for YHWH has dealt bountifully with you.
For you have delivered my soul from death,
    my eyes from tears,
    and my feet from falling.
I will walk before YHWH in the land of the living.
I believed, therefore I said,
    "I was greatly afflicted."
I said in my haste,
    "All people are liars."
What will I give to YHWH for all his benefits toward me?
    I will take the cup of salvation, and call on YHWH's name.
I will pay my vows to YHWH,
    yes, in the presence of all his people.

Precious in YHWH's *sight is the death of his saints.*
YHWH, *truly I am your servant.*
    I am your servant, the son of your servant girl.
    You have freed me from my chains.
I will offer to you the sacrifice of thanksgiving,
    and will call on YHWH's *name.*
I will pay my vows to YHWH,
    yes, in the presence of all his people,
in the courts of YHWH's *house,*
    in the middle of you, Jerusalem.
Praise Yah!

....

Praise YHWH, *all you nations!*
    Extol him, all you peoples!
For his loving kindness is great toward us.
    YHWH's *faithfulness endures forever.*
Praise Yah!

....

Give thanks to YHWH, *for he is good,*
    for his loving kindness endures forever.
Let Israel now say
    that his loving kindness endures forever.
Let the house of Aaron now say
    that his loving kindness endures forever.
Now let those who fear YHWH *say*
    that his loving kindness endures forever.
Out of my distress, I called on Yah.
    Yah answered me with freedom.
YHWH *is on my side. I will not be afraid.*
    What can man do to me?
YHWH *is on my side among those who help me.*
    Therefore I will look in triumph at those who hate me.
It is better to take refuge in YHWH,
    than to put confidence in man.
It is better to take refuge in YHWH,
    than to put confidence in princes.
All the nations surrounded me,
    but in YHWH's *name, I cut them off.*

They surrounded me, yes, they surrounded me.
    In YHWH's name I indeed cut them off.
They surrounded me like bees.
        They are quenched like the burning thorns.
    In YHWH's name I cut them off.
You pushed me back hard, to make me fall,
    but YHWH helped me.
Yah is my strength and song.
    He has become my salvation.
The voice of rejoicing and salvation is in the tents of the righteous.
    "The right hand of YHWH does valiantly.
The right hand of YHWH is exalted!
        The right hand of YHWH does valiantly!"
I will not die, but live,
    and declare Yah's works.
Yah has punished me severely,
    but he has not given me over to death.
Open to me the gates of righteousness.
    I will enter into them.
    I will give thanks to Yah.
This is the gate of YHWH;
    the righteous will enter into it.
I will give thanks to you, for you have answered me,
    and have become my salvation.
The stone which the builders rejected
    has become the cornerstone.
This is YHWH's doing.
    It is marvelous in our eyes.
This is the day that YHWH has made.
    We will rejoice and be glad in it!
Save us now, we beg you, YHWH!
    YHWH, we beg you, send prosperity now.
Blessed is he who comes in YHWH's name!
    We have blessed you out of YHWH's house.
YHWH is God, and he has given us light.
    Bind the sacrifice with cords, even to the horns of the altar.
You are my God, and I will give thanks to you.
    You are my God, I will exalt you.
Oh give thanks to YHWH, for he is good,
    for his loving kindness endures forever.

....

ALEPH Blessed are those whose ways are blameless,
    who walk according to YHWH's *law.*
Blessed are those who keep his statutes,
    who seek him with their whole heart.
Yes, they do nothing wrong.
    They walk in his ways.
You have commanded your precepts,
    that we should fully obey them.
Oh that my ways were steadfast
    to obey your statutes!
Then I wouldn't be disappointed,
    when I consider all of your commandments.
I will give thanks to you with uprightness of heart,
    when I learn your righteous judgments.
I will observe your statutes.
    Don't utterly forsake me.
BET How can a young man keep his way pure?
    By living according to your word.
With my whole heart, I have sought you.
    Don't let me wander from your commandments.
I have hidden your word in my heart,
    that I might not sin against you.
Blessed are you, YHWH.
    Teach me your statutes.
With my lips,
    I have declared all the ordinances of your mouth.
I have rejoiced in the way of your testimonies,
    as much as in all riches.
I will meditate on your precepts,
    and consider your ways.
I will delight myself in your statutes.
    I will not forget your word.
GIMEL Do good to your servant.
    I will live and I will obey your word.
Open my eyes,
    that I may see wondrous things out of your law.
I am a stranger on the earth.
    Don't hide your commandments from me.

My soul is consumed with longing for your ordinances at all times.
You have rebuked the proud who are cursed,
*   who wander from your commandments.*
Take reproach and contempt away from me,
*   for I have kept your statutes.*
Though princes sit and slander me,
*   your servant will meditate on your statutes.*
Indeed your statutes are my delight,
*   and my counselors.*
DALED My soul is laid low in the dust.
*   Revive me according to your word!*
I declared my ways, and you answered me.
*   Teach me your statutes.*
Let me understand the teaching of your precepts!
*   Then I will meditate on your wondrous works.*
My soul is weary with sorrow:
*   strengthen me according to your word.*
Keep me from the way of deceit.
*   Grant me your law graciously!*
I have chosen the way of truth.
*   I have set your ordinances before me.*
I cling to your statutes, YHWH.
*   Don't let me be disappointed.*
I run in the path of your commandments,
*   for you have set my heart free.*
HEY Teach me, YHWH, the way of your statutes.
*   I will keep them to the end.*
Give me understanding, and I will keep your law.
*   Yes, I will obey it with my whole heart.*
Direct me in the path of your commandments,
*   for I delight in them.*
Turn my heart toward your statutes,
*   not toward selfish gain.*
Turn my eyes away from looking at worthless things.
*   Revive me in your ways.*
Fulfill your promise to your servant,
*   that you may be feared.*
Take away my disgrace that I dread,
*   for your ordinances are good.*
Behold, I long for your precepts!

Revive me in your righteousness.
WAW Let your loving kindness also come to me, YHWH,
    your salvation, according to your word.
So I will have an answer for him who reproaches me,
    for I trust in your word.
Don't snatch the word of truth out of my mouth,
    for I put my hope in your ordinances.
So I will obey your law continually,
    forever and ever.
I will walk in liberty,
    for I have sought your precepts.
I will also speak of your statutes before kings,
    and will not be disappointed.
I will delight myself in your commandments,
    because I love them.
I reach out my hands for your commandments, which I love.
    I will meditate on your statutes.
ZAYIN Remember your word to your servant,
    because you gave me hope.
This is my comfort in my affliction,
    for your word has revived me.
The arrogant mock me excessively,
    but I don't swerve from your law.
I remember your ordinances of old, YHWH,
    and have comforted myself.
Indignation has taken hold on me,
    because of the wicked who forsake your law.
Your statutes have been my songs
    in the house where I live.
I have remembered your name, YHWH, in the night,
    and I obey your law.
This is my way,
    that I keep your precepts.
CHET YHWH is my portion.
    I promised to obey your words.
I sought your favor with my whole heart.
    Be merciful to me according to your word.
I considered my ways,
    and turned my steps to your statutes.
I will hurry, and not delay,

to obey your commandments.
The ropes of the wicked bind me,
    but I won't forget your law.
At midnight I will rise to give thanks to you,
    because of your righteous ordinances.
I am a friend of all those who fear you,
    of those who observe your precepts.
The earth is full of your loving kindness, YHWH.
    Teach me your statutes.
TET Do good to your servant,
    according to your word, YHWH.
Teach me good judgment and knowledge,
    for I believe in your commandments.
Before I was afflicted, I went astray;
    but now I observe your word.
You are good, and do good.
    Teach me your statutes.
The proud have smeared a lie upon me.
    With my whole heart, I will keep your precepts.
Their heart is as callous as the fat,
    but I delight in your law.
It is good for me that I have been afflicted,
    that I may learn your statutes.
The law of your mouth is better to me than thousands of pieces of
gold and silver.
YUD Your hands have made me and formed me.
    Give me understanding, that I may learn your command-
    ments.
Those who fear you will see me and be glad,
    because I have put my hope in your word.
YHWH, I know that your judgments are righteous,
    that in faithfulness you have afflicted me.
Please let your loving kindness be for my comfort,
    according to your word to your servant.
Let your tender mercies come to me, that I may live;
    for your law is my delight.
Let the proud be disappointed, for they have overthrown me
wrongfully.
    I will meditate on your precepts.
Let those who fear you turn to me.

They will know your statutes.
Let my heart be blameless toward your decrees,
*   that I may not be disappointed.*
KAF My soul faints for your salvation.
*   I hope in your word.*
My eyes fail for your word.
*   I say, "When will you comfort me?"*
For I have become like a wineskin in the smoke.
*   I don't forget your statutes.*
How many are the days of your servant?
*   When will you execute judgment on those who persecute me?*
The proud have dug pits for me,
*   contrary to your law.*
All of your commandments are faithful.
*   They persecute me wrongfully.*
*   Help me!*
They had almost wiped me from the earth,
*   but I didn't forsake your precepts.*
Preserve my life according to your loving kindness,
*   so I will obey the statutes of your mouth.*
LAMED YHWH, your word is settled in heaven forever.
Your faithfulness is to all generations.
*   You have established the earth, and it remains.*
Your laws remain to this day,
*   for all things serve you.*
Unless your law had been my delight,
*   I would have perished in my affliction.*
I will never forget your precepts,
*   for with them, you have revived me.*
I am yours.
*   Save me, for I have sought your precepts.*
The wicked have waited for me, to destroy me.
*   I will consider your statutes.*
I have seen a limit to all perfection,
*   but your commands are boundless.*
MEM How I love your law!
*   It is my meditation all day.*
Your commandments make me wiser than my enemies,
*   for your commandments are always with me.*
I have more understanding than all my teachers,

for your testimonies are my meditation.
I understand more than the aged,
  because I have kept your precepts.
I have kept my feet from every evil way,
  that I might observe your word.
I have not turned away from your ordinances,
  for you have taught me.
How sweet are your promises to my taste,
  more than honey to my mouth!
Through your precepts, I get understanding;
  therefore I hate every false way.
NUN Your word is a lamp to my feet,
  and a light for my path.
I have sworn, and have confirmed it,
  that I will obey your righteous ordinances.
I am afflicted very much.
  Revive me, YHWH, according to your word.
Accept, I beg you, the willing offerings of my mouth.
  YHWH, teach me your ordinances.
My soul is continually in my hand,
  yet I won't forget your law.
The wicked have laid a snare for me,
  yet I haven't gone astray from your precepts.
I have taken your testimonies as a heritage forever,
  for they are the joy of my heart.
I have set my heart to perform your statutes forever,
  even to the end.
SAMEKH I hate double-minded men,
  but I love your law.
You are my hiding place and my shield.
  I hope in your word.
Depart from me, you evildoers,
  that I may keep the commandments of my God.
Uphold me according to your word, that I may live.
  Let me not be ashamed of my hope.
Hold me up, and I will be safe,
  and will have respect for your statutes continually.
You reject all those who stray from your statutes,
  for their deceit is in vain.
You put away all the wicked of the earth like dross.

Therefore I love your testimonies.
My flesh trembles for fear of you.
I am afraid of your judgments.
AYIN I have done what is just and righteous.
Don't leave me to my oppressors.
Ensure your servant's well-being.
Don't let the proud oppress me.
My eyes fail looking for your salvation,
for your righteous word.
Deal with your servant according to your loving kindness.
Teach me your statutes.
I am your servant. Give me understanding,
that I may know your testimonies.
It is time to act, YHWH,
for they break your law.
Therefore I love your commandments more than gold,
yes, more than pure gold.
Therefore I consider all of your precepts to be right.
I hate every false way.
PEY Your testimonies are wonderful,
therefore my soul keeps them.
The entrance of your words gives light.
It gives understanding to the simple.
I opened my mouth wide and panted,
for I longed for your commandments.
Turn to me, and have mercy on me,
as you always do to those who love your name.
Establish my footsteps in your word.
Don't let any iniquity have dominion over me.
Redeem me from the oppression of man,
so I will observe your precepts.
Make your face shine on your servant.
Teach me your statutes.
Streams of tears run down my eyes,
because they don't observe your law.
TZADI You are righteous, YHWH.
Your judgments are upright.
You have commanded your statutes in righteousness.
They are fully trustworthy.
My zeal wears me out,

because my enemies ignore your words.
Your promises have been thoroughly tested,
  and your servant loves them.
I am small and despised.
  I don't forget your precepts.
Your righteousness is an everlasting righteousness.
  Your law is truth.
Trouble and anguish have taken hold of me.
  Your commandments are my delight.
Your testimonies are righteous forever.
  Give me understanding, that I may live.
KUF I have called with my whole heart.
  Answer me, YHWH!
  I will keep your statutes.
I have called to you. Save me!
  I will obey your statutes.
I rise before dawn and cry for help.
  I put my hope in your words.
My eyes stay open through the night watches,
  that I might meditate on your word.
Hear my voice according to your loving kindness.
  Revive me, YHWH, according to your ordinances.
They draw near who follow after wickedness.
  They are far from your law.
You are near, YHWH.
  All your commandments are truth.
Of old I have known from your testimonies,
  that you have founded them forever.
RESH Consider my affliction, and deliver me,
  for I don't forget your law.
Plead my cause, and redeem me!
  Revive me according to your promise.
Salvation is far from the wicked,
  for they don't seek your statutes.
Great are your tender mercies, YHWH.
  Revive me according to your ordinances.
Many are my persecutors and my adversaries.
  I haven't swerved from your testimonies.
I look at the faithless with loathing,
  because they don't observe your word.

Consider how I love your precepts.
Revive me, YHWH, according to your loving kindness.
All of your words are truth.
Every one of your righteous ordinances endures forever.
SIN AND SHIN Princes have persecuted me without a cause,
but my heart stands in awe of your words.
I rejoice at your word,
as one who finds great plunder.
I hate and abhor falsehood.
I love your law.
Seven times a day, I praise you,
because of your righteous ordinances.
Those who love your law have great peace.
Nothing causes them to stumble.
I have hoped for your salvation, YHWH.
I have done your commandments.
My soul has observed your testimonies.
I love them exceedingly.
I have obeyed your precepts and your testimonies,
for all my ways are before you.
TAV Let my cry come before you, YHWH.
Give me understanding according to your word.
Let my supplication come before you.
Deliver me according to your word.
Let my lips utter praise,
for you teach me your statutes.
Let my tongue sing of your word,
for all your commandments are righteousness.
Let your hand be ready to help me,
for I have chosen your precepts.
I have longed for your salvation, YHWH.
Your law is my delight.
Let my soul live, that I may praise you.
Let your ordinances help me.
I have gone astray like a lost sheep.
Seek your servant, for I don't forget your commandments.

....

A Song of Ascents. In my distress, I cried to YHWH.
He answered me.

Deliver my soul, YHWH, from lying lips,
    from a deceitful tongue.
What will be given to you, and what will be done more to you,
    you deceitful tongue?
Sharp arrows of the mighty,
    with coals of juniper.
Woe is me, that I live in Meshech,
    that I dwell among the tents of Kedar!
My soul has had her dwelling too long
    with him who hates peace.
I am for peace,
    but when I speak, they are for war.

....

A Song of Ascents. I will lift up my eyes to the hills.
    Where does my help come from?
My help comes from YHWH,
    who made heaven and earth.

He will not allow your foot to be moved.
    He who keeps you will not slumber.
Behold, he who keeps Israel
    will neither slumber nor sleep.
YHWH is your keeper.
    YHWH is your shade on your right hand.
The sun will not harm you by day,
    nor the moon by night.
YHWH will keep you from all evil.
    He will keep your soul.
YHWH will keep your going out and your coming in,
    from this time forward, and forever more.

....

A Song of Ascents. By David. I was glad when they said to me,
    "Let's go to YHWH's house!"
Our feet are standing within your gates, Jerusalem,
    Jerusalem, that is built as a city that is compact together,
where the tribes go up, even Yah's tribes,
    according to an ordinance for Israel,
    to give thanks to YHWH's name.

For there are set thrones for judgment,
   the thrones of David's house.
Pray for the peace of Jerusalem.
   Those who love you will prosper.
Peace be within your walls,
   and prosperity within your palaces.
For my brothers' and companions' sakes,
   I will now say, "Peace be within you."
For the sake of the house of YHWH *our God,*
   I will seek your good.

....

A Song of Ascents. I lift up my eyes to you,
   you who sit in the heavens.
Behold, as the eyes of servants look to the hand of their master,
   as the eyes of a maid to the hand of her mistress;
   so our eyes look to YHWH, *our God,*
   until he has mercy on us.
Have mercy on us, YHWH, *have mercy on us,*
   for we have endured much contempt.
Our soul is exceedingly filled with the scoffing of those who are at ease,
   with the contempt of the proud.

....

A Song of Ascents. By David. If it had not been YHWH *who was on our side,*
   let Israel now say,
if it had not been YHWH *who was on our side,*
   when men rose up against us;
then they would have swallowed us up alive,
   when their wrath was kindled against us;
then the waters would have overwhelmed us,
   the stream would have gone over our soul;
then the proud waters would have gone over our soul.
Blessed be YHWH,
   who has not given us as a prey to their teeth.
Our soul has escaped like a bird out of the fowler's snare.
   The snare is broken, and we have escaped.
Our help is in YHWH's *name,*

who made heaven and earth.

....

A Song of Ascents. Those who trust in YHWH *are as Mount Zion,*
which can't be moved, but remains forever.
As the mountains surround Jerusalem,
so YHWH *surrounds his people from this time forward and*
forever more.
For the scepter of wickedness won't remain over the allotment of
the righteous;
so that the righteous won't use their hands to do evil.
Do good, YHWH, *to those who are good,*
to those who are upright in their hearts.
But as for those who turn away to their crooked ways,
YHWH *will lead them away with the workers of iniquity.*
Peace be on Israel.

....

A Song of Ascents. When YHWH *brought back those who returned*
to Zion,
we were like those who dream.
Then our mouth was filled with laughter,
and our tongue with singing.
Then they said among the nations,
*"*YHWH *has done great things for them."*
YHWH *has done great things for us,*
and we are glad.
Restore our fortunes again, YHWH,
like the streams in the Negev.
Those who sow in tears will reap in joy.
He who goes out weeping, carrying seed for sowing,
will certainly come again with joy, carrying his sheaves.

....

A Song of Ascents. By Solomon. Unless YHWH *builds the house,*
they who build it labor in vain.
Unless YHWH *watches over the city,*
the watchman guards it in vain.
It is vain for you to rise up early,
to stay up late,

eating the bread of toil,
  for he gives sleep to his loved ones.
Behold, children are a heritage of YHWH.
  The fruit of the womb is his reward.
As arrows in the hand of a mighty man,
  so are the children of youth.
Happy is the man who has his quiver full of them.
  They won't be disappointed when they speak with their ene-
  mies in the gate.

....

A Song of Ascents. Blessed is everyone who fears YHWH,
  who walks in his ways.
For you will eat the labor of your hands.
  You will be happy, and it will be well with you.
Your wife will be as a fruitful vine in the innermost parts of your
house,
  your children like olive plants around your table.
Behold, thus is the man blessed who fears YHWH.
  May YHWH bless you out of Zion,
  and may you see the good of Jerusalem all the days of your life.
Yes, may you see your children's children.
  Peace be upon Israel.

....

A Song of Ascents. Many times they have afflicted me from my
youth up.
  Let Israel now say,
many times they have afflicted me from my youth up,
  yet they have not prevailed against me.
The plowers plowed on my back.
  They made their furrows long.
YHWH is righteous.
  He has cut apart the cords of the wicked.
Let them be disappointed and turned backward,
  all those who hate Zion.
Let them be as the grass on the housetops,
  which withers before it grows up,
with which the reaper doesn't fill his hand,
  nor he who binds sheaves, his bosom.

Neither do those who go by say,
　"The blessing of YHWH be on you.
　We bless you in YHWH's name."

....

A Song of Ascents. Out of the depths I have cried to you, YHWH.
Lord, hear my voice.
　Let your ears be attentive to the voice of my petitions.
If you, Yah, kept a record of sins,
　Lord, who could stand?
But there is forgiveness with you,
　therefore you are feared.
I wait for YHWH.
　My soul waits.
　I hope in his word.
My soul longs for the Lord more than watchmen long for the
morning,
　more than watchmen for the morning.
Israel, hope in YHWH,
　for there is loving kindness with YHWH.
　Abundant redemption is with him.
He will redeem Israel from all their sins.

....

A Song of Ascents. By David. YHWH, my heart isn't arrogant, nor
my eyes lofty;
　nor do I concern myself with great matters,
　or things too wonderful for me.
Surely I have stilled and quieted my soul,
　like a weaned child with his mother,
　like a weaned child is my soul within me.
Israel, hope in YHWH,
　from this time forward and forever more.

....

A Song of Ascents. YHWH, remember David and all his affliction,
how he swore to YHWH,
　and vowed to the Mighty One of Jacob:
"Surely I will not come into the structure of my house,
　nor go up into my bed;

214

I will not give sleep to my eyes,
      or slumber to my eyelids;
until I find out a place for YHWH,
      a dwelling for the Mighty One of Jacob."
Behold, we heard of it in Ephrathah.
      We found it in the field of Jaar:
"We will go into his dwelling place.
      We will worship at his footstool.
Arise, YHWH, into your resting place,
      you, and the ark of your strength.
Let your priests be clothed with righteousness.
      Let your saints shout for joy!"
For your servant David's sake,
      don't turn away the face of your anointed one.
YHWH has sworn to David in truth.
      He will not turn from it:
      "I will set the fruit of your body on your throne.
If your children will keep my covenant,
      my testimony that I will teach them,
      their children also will sit on your throne forever more."
For YHWH has chosen Zion.
      He has desired it for his habitation.
"This is my resting place forever.
      I will live here, for I have desired it.
I will abundantly bless her provision.
      I will satisfy her poor with bread.
I will also clothe her priests with salvation.
      Her saints will shout aloud for joy.
I will make the horn of David to bud there.
      I have ordained a lamp for my anointed.
I will clothe his enemies with shame,
      but on himself, his crown will shine."

....

A Song of Ascents. By David. See how good and how pleasant it is
      for brothers to live together in unity!
It is like the precious oil on the head,
      that ran down on the beard,
      even Aaron's beard,
      that came down on the edge of his robes,

like the dew of Hermon,
   that comes down on the hills of Zion;
   for there YHWH *gives the blessing,*
   even life forever more.

....

A Song of Ascents. Look! Praise YHWH, *all you servants of* YHWH,
   who stand by night in YHWH'*s house!*
Lift up your hands in the sanctuary.
   Praise YHWH!
May YHWH *bless you from Zion,*
   even he who made heaven and earth.

....

Praise Yah!
   Praise YHWH'*s name!*
   Praise him, you servants of YHWH,
you who stand in YHWH'*s house,*
   in the courts of our God's house.
Praise Yah, for YHWH *is good.*
   Sing praises to his name, for that is pleasant.
For Yah has chosen Jacob for himself,
   Israel for his own possession.
For I know that YHWH *is great,*
   that our Lord is above all gods.
Whatever YHWH *pleased, that he has done,*
   in heaven and in earth, in the seas and in all deeps.
He causes the clouds to rise from the ends of the earth.
   He makes lightnings with the rain.
   He brings the wind out of his treasuries.
He struck the firstborn of Egypt,
   both of man and animal.
He sent signs and wonders into the middle of you, Egypt,
   on Pharaoh, and on all his servants.
He struck many nations,
   and killed mighty kings,
Sihon king of the Amorites,
   Og king of Bashan,
   and all the kingdoms of Canaan,
and gave their land for a heritage,

a heritage to Israel, his people.
Your name, YHWH, endures forever;
    your renown, YHWH, throughout all generations.
For YHWH will judge his people
    and have compassion on his servants.

The idols of the nations are silver and gold,
    the work of men's hands.
They have mouths, but they can't speak.
    They have eyes, but they can't see.
They have ears, but they can't hear,
    neither is there any breath in their mouths.
Those who make them will be like them,
    yes, everyone who trusts in them.
House of Israel, praise YHWH!
    House of Aaron, praise YHWH!
House of Levi, praise YHWH!
    You who fear YHWH, praise YHWH!
Blessed be YHWH from Zion,
    who dwells at Jerusalem.
Praise Yah!

....

Give thanks to YHWH, for he is good;
    for his loving kindness endures forever.
Give thanks to the God of gods;
    for his loving kindness endures forever.
Give thanks to the Lord of lords;
    for his loving kindness endures forever:
to him who alone does great wonders;
    for his loving kindness endures forever:
to him who by understanding made the heavens;
    for his loving kindness endures forever:
to him who spread out the earth above the waters;
    for his loving kindness endures forever:
to him who made the great lights;
    for his loving kindness endures forever:
the sun to rule by day;
    for his loving kindness endures forever;
the moon and stars to rule by night;

for his loving kindness endures forever:
to him who struck down the Egyptian firstborn;
  for his loving kindness endures forever;
and brought out Israel from among them;
  for his loving kindness endures forever;
with a strong hand, and with an outstretched arm;
  for his loving kindness endures forever:
to him who divided the Red Sea apart;
  for his loving kindness endures forever;
and made Israel to pass through the middle of it;
  for his loving kindness endures forever;
but overthrew Pharaoh and his army in the Red Sea;
  for his loving kindness endures forever:
to him who led his people through the wilderness;
  for his loving kindness endures forever:
to him who struck great kings;
  for his loving kindness endures forever;
and killed mighty kings;
  for his loving kindness endures forever:
Sihon king of the Amorites;
  for his loving kindness endures forever;
Og king of Bashan;
  for his loving kindness endures forever;
and gave their land as an inheritance;
  for his loving kindness endures forever;
even a heritage to Israel his servant;
  for his loving kindness endures forever:
who remembered us in our low estate;
  for his loving kindness endures forever;
and has delivered us from our adversaries;
  for his loving kindness endures forever:
who gives food to every creature;
  for his loving kindness endures forever.
Oh give thanks to the God of heaven;
  for his loving kindness endures forever.

....

By the rivers of Babylon, there we sat down.
  Yes, we wept, when we remembered Zion.
On the willows in that land,

we hung up our harps.
For there, those who led us captive asked us for songs.
    Those who tormented us demanded songs of joy:
    "Sing us one of the songs of Zion!"
How can we sing YHWH's song in a foreign land?
If I forget you, Jerusalem,
    let my right hand forget its skill.
Let my tongue stick to the roof of my mouth if I don't remember you,
    if I don't prefer Jerusalem above my chief joy.
Remember, YHWH, against the children of Edom in the day of Jerusalem,
    who said, "Raze it!
    Raze it even to its foundation!"
Daughter of Babylon, doomed to destruction,
    he will be happy who repays you,
    as you have done to us.
Happy shall he be,
    who takes and dashes your little ones against the rock.

....

By David. I will give you thanks with my whole heart.
    Before the gods, I will sing praises to you.
I will bow down toward your holy temple,
    and give thanks to your Name for your loving kindness and for your truth;
    for you have exalted your Name and your Word above all.
In the day that I called, you answered me.
    You encouraged me with strength in my soul.
All the kings of the earth will give you thanks, YHWH,
    for they have heard the words of your mouth.
Yes, they will sing of the ways of YHWH,
    for YHWH's glory is great!
For though YHWH is high, yet he looks after the lowly;
    but he knows the proud from afar.
Though I walk in the middle of trouble, you will revive me.
    You will stretch out your hand against the wrath of my enemies.
    Your right hand will save me.
YHWH will fulfill that which concerns me.

Your loving kindness, YHWH, endures forever.
Don't forsake the works of your own hands.

....

For the Chief Musician. A Psalm by David. YHWH, you have
searched me,
*   and you know me.*
You know my sitting down and my rising up.
*   You perceive my thoughts from afar.*
You search out my path and my lying down,
*   and are acquainted with all my ways.*
For there is not a word on my tongue,
*   but, behold, YHWH, you know it altogether.*
You hem me in behind and before.
*   You laid your hand on me.*
This knowledge is beyond me.
*   It's lofty.*
*   I can't attain it.*
Where could I go from your Spirit?
*   Or where could I flee from your presence?*
If I ascend up into heaven, you are there.
*   If I make my bed in Sheol, behold, you are there!*
If I take the wings of the dawn,
*   and settle in the uttermost parts of the sea,*
even there your hand will lead me,
*   and your right hand will hold me.*
If I say, "Surely the darkness will overwhelm me.
*   The light around me will be night,"*
even the darkness doesn't hide from you,
*   but the night shines as the day.*
*   The darkness is like light to you.*
For you formed my inmost being.
*   You knit me together in my mother's womb.*
I will give thanks to you,
*   for I am fearfully and wonderfully made.*
Your works are wonderful.
*   My soul knows that very well.*
My frame wasn't hidden from you,
*   when I was made in secret,*
*   woven together in the depths of the earth.*

Your eyes saw my body.
In your book they were all written,
the days that were ordained for me,
when as yet there were none of them.
How precious to me are your thoughts, God!
How vast is their sum!
If I would count them, they are more in number than the sand.
When I wake up, I am still with you.
If only you, God, would kill the wicked.
Get away from me, you bloodthirsty men!
For they speak against you wickedly.
Your enemies take your name in vain.
YHWH, don't I hate those who hate you?
Am I not grieved with those who rise up against you?
I hate them with perfect hatred.
They have become my enemies.
Search me, God, and know my heart.
Try me, and know my thoughts.
See if there is any wicked way in me,
and lead me in the everlasting way.

....

For the Chief Musician. A Psalm by David. Deliver me, YHWH,
from the evil man.
Preserve me from the violent man:
those who devise mischief in their hearts.
They continually gather themselves together for war.
They have sharpened their tongues like a serpent.
Viper's poison is under their lips. Selah.
YHWH, keep me from the hands of the wicked.
Preserve me from the violent men who have determined to trip
my feet.
The proud have hidden a snare for me,
they have spread the cords of a net by the path.
They have set traps for me. Selah.
I said to YHWH, "You are my God."
Listen to the cry of my petitions, YHWH.
YHWH, the Lord, the strength of my salvation,
you have covered my head in the day of battle.
YHWH, don't grant the desires of the wicked.

Don't let their evil plans succeed, or they will become proud.
Selah.
As for the head of those who surround me,
let the mischief of their own lips cover them.
Let burning coals fall on them.
Let them be thrown into the fire,
into miry pits, from where they never rise.
An evil speaker won't be established in the earth.
Evil will hunt the violent man to overthrow him.
I know that YHWH will maintain the cause of the afflicted,
and justice for the needy.
Surely the righteous will give thanks to your name.
The upright will dwell in your presence.

....

A Psalm by David. YHWH, I have called on you.
Come to me quickly!
Listen to my voice when I call to you.
Let my prayer be set before you like incense;
the lifting up of my hands like the evening sacrifice.
Set a watch, YHWH, before my mouth.
Keep the door of my lips.
Don't incline my heart to any evil thing,
to practice deeds of wickedness with men who work iniquity.
Don't let me eat of their delicacies.
Let the righteous strike me, it is kindness;
let him reprove me, it is like oil on the head;
don't let my head refuse it;
Yet my prayer is always against evil deeds.
Their judges are thrown down by the sides of the rock.
They will hear my words, for they are well spoken.
"As when one plows and breaks up the earth,
our bones are scattered at the mouth of Sheol."
For my eyes are on you, YHWH, the Lord.
In you, I take refuge.
Don't leave my soul destitute.
Keep me from the snare which they have laid for me,
from the traps of the workers of iniquity.
Let the wicked fall together into their own nets
while I pass by.

....

*A contemplation by David, when he was in the cave. A Prayer. I
cry with my voice to YHWH.*
> *With my voice, I ask YHWH for mercy.*
I pour out my complaint before him.
> *I tell him my troubles.*
When my spirit was overwhelmed within me,
> *you knew my route.*
On the path in which I walk,
> *they have hidden a snare for me.*
Look on my right, and see;
> *for there is no one who is concerned for me.*
> *Refuge has fled from me.*
> *No one cares for my soul.*
I cried to you, YHWH.
> *I said, "You are my refuge,*
> *my portion in the land of the living."*
Listen to my cry,
> *for I am in desperate need.*
Deliver me from my persecutors,
> *for they are too strong for me.*
Bring my soul out of prison,
> *that I may give thanks to your name.*
The righteous will surround me,
> *for you will be good to me.*

....

A Psalm by David. Hear my prayer, YHWH.
> *Listen to my petitions.*
> *In your faithfulness and righteousness, relieve me.*
Don't enter into judgment with your servant,
> *for in your sight no man living is righteous.*
For the enemy pursues my soul.
> *He has struck my life down to the ground.*
> *He has made me live in dark places, as those who have been
> long dead.*
Therefore my spirit is overwhelmed within me.
> *My heart within me is desolate.*
I remember the days of old.

I meditate on all your doings.
    I contemplate the work of your hands.
I spread out my hands to you.
    My soul thirsts for you, like a parched land. Selah.
Hurry to answer me, YHWH.
    My spirit fails.
Don't hide your face from me,
    so that I don't become like those who go down into the pit.
Cause me to hear your loving kindness in the morning,
    for I trust in you.
Cause me to know the way in which I should walk,
    for I lift up my soul to you.
Deliver me, YHWH, from my enemies.
    I flee to you to hide me.
Teach me to do your will,
    for you are my God.
Your Spirit is good.
    Lead me in the land of uprightness.
Revive me, YHWH, for your name's sake.
    In your righteousness, bring my soul out of trouble.
In your loving kindness, cut off my enemies,
    and destroy all those who afflict my soul,
    For I am your servant.

....

By David. Blessed be YHWH, my rock,
    who teaches my hands to war,
    and my fingers to battle:
my loving kindness, my fortress,
    my high tower, my deliverer,
    my shield, and he in whom I take refuge,
    who subdues my people under me.
YHWH, what is man, that you care for him?
    Or the son of man, that you think of him?
Man is like a breath.
    His days are like a shadow that passes away.
Part your heavens, YHWH, and come down.
    Touch the mountains, and they will smoke.
Throw out lightning, and scatter them.
    Send out your arrows, and rout them.

Stretch out your hand from above,
rescue me, and deliver me out of great waters,
out of the hands of foreigners,
whose mouths speak deceit,
whose right hand is a right hand of falsehood.
I will sing a new song to you, God.
On a ten-stringed lyre, I will sing praises to you.
You are he who gives salvation to kings,
who rescues David, his servant, from the deadly sword.
Rescue me, and deliver me out of the hands of foreigners,
whose mouths speak deceit,
whose right hand is a right hand of falsehood.

Then our sons will be like well-nurtured plants,
our daughters like pillars carved to adorn a palace.
Our barns are full, filled with all kinds of provision.
Our sheep produce thousands and ten thousands in our fields.
Our oxen will pull heavy loads.
There is no breaking in, and no going away,
and no outcry in our streets.
Happy are the people who are in such a situation.
Happy are the people whose God is YHWH.

....

A praise psalm by David. I will exalt you, my God, the King.
I will praise your name forever and ever.
Every day I will praise you.
I will extol your name forever and ever.
Great is YHWH, and greatly to be praised!
His greatness is unsearchable.
One generation will commend your works to another,
and will declare your mighty acts.
I will meditate on the glorious majesty of your honor,
on your wondrous works.
Men will speak of the might of your awesome acts.
I will declare your greatness.
They will utter the memory of your great goodness,
and will sing of your righteousness.
YHWH is gracious, merciful,
slow to anger, and of great loving kindness.

YHWH is good to all.
His tender mercies are over all his works.
All your works will give thanks to you, YHWH.
Your saints will extol you.
They will speak of the glory of your kingdom,
and talk about your power,
to make known to the sons of men his mighty acts,
the glory of the majesty of his kingdom.
Your kingdom is an everlasting kingdom.
Your dominion endures throughout all generations.
YHWH is faithful in all his words,
and loving in all his deeds.
YHWH upholds all who fall,
and raises up all those who are bowed down.
The eyes of all wait for you.
You give them their food in due season.
You open your hand,
and satisfy the desire of every living thing.
YHWH is righteous in all his ways,
and gracious in all his works.
YHWH is near to all those who call on him,
to all who call on him in truth.
He will fulfill the desire of those who fear him.
He also will hear their cry, and will save them.
YHWH preserves all those who love him,
but he will destroy all the wicked.
My mouth will speak the praise of YHWH.
Let all flesh bless his holy name forever and ever.

....

Praise Yah!
Praise YHWH, my soul.
While I live, I will praise YHWH.
I will sing praises to my God as long as I exist.
Don't put your trust in princes,
each a son of man in whom there is no help.
His spirit departs, and he returns to the earth.
In that very day, his thoughts perish.
Happy is he who has the God of Jacob for his help,

whose hope is in YHWH, *his God:*
who made heaven and earth,
   the sea, and all that is in them;
   who keeps truth forever;
who executes justice for the oppressed;
   who gives food to the hungry.
YHWH *frees the prisoners.*
   YHWH *opens the eyes of the blind.*
   YHWH *raises up those who are bowed down.*
   YHWH *loves the righteous.*
YHWH *preserves the foreigners.*
   He upholds the fatherless and widow,
   but he turns the way of the wicked upside down.
YHWH *will reign forever;*
   your God, O Zion, to all generations.
Praise Yah!

....

Praise Yah,
   for it is good to sing praises to our God;
   for it is pleasant and fitting to praise him.
YHWH *builds up Jerusalem.*
   He gathers together the outcasts of Israel.
He heals the broken in heart,
   and binds up their wounds.
He counts the number of the stars.
   He calls them all by their names.
Great is our Lord, and mighty in power.
   His understanding is infinite.
YHWH *upholds the humble.*
   He brings the wicked down to the ground.
Sing to YHWH *with thanksgiving.*
   Sing praises on the harp to our God,
who covers the sky with clouds,
   who prepares rain for the earth,
   who makes grass grow on the mountains.
He provides food for the livestock,
   and for the young ravens when they call.
He doesn't delight in the strength of the horse.

He takes no pleasure in the legs of a man.
YHWH takes pleasure in those who fear him,
in those who hope in his loving kindness.
Praise YHWH, Jerusalem!
Praise your God, Zion!
For he has strengthened the bars of your gates.
He has blessed your children within you.
He makes peace in your borders.
He fills you with the finest of the wheat.
He sends out his commandment to the earth.
His word runs very swiftly.
He gives snow like wool,
and scatters frost like ashes.
He hurls down his hail like pebbles.
Who can stand before his cold?
He sends out his word, and melts them.
He causes his wind to blow, and the waters flow.
He shows his word to Jacob,
his statutes and his ordinances to Israel.
He has not done this for just any nation.
They don't know his ordinances.
Praise Yah!

....

Praise Yah!
Praise YHWH from the heavens!
Praise him in the heights!
Praise him, all his angels!
Praise him, all his army!
Praise him, sun and moon!
Praise him, all you shining stars!
Praise him, you heavens of heavens,
you waters that are above the heavens.
Let them praise YHWH's name,
for he commanded, and they were created.
He has also established them forever and ever.
He has made a decree which will not pass away.
Praise YHWH from the earth,
you great sea creatures, and all depths;

lightning and hail, snow and clouds;
    stormy wind, fulfilling his word;
mountains and all hills;
    fruit trees and all cedars;
wild animals and all livestock;
    small creatures and flying birds;
kings of the earth and all peoples;
    princes and all judges of the earth;
both young men and maidens;
    old men and children:
let them praise YHWH's *name,*
    for his name alone is exalted.
    His glory is above the earth and the heavens.
He has lifted up the horn of his people,
    the praise of all his saints,
    even of the children of Israel, a people near to him.
Praise Yah!

....

Praise YHWH!
    Sing to YHWH *a new song,*
    his praise in the assembly of the saints.
Let Israel rejoice in him who made them.
    Let the children of Zion be joyful in their King.
Let them praise his name in the dance!
    Let them sing praises to him with tambourine and harp!
For YHWH *takes pleasure in his people.*
    He crowns the humble with salvation.
Let the saints rejoice in honor.
    Let them sing for joy on their beds.
May the high praises of God be in their mouths,
    and a two-edged sword in their hand,
to execute vengeance on the nations,
    and punishments on the peoples;
to bind their kings with chains,
    and their nobles with fetters of iron;
to execute on them the written judgment.
    All his saints have this honor.
Praise Yah!

....

Praise Yah!
    Praise God in his sanctuary!
    Praise him in his heavens for his acts of power!
Praise him for his mighty acts!
    Praise him according to his excellent greatness!
Praise him with the sounding of the trumpet!
    Praise him with harp and lyre!
Praise him with tambourine and dancing!
    Praise him with stringed instruments and flute!
Praise him with loud cymbals!
    Praise him with resounding cymbals!
Let everything that has breath praise Yah!
    Praise Yah!

THE

PROVERBS

1 HR 17 MIN

The proverbs of Solomon, the son of David, king of Israel:
to know wisdom and instruction;
to discern the words of understanding;
to receive instruction in wise dealing,
in righteousness, justice, and equity;
to give prudence to the simple,
knowledge and discretion to the young man:
that the wise man may hear, and increase in learning;
that the man of understanding may attain to sound counsel:
to understand a proverb, and parables,
the words and riddles of the wise.

The fear of YHWH is the beginning of knowledge;
but the foolish despise wisdom and instruction.
My son, listen to your father's instruction,
and don't forsake your mother's teaching:
for they will be a garland to grace your head,
and chains around your neck.
My son, if sinners entice you,
don't consent.
If they say, "Come with us.
Let's lay in wait for blood.
Let's lurk secretly for the innocent without cause.
Let's swallow them up alive like Sheol,
and whole, like those who go down into the pit.
We'll find all valuable wealth.
We'll fill our houses with plunder.
You shall cast your lot among us.
We'll all have one purse."
My son, don't walk on the path with them.
Keep your foot from their path,
for their feet run to evil.
They hurry to shed blood.
For the net is spread in vain in the sight of any bird;
but these lay in wait for their own blood.
They lurk secretly for their own lives.
So are the ways of everyone who is greedy for gain.
It takes away the life of its owners.

Wisdom calls aloud in the street.
  She utters her voice in the public squares.
She calls at the head of noisy places.
  At the entrance of the city gates, she utters her words:
"How long, you simple ones, will you love simplicity?
  How long will mockers delight themselves in mockery,
    and fools hate knowledge?
Turn at my reproof.
  Behold, I will pour out my spirit on you.
  I will make known my words to you.
Because I have called, and you have refused;
  I have stretched out my hand, and no one has paid attention;
but you have ignored all my counsel,
  and wanted none of my reproof;
I also will laugh at your disaster.
  I will mock when calamity overtakes you,
when calamity overtakes you like a storm,
  when your disaster comes on like a whirlwind,
  when distress and anguish come on you.
Then they will call on me, but I will not answer.
  They will seek me diligently, but they will not find me;
because they hated knowledge,
  and didn't choose the fear of YHWH.
They wanted none of my counsel.
  They despised all my reproof.
Therefore they will eat of the fruit of their own way,
  and be filled with their own schemes.
For the backsliding of the simple will kill them.
  The careless ease of fools will destroy them.
But whoever listens to me will dwell securely,
  and will be at ease, without fear of harm."

....

My son, if you will receive my words,
  and store up my commandments within you,
so as to turn your ear to wisdom,
  and apply your heart to understanding;
yes, if you call out for discernment,
  and lift up your voice for understanding;
if you seek her as silver,

and search for her as for hidden treasures:
then you will understand the fear of YHWH,
    and find the knowledge of God.
For YHWH *gives wisdom.*
    Out of his mouth comes knowledge and understanding.
He lays up sound wisdom for the upright.
    He is a shield to those who walk in integrity,
that he may guard the paths of justice,
    and preserve the way of his saints.
Then you will understand righteousness and justice,
    equity and every good path.
For wisdom will enter into your heart.
    Knowledge will be pleasant to your soul.
Discretion will watch over you.
    Understanding will keep you,
to deliver you from the way of evil,
    from the men who speak perverse things,
who forsake the paths of uprightness,
    to walk in the ways of darkness,
who rejoice to do evil,
    and delight in the perverseness of evil,
who are crooked in their ways,
    and wayward in their paths,
to deliver you from the strange woman,
    even from the foreigner who flatters with her words,
who forsakes the friend of her youth,
    and forgets the covenant of her God;
for her house leads down to death,
    her paths to the departed spirits.
None who go to her return again,
    neither do they attain to the paths of life.
So you may walk in the way of good men,
    and keep the paths of the righteous.
For the upright will dwell in the land.
    The perfect will remain in it.
But the wicked will be cut off from the land.
    The treacherous will be rooted out of it.

        ....

My son, don't forget my teaching;

but let your heart keep my commandments:
for they will add to you length of days,
    years of life, and peace.
Don't let kindness and truth forsake you.
    Bind them around your neck.
    Write them on the tablet of your heart.
So you will find favor,
    and good understanding in the sight of God and man.
Trust in YHWH with all your heart,
    and don't lean on your own understanding.
In all your ways acknowledge him,
    and he will make your paths straight.
Don't be wise in your own eyes.
    Fear YHWH, and depart from evil.
It will be health to your body,
    and nourishment to your bones.
Honor YHWH with your substance,
    with the first fruits of all your increase:
so your barns will be filled with plenty,
    and your vats will overflow with new wine.
My son, don't despise YHWH's discipline,
    neither be weary of his correction;
for whom YHWH loves, he corrects,
    even as a father reproves the son in whom he delights.

Happy is the man who finds wisdom,
    the man who gets understanding.
For her good profit is better than getting silver,
    and her return is better than fine gold.
She is more precious than rubies.
    None of the things you can desire are to be compared to her.
Length of days is in her right hand.
    In her left hand are riches and honor.
Her ways are ways of pleasantness.
    All her paths are peace.
She is a tree of life to those who lay hold of her.
    Happy is everyone who retains her.
By wisdom YHWH founded the earth.
    By understanding, he established the heavens.
By his knowledge, the depths were broken up,

and the skies drop down the dew.
My son, let them not depart from your eyes.
 Keep sound wisdom and discretion:
so they will be life to your soul,
 and grace for your neck.
Then you shall walk in your way securely.
 Your foot won't stumble.
When you lie down, you will not be afraid.
 Yes, you will lie down, and your sleep will be sweet.
Don't be afraid of sudden fear,
 neither of the desolation of the wicked, when it comes;
for YHWH will be your confidence,
 and will keep your foot from being taken.

Don't withhold good from those to whom it is due,
 when it is in the power of your hand to do it.
Don't say to your neighbor, "Go, and come again;
 tomorrow I will give it to you,"
 when you have it by you.
Don't devise evil against your neighbor,
 since he dwells securely by you.
Don't strive with a man without cause,
 if he has done you no harm.
Don't envy the man of violence.
 Choose none of his ways.
For the perverse is an abomination to YHWH,
 but his friendship is with the upright.
YHWH's curse is in the house of the wicked,
 but he blesses the habitation of the righteous.
Surely he mocks the mockers,
 but he gives grace to the humble.
The wise will inherit glory,
 but shame will be the promotion of fools.

   ....

Listen, sons, to a father's instruction.
 Pay attention and know understanding;
for I give you sound learning.
 Don't forsake my law.
For I was a son to my father,

tender and an only child in the sight of my mother.
He taught me, and said to me:
"Let your heart retain my words.
Keep my commandments, and live.
Get wisdom.
Get understanding.
Don't forget, and don't deviate from the words of my mouth.
Don't forsake her, and she will preserve you.
Love her, and she will keep you.
Wisdom is supreme.
Get wisdom.
Yes, though it costs all your possessions, get understanding.
Esteem her, and she will exalt you.
She will bring you to honor when you embrace her.
She will give to your head a garland of grace.
She will deliver a crown of splendor to you."

Listen, my son, and receive my sayings.
The years of your life will be many.
I have taught you in the way of wisdom.
I have led you in straight paths.
When you go, your steps will not be hampered.
When you run, you will not stumble.
Take firm hold of instruction.
Don't let her go.
Keep her, for she is your life.
Don't enter into the path of the wicked.
Don't walk in the way of evil men.
Avoid it, and don't pass by it.
Turn from it, and pass on.
For they don't sleep unless they do evil.
Their sleep is taken away, unless they make someone fall.
For they eat the bread of wickedness
and drink the wine of violence.
But the path of the righteous is like the dawning light
that shines more and more until the perfect day.
The way of the wicked is like darkness.
They don't know what they stumble over.

My son, attend to my words.

Turn your ear to my sayings.
Let them not depart from your eyes.
Keep them in the center of your heart.
For they are life to those who find them,
and health to their whole body.
Keep your heart with all diligence,
for out of it is the wellspring of life.
Put away from yourself a perverse mouth.
Put corrupt lips far from you.
Let your eyes look straight ahead.
Fix your gaze directly before you.
Make the path of your feet level.
Let all of your ways be established.
Don't turn to the right hand nor to the left.
Remove your foot from evil.

....

My son, pay attention to my wisdom.
Turn your ear to my understanding,
that you may maintain discretion,
that your lips may preserve knowledge.
For the lips of an adulteress drip honey.
Her mouth is smoother than oil,
but in the end she is as bitter as wormwood,
and as sharp as a two-edged sword.
Her feet go down to death.
Her steps lead straight to Sheol.
She gives no thought to the way of life.
Her ways are crooked, and she doesn't know it.

Now therefore, my sons, listen to me.
Don't depart from the words of my mouth.
Remove your way far from her.
Don't come near the door of her house,
lest you give your honor to others,
and your years to the cruel one;
lest strangers feast on your wealth,
and your labors enrich another man's house.
You will groan at your latter end,
when your flesh and your body are consumed,

and say, "How I have hated instruction,
    and my heart despised reproof;
neither have I obeyed the voice of my teachers,
    nor turned my ear to those who instructed me!
I have come to the brink of utter ruin,
    among the gathered assembly."

Drink water out of your own cistern,
    running water out of your own well.
Should your springs overflow in the streets,
    streams of water in the public squares?
Let them be for yourself alone,
    not for strangers with you.
Let your spring be blessed.
    Rejoice in the wife of your youth.
A loving doe and a graceful deer—
    let her breasts satisfy you at all times.
    Be captivated always with her love.
For why should you, my son, be captivated with an adulteress?
    Why embrace the bosom of another?
For the ways of man are before YHWH's eyes.
    He examines all his paths.
The evil deeds of the wicked ensnare him.
    The cords of his sin hold him firmly.
He will die for lack of instruction.
    In the greatness of his folly, he will go astray.

My son, if you have become collateral for your neighbor,
    if you have struck your hands in pledge for a stranger,
you are trapped by the words of your mouth;
    you are ensnared with the words of your mouth.
Do this now, my son, and deliver yourself,
    since you have come into the hand of your neighbor.
Go, humble yourself.
    Press your plea with your neighbor.
Give no sleep to your eyes,
    nor slumber to your eyelids.
Free yourself, like a gazelle from the hand of the hunter,
    like a bird from the snare of the fowler.

Go to the ant, you sluggard.
Consider her ways, and be wise;
which having no chief, overseer, or ruler,
provides her bread in the summer,
and gathers her food in the harvest.
How long will you sleep, sluggard?
When will you arise out of your sleep?
A little sleep, a little slumber,
a little folding of the hands to sleep:
so your poverty will come as a robber,
and your scarcity as an armed man.

A worthless person, a man of iniquity,
is he who walks with a perverse mouth,
who winks with his eyes, who signals with his feet,
who motions with his fingers,
in whose heart is perverseness,
who devises evil continually,
who always sows discord.
Therefore his calamity will come suddenly.
He will be broken suddenly, and that without remedy.

There are six things which YHWH hates;
yes, seven which are an abomination to him:
arrogant eyes, a lying tongue,
hands that shed innocent blood,
a heart that devises wicked schemes,
feet that are swift in running to mischief,
a false witness who utters lies,
and he who sows discord among brothers.

My son, keep your father's commandment,
and don't forsake your mother's teaching.
Bind them continually on your heart.
Tie them around your neck.
When you walk, it will lead you.
When you sleep, it will watch over you.
When you awake, it will talk with you.
For the commandment is a lamp,

and the law is light.
    Reproofs of instruction are the way of life,
to keep you from the immoral woman,
    from the flattery of the wayward wife's tongue.
Don't lust after her beauty in your heart,
    neither let her captivate you with her eyelids.
For a prostitute reduces you to a piece of bread.
    The adulteress hunts for your precious life.
Can a man scoop fire into his lap,
    and his clothes not be burned?
Or can one walk on hot coals,
    and his feet not be scorched?
So is he who goes in to his neighbor's wife.
    Whoever touches her will not be unpunished.
Men don't despise a thief
    if he steals to satisfy himself when he is hungry;
but if he is found, he shall restore seven times.
    He shall give all the wealth of his house.
He who commits adultery with a woman is void of understanding.
    He who does it destroys his own soul.
He will get wounds and dishonor.
    His reproach will not be wiped away.
For jealousy arouses the fury of the husband.
    He won't spare in the day of vengeance.
He won't regard any ransom,
    neither will he rest content, though you give many gifts.

....

My son, keep my words.
    Lay up my commandments within you.
Keep my commandments and live!
    Guard my teaching as the apple of your eye.
Bind them on your fingers.
    Write them on the tablet of your heart.
Tell wisdom, "You are my sister."
    Call understanding your relative,
that they may keep you from the strange woman,
    from the foreigner who flatters with her words.
For at the window of my house,

I looked out through my lattice.
I saw among the simple ones.
 I discerned among the youths a young man void of under-
  standing,
passing through the street near her corner,
 he went the way to her house,
in the twilight, in the evening of the day,
 in the middle of the night and in the darkness.
Behold, there a woman met him with the attire of a prostitute,
 and with crafty intent.
She is loud and defiant.
 Her feet don't stay in her house.
Now she is in the streets, now in the squares,
 and lurking at every corner.
So she caught him, and kissed him.
 With an impudent face she said to him:
"Sacrifices of peace offerings are with me.
 Today I have paid my vows.
Therefore I came out to meet you,
 to diligently seek your face,
 and I have found you.
I have spread my couch with carpets of tapestry,
 with striped cloths of the yarn of Egypt.
I have perfumed my bed with myrrh, aloes, and cinnamon.
Come, let's take our fill of loving until the morning.
 Let's solace ourselves with loving.
For my husband isn't at home.
 He has gone on a long journey.
He has taken a bag of money with him.
 He will come home at the full moon."
With persuasive words, she led him astray.
 With the flattering of her lips, she seduced him.
He followed her immediately,
 as an ox goes to the slaughter,
 as a fool stepping into a noose.
Until an arrow strikes through his liver,
 as a bird hurries to the snare,
 and doesn't know that it will cost his life.

Now therefore, sons, listen to me.

Pay attention to the words of my mouth.
Don't let your heart turn to her ways.
Don't go astray in her paths,
for she has thrown down many wounded.
Yes, all her slain are a mighty army.
Her house is the way to Sheol,
going down to the rooms of death.

....

Doesn't wisdom cry out?
Doesn't understanding raise her voice?
On the top of high places by the way,
where the paths meet, she stands.
Beside the gates, at the entry of the city,
at the entry doors, she cries aloud:
"I call to you men!
I send my voice to the sons of mankind.
You simple, understand prudence!
You fools, be of an understanding heart!
Hear, for I will speak excellent things.
The opening of my lips is for right things.
For my mouth speaks truth.
Wickedness is an abomination to my lips.
All the words of my mouth are in righteousness.
There is nothing crooked or perverse in them.
They are all plain to him who understands,
right to those who find knowledge.
Receive my instruction rather than silver,
knowledge rather than choice gold.
For wisdom is better than rubies.
All the things that may be desired can't be compared to it.

"I, wisdom, have made prudence my dwelling.
Find out knowledge and discretion.
The fear of YHWH is to hate evil.
I hate pride, arrogance, the evil way, and the perverse mouth.
Counsel and sound knowledge are mine.
I have understanding and power.
By me kings reign,
and princes decree justice.

By me princes rule,
  nobles, and all the righteous rulers of the earth.
I love those who love me.
  Those who seek me diligently will find me.
With me are riches, honor,
  enduring wealth, and prosperity.
My fruit is better than gold, yes, than fine gold,
  my yield than choice silver.
I walk in the way of righteousness,
  in the middle of the paths of justice,
that I may give wealth to those who love me.
  I fill their treasuries.

"YHWH possessed me in the beginning of his work,
  before his deeds of old.
I was set up from everlasting, from the beginning,
  before the earth existed.
When there were no depths, I was born,
  when there were no springs abounding with water.
Before the mountains were settled in place,
  before the hills, I was born;
while as yet he had not made the earth, nor the fields,
  nor the beginning of the dust of the world.
When he established the heavens, I was there.
  When he set a circle on the surface of the deep,
when he established the clouds above,
  when the springs of the deep became strong,
when he gave to the sea its boundary,
  that the waters should not violate his commandment,
  when he marked out the foundations of the earth,
then I was the craftsman by his side.
  I was a delight day by day,
  always rejoicing before him,
rejoicing in his whole world.
  My delight was with the sons of men.

"Now therefore, my sons, listen to me,
  for blessed are those who keep my ways.
Hear instruction, and be wise.
  Don't refuse it.

Blessed is the man who hears me,
  watching daily at my gates,
  waiting at my door posts.
For whoever finds me, finds life,
  and will obtain favor from YHWH.
But he who sins against me wrongs his own soul.
  All those who hate me love death."

....

Wisdom has built her house.
  She has carved out her seven pillars.
She has prepared her meat.
  She has mixed her wine.
  She has also set her table.
She has sent out her maidens.
  She cries from the highest places of the city:
"Whoever is simple, let him turn in here!"
  As for him who is void of understanding, she says to him,
"Come, eat some of my bread,
  Drink some of the wine which I have mixed!
Leave your simple ways, and live.
  Walk in the way of understanding."

One who corrects a mocker invites insult.
  One who reproves a wicked man invites abuse.
Don't reprove a scoffer, lest he hate you.
  Reprove a wise person, and he will love you.
Instruct a wise person, and he will be still wiser.
  Teach a righteous person, and he will increase in learning.
The fear of YHWH is the beginning of wisdom.
  The knowledge of the Holy One is understanding.
For by me your days will be multiplied.
  The years of your life will be increased.
If you are wise, you are wise for yourself.
  If you mock, you alone will bear it.

The foolish woman is loud,
  undisciplined, and knows nothing.
She sits at the door of her house,
  on a seat in the high places of the city,

to call to those who pass by,
    who go straight on their ways,
"Whoever is simple, let him turn in here."
    as for him who is void of understanding, she says to him,
"Stolen water is sweet.
    Food eaten in secret is pleasant."
But he doesn't know that the departed spirits are there,
    that her guests are in the depths of Sheol.

....

The proverbs of Solomon.
A wise son makes a glad father;
    but a foolish son brings grief to his mother.
Treasures of wickedness profit nothing,
    but righteousness delivers from death.
YHWH will not allow the soul of the righteous to go hungry,
    but he thrusts away the desire of the wicked.
He becomes poor who works with a lazy hand,
    but the hand of the diligent brings wealth.
He who gathers in summer is a wise son,
    but he who sleeps during the harvest is a son who causes
    shame.
Blessings are on the head of the righteous,
    but violence covers the mouth of the wicked.
The memory of the righteous is blessed,
    but the name of the wicked will rot.
The wise in heart accept commandments,
    but a chattering fool will fall.
He who walks blamelessly walks surely,
    but he who perverts his ways will be found out.
One winking with the eye causes sorrow,
    but a chattering fool will fall.
The mouth of the righteous is a spring of life,
    but violence covers the mouth of the wicked.
Hatred stirs up strife,
    but love covers all wrongs.
Wisdom is found on the lips of him who has discernment,
    but a rod is for the back of him who is void of understanding.
Wise men lay up knowledge,
    but the mouth of the foolish is near ruin.

The rich man's wealth is his strong city.
　　The destruction of the poor is their poverty.
The labor of the righteous leads to life.
　　The increase of the wicked leads to sin.
He is in the way of life who heeds correction,
　　but he who forsakes reproof leads others astray.
He who hides hatred has lying lips.
　　He who utters a slander is a fool.
In the multitude of words there is no lack of disobedience,
　　but he who restrains his lips does wisely.
The tongue of the righteous is like choice silver.
　　The heart of the wicked is of little worth.
The lips of the righteous feed many,
　　but the foolish die for lack of understanding.
YHWH's blessing brings wealth,
　　and he adds no trouble to it.
It is a fool's pleasure to do wickedness,
　　but wisdom is a man of understanding's pleasure.
What the wicked fear, will overtake them,
　　but the desire of the righteous will be granted.
When the whirlwind passes, the wicked is no more;
　　but the righteous stand firm forever.
As vinegar to the teeth, and as smoke to the eyes,
　　so is the sluggard to those who send him.
The fear of YHWH prolongs days,
　　but the years of the wicked shall be shortened.
The prospect of the righteous is joy,
　　but the hope of the wicked will perish.
The way of YHWH is a stronghold to the upright,
　　but it is a destruction to the workers of iniquity.
The righteous will never be removed,
　　but the wicked will not dwell in the land.
The mouth of the righteous produces wisdom,
　　but the perverse tongue will be cut off.
The lips of the righteous know what is acceptable,
　　but the mouth of the wicked is perverse.

A false balance is an abomination to YHWH,
　　but accurate weights are his delight.

When pride comes, then comes shame,
    but with humility comes wisdom.
The integrity of the upright shall guide them,
    but the perverseness of the treacherous shall destroy them.
Riches don't profit in the day of wrath,
    but righteousness delivers from death.
The righteousness of the blameless will direct his way,
    but the wicked shall fall by his own wickedness.
The righteousness of the upright shall deliver them,
    but the unfaithful will be trapped by evil desires.
When a wicked man dies, hope perishes,
    and expectation of power comes to nothing.
A righteous person is delivered out of trouble,
    and the wicked takes his place.
With his mouth the godless man destroys his neighbor,
    but the righteous will be delivered through knowledge.
When it goes well with the righteous, the city rejoices.
    When the wicked perish, there is shouting.
By the blessing of the upright, the city is exalted,
    but it is overthrown by the mouth of the wicked.
One who despises his neighbor is void of wisdom,
    but a man of understanding holds his peace.
One who brings gossip betrays a confidence,
    but one who is of a trustworthy spirit is one who keeps a secret.
Where there is no wise guidance, the nation falls,
    but in the multitude of counselors there is victory.
He who is collateral for a stranger will suffer for it,
    but he who refuses pledges of collateral is secure.
A gracious woman obtains honor,
    but violent men obtain riches.
The merciful man does good to his own soul,
    but he who is cruel troubles his own flesh.
Wicked people earn deceitful wages,
    but one who sows righteousness reaps a sure reward.
He who is truly righteous gets life.
    He who pursues evil gets death.
Those who are perverse in heart are an abomination to YHWH,
    but those whose ways are blameless are his delight.
Most certainly, the evil man will not be unpunished,
    but the offspring of the righteous will be delivered.

Like a gold ring in a pig's snout,
  is a beautiful woman who lacks discretion.
The desire of the righteous is only good.
  The expectation of the wicked is wrath.
There is one who scatters, and increases yet more.
    There is one who withholds more than is appropriate, but
    gains poverty.
The liberal soul shall be made fat.
  He who waters shall be watered also himself.
People curse someone who withholds grain,
  but blessing will be on the head of him who sells it.
He who diligently seeks good seeks favor,
  but he who searches after evil, it shall come to him.
He who trusts in his riches will fall,
  but the righteous shall flourish as the green leaf.
He who troubles his own house shall inherit the wind.
  The foolish shall be servant to the wise of heart.
The fruit of the righteous is a tree of life.
  He who is wise wins souls.
Behold, the righteous shall be repaid in the earth,
  how much more the wicked and the sinner!

....

Whoever loves correction loves knowledge,
  but he who hates reproof is stupid.
A good man shall obtain favor from YHWH,
  but he will condemn a man of wicked plans.
A man shall not be established by wickedness,
  but the root of the righteous shall not be moved.
A worthy woman is the crown of her husband,
  but a disgraceful wife is as rottenness in his bones.
The thoughts of the righteous are just,
  but the advice of the wicked is deceitful.
The words of the wicked are about lying in wait for blood,
  but the speech of the upright rescues them.
The wicked are overthrown, and are no more,
  but the house of the righteous shall stand.
A man shall be commended according to his wisdom,
  but he who has a warped mind shall be despised.
Better is he who is little known, and has a servant,

than he who honors himself, and lacks bread.
A righteous man respects the life of his animal,
    but the tender mercies of the wicked are cruel.
He who tills his land shall have plenty of bread,
    but he who chases fantasies is void of understanding.
The wicked desires the plunder of evil men,
    but the root of the righteous flourishes.
An evil man is trapped by sinfulness of lips,
    but the righteous shall come out of trouble.
A man shall be satisfied with good by the fruit of his mouth.
    The work of a man's hands shall be rewarded to him.
The way of a fool is right in his own eyes,
    but he who is wise listens to counsel.
A fool shows his annoyance the same day,
    but one who overlooks an insult is prudent.
He who is truthful testifies honestly,
    but a false witness lies.
There is one who speaks rashly like the piercing of a sword,
    but the tongue of the wise heals.
Truth's lips will be established forever,
    but a lying tongue is only momentary.
Deceit is in the heart of those who plot evil,
    but joy comes to the promoters of peace.
No mischief shall happen to the righteous,
    but the wicked shall be filled with evil.
Lying lips are an abomination to YHWH,
    but those who do the truth are his delight.
A prudent man keeps his knowledge,
    but the hearts of fools proclaim foolishness.
The hands of the diligent ones shall rule,
    but laziness ends in slave labor.
Anxiety in a man's heart weighs it down,
    but a kind word makes it glad.
A righteous person is cautious in friendship,
    but the way of the wicked leads them astray.
The slothful man doesn't roast his game,
    but the possessions of diligent men are prized.
In the way of righteousness is life;
    in its path there is no death.

....

A wise son listens to his father's instruction,
    but a scoffer doesn't listen to rebuke.
By the fruit of his lips, a man enjoys good things,
    but the unfaithful crave violence.
He who guards his mouth guards his soul.
    One who opens wide his lips comes to ruin.
The soul of the sluggard desires, and has nothing,
    but the desire of the diligent shall be fully satisfied.
A righteous man hates lies,
    but a wicked man brings shame and disgrace.
Righteousness guards the way of integrity,
    but wickedness overthrows the sinner.
There are some who pretend to be rich, yet have nothing.
    There are some who pretend to be poor, yet have great wealth.
The ransom of a man's life is his riches,
    but the poor hear no threats.
The light of the righteous shines brightly,
    but the lamp of the wicked is snuffed out.
Pride only breeds quarrels,
    but wisdom is with people who take advice.
Wealth gained dishonestly dwindles away,
    but he who gathers by hand makes it grow.
Hope deferred makes the heart sick,
    but when longing is fulfilled, it is a tree of life.
Whoever despises instruction will pay for it,
    but he who respects a command will be rewarded.
The teaching of the wise is a spring of life,
    to turn from the snares of death.
Good understanding wins favor,
    but the way of the unfaithful is hard.
Every prudent man acts from knowledge,
    but a fool exposes folly.
A wicked messenger falls into trouble,
    but a trustworthy envoy gains healing.
Poverty and shame come to him who refuses discipline,
    but he who heeds correction shall be honored.
Longing fulfilled is sweet to the soul,
    but fools detest turning from evil.
One who walks with wise men grows wise,
    but a companion of fools suffers harm.

Misfortune pursues sinners,
    but prosperity rewards the righteous.
A good man leaves an inheritance to his children's children,
    but the wealth of the sinner is stored for the righteous.
An abundance of food is in poor people's fields,
    but injustice sweeps it away.
One who spares the rod hates his son,
    but one who loves him is careful to discipline him.
The righteous one eats to the satisfying of his soul,
    but the belly of the wicked goes hungry.

....

Every wise woman builds her house,
    but the foolish one tears it down with her own hands.
He who walks in his uprightness fears YHWH,
    but he who is perverse in his ways despises him.
The fool's talk brings a rod to his back,
    but the lips of the wise protect them.
Where no oxen are, the crib is clean,
    but much increase is by the strength of the ox.
A truthful witness will not lie,
    but a false witness pours out lies.
A scoffer seeks wisdom, and doesn't find it,
    but knowledge comes easily to a discerning person.
Stay away from a foolish man,
    for you won't find knowledge on his lips.
The wisdom of the prudent is to think about his way,
    but the folly of fools is deceit.
Fools mock at making atonement for sins,
    but among the upright there is good will.
The heart knows its own bitterness and joy;
    he will not share these with a stranger.
The house of the wicked will be overthrown,
    but the tent of the upright will flourish.
There is a way which seems right to a man,
    but in the end it leads to death.
Even in laughter the heart may be sorrowful,
    and mirth may end in heaviness.
The unfaithful will be repaid for his own ways;
    likewise a good man will be rewarded for his ways.

A simple man believes everything,
    but the prudent man carefully considers his ways.
A wise man fears and shuns evil,
    but the fool is hot headed and reckless.
He who is quick to become angry will commit folly,
    and a crafty man is hated.
The simple inherit folly,
    but the prudent are crowned with knowledge.
The evil bow down before the good,
    and the wicked at the gates of the righteous.
The poor person is shunned even by his own neighbor,
    but the rich person has many friends.
He who despises his neighbor sins,
    but he who has pity on the poor is blessed.
Don't they go astray who plot evil?
    But love and faithfulness belong to those who plan good.
In all hard work there is profit,
    but the talk of the lips leads only to poverty.
The crown of the wise is their riches,
    but the folly of fools crowns them with folly.
A truthful witness saves souls,
    but a false witness is deceitful.
In the fear of YHWH is a secure fortress,
    and he will be a refuge for his children.
The fear of YHWH is a fountain of life,
    turning people from the snares of death.
In the multitude of people is the king's glory,
    but in the lack of people is the destruction of the prince.
He who is slow to anger has great understanding,
    but he who has a quick temper displays folly.
The life of the body is a heart at peace,
    but envy rots the bones.
He who oppresses the poor shows contempt for his Maker,
    but he who is kind to the needy honors him.
The wicked is brought down in his calamity,
    but in death, the righteous has a refuge.
Wisdom rests in the heart of one who has understanding,
    and is even made known in the inward part of fools.
Righteousness exalts a nation,
    but sin is a disgrace to any people.

The king's favor is toward a servant who deals wisely,
but his wrath is toward one who causes shame.

. . . .

A gentle answer turns away wrath,
but a harsh word stirs up anger.
The tongue of the wise commends knowledge,
but the mouth of fools gush out folly.
YHWH's eyes are everywhere,
keeping watch on the evil and the good.
A gentle tongue is a tree of life,
but deceit in it crushes the spirit.
A fool despises his father's correction,
but he who heeds reproof shows prudence.
In the house of the righteous is much treasure,
but the income of the wicked brings trouble.
The lips of the wise spread knowledge;
not so with the heart of fools.
The sacrifice made by the wicked is an abomination to YHWH,
but the prayer of the upright is his delight.
The way of the wicked is an abomination to YHWH,
but he loves him who follows after righteousness.
There is stern discipline for one who forsakes the way:
whoever hates reproof shall die.
Sheol and Abaddon are before YHWH—
how much more then the hearts of the children of men!
A scoffer doesn't love to be reproved;
he will not go to the wise.
A glad heart makes a cheerful face,
but an aching heart breaks the spirit.
The heart of one who has understanding seeks knowledge,
but the mouths of fools feed on folly.
All the days of the afflicted are wretched,
but one who has a cheerful heart enjoys a continual feast.
Better is little, with the fear of YHWH,
than great treasure with trouble.
Better is a dinner of herbs, where love is,
than a fattened calf with hatred.
A wrathful man stirs up contention,
but one who is slow to anger appeases strife.

The way of the sluggard is like a thorn patch,
  but the path of the upright is a highway.
A wise son makes a father glad,
  but a foolish man despises his mother.
Folly is joy to one who is void of wisdom,
  but a man of understanding keeps his way straight.
Where there is no counsel, plans fail;
  but in a multitude of counselors they are established.
Joy comes to a man with the reply of his mouth.
  How good is a word at the right time!
The path of life leads upward for the wise,
  to keep him from going downward to Sheol.
YHWH will uproot the house of the proud,
  but he will keep the widow's borders intact.
YHWH detests the thoughts of the wicked,
  but the thoughts of the pure are pleasing.
He who is greedy for gain troubles his own house,
  but he who hates bribes will live.
The heart of the righteous weighs answers,
  but the mouth of the wicked gushes out evil.
YHWH is far from the wicked,
  but he hears the prayer of the righteous.
The light of the eyes rejoices the heart.
  Good news gives health to the bones.
The ear that listens to reproof lives,
  and will be at home among the wise.
He who refuses correction despises his own soul,
  but he who listens to reproof gets understanding.
The fear of YHWH teaches wisdom.
  Before honor is humility.

....

The plans of the heart belong to man,
  but the answer of the tongue is from YHWH.
All the ways of a man are clean in his own eyes;
  but YHWH weighs the motives.
Commit your deeds to YHWH,
  and your plans shall succeed.
YHWH has made everything for its own end—
  yes, even the wicked for the day of evil.

Everyone who is proud in heart is an abomination to YHWH:
they shall certainly not be unpunished.
By mercy and truth iniquity is atoned for.
By the fear of YHWH *men depart from evil.*
When a man's ways please YHWH,
he makes even his enemies to be at peace with him.
Better is a little with righteousness,
than great revenues with injustice.
A man's heart plans his course,
but YHWH *directs his steps.*
Inspired judgments are on the lips of the king.
He shall not betray his mouth.
Honest balances and scales are YHWH's;
all the weights in the bag are his work.
It is an abomination for kings to do wrong,
for the throne is established by righteousness.
Righteous lips are the delight of kings.
They value one who speaks the truth.
The king's wrath is a messenger of death,
but a wise man will pacify it.
In the light of the king's face is life.
His favor is like a cloud of the spring rain.
How much better it is to get wisdom than gold!
Yes, to get understanding is to be chosen rather than silver.
The highway of the upright is to depart from evil.
He who keeps his way preserves his soul.
Pride goes before destruction,
and an arrogant spirit before a fall.
It is better to be of a lowly spirit with the poor,
than to divide the plunder with the proud.
He who heeds the Word finds prosperity.
Whoever trusts in YHWH *is blessed.*
The wise in heart shall be called prudent.
Pleasantness of the lips promotes instruction.
Understanding is a fountain of life to one who has it,
but the punishment of fools is their folly.
The heart of the wise instructs his mouth,
and adds learning to his lips.
Pleasant words are a honeycomb,
sweet to the soul, and health to the bones.

There is a way which seems right to a man,
    but in the end it leads to death.
The appetite of the laboring man labors for him;
    for his mouth urges him on.
A worthless man devises mischief.
    His speech is like a scorching fire.
A perverse man stirs up strife.
    A whisperer separates close friends.
A man of violence entices his neighbor,
    and leads him in a way that is not good.
One who winks his eyes to plot perversities,
    one who compresses his lips, is bent on evil.
Gray hair is a crown of glory.
    It is attained by a life of righteousness.
One who is slow to anger is better than the mighty;
    one who rules his spirit, than he who takes a city.
The lot is cast into the lap,
    but its every decision is from YHWH.

....

Better is a dry morsel with quietness,
    than a house full of feasting with strife.
A servant who deals wisely will rule over a son who causes shame,
    and shall have a part in the inheritance among the brothers.
The refining pot is for silver, and the furnace for gold,
    but YHWH *tests the hearts.*
An evildoer heeds wicked lips.
    A liar gives ear to a mischievous tongue.
Whoever mocks the poor reproaches his Maker.
    He who is glad at calamity shall not be unpunished.
Children's children are the crown of old men;
    the glory of children are their parents.
Arrogant speech isn't fitting for a fool,
    much less do lying lips fit a prince.
A bribe is a precious stone in the eyes of him who gives it;
    wherever he turns, he prospers.
He who covers an offense promotes love;
    but he who repeats a matter separates best friends.
A rebuke enters deeper into one who has understanding
    than a hundred lashes into a fool.

An evil man seeks only rebellion;
    therefore a cruel messenger shall be sent against him.
Let a bear robbed of her cubs meet a man,
    rather than a fool in his folly.
Whoever rewards evil for good,
    evil shall not depart from his house.
The beginning of strife is like breaching a dam,
    therefore stop contention before quarreling breaks out.
He who justifies the wicked, and he who condemns the righteous,
    both of them alike are an abomination to YHWH.
Why is there money in the hand of a fool to buy wisdom,
    since he has no understanding?
A friend loves at all times;
    and a brother is born for adversity.
A man void of understanding strikes hands,
    and becomes collateral in the presence of his neighbor.
He who loves disobedience loves strife.
    One who builds a high gate seeks destruction.
One who has a perverse heart doesn't find prosperity,
    and one who has a deceitful tongue falls into trouble.
He who becomes the father of a fool grieves.
    The father of a fool has no joy.
A cheerful heart makes good medicine,
    but a crushed spirit dries up the bones.
A wicked man receives a bribe in secret,
    to pervert the ways of justice.
Wisdom is before the face of one who has understanding,
    but the eyes of a fool wander to the ends of the earth.
A foolish son brings grief to his father,
    and bitterness to her who bore him.
Also to punish the righteous is not good,
    nor to flog officials for their integrity.
He who spares his words has knowledge.
    He who is even tempered is a man of understanding.
Even a fool, when he keeps silent, is counted wise.
    When he shuts his lips, he is thought to be discerning.

....

A man who isolates himself pursues selfishness,
    and defies all sound judgment.

A fool has no delight in understanding,
  but only in revealing his own opinion.
When wickedness comes, contempt also comes,
  and with shame comes disgrace.
The words of a man's mouth are like deep waters.
  The fountain of wisdom is like a flowing brook.
To be partial to the faces of the wicked is not good,
  nor to deprive the innocent of justice.
A fool's lips come into strife,
  and his mouth invites beatings.
A fool's mouth is his destruction,
  and his lips are a snare to his soul.
The words of a gossip are like dainty morsels:
  they go down into a person's innermost parts.
One who is slack in his work
  is brother to him who is a master of destruction.
YHWH's name is a strong tower:
  the righteous run to him, and are safe.
The rich man's wealth is his strong city,
  like an unscalable wall in his own imagination.
Before destruction the heart of man is proud,
  but before honor is humility.
He who answers before he hears,
  that is folly and shame to him.
A man's spirit will sustain him in sickness,
  but a crushed spirit, who can bear?
The heart of the discerning gets knowledge.
  The ear of the wise seeks knowledge.
A man's gift makes room for him,
  and brings him before great men.
He who pleads his cause first seems right;
  until another comes and questions him.
The lot settles disputes,
  and keeps strong ones apart.
A brother offended is more difficult than a fortified city.
  Disputes are like the bars of a fortress.
A man's stomach is filled with the fruit of his mouth.
  With the harvest of his lips he is satisfied.
Death and life are in the power of the tongue;
  those who love it will eat its fruit.

Whoever finds a wife finds a good thing,
    and obtains favor of YHWH.
The poor plead for mercy,
    but the rich answer harshly.
A man of many companions may be ruined,
    but there is a friend who sticks closer than a brother.

       ....

Better is the poor who walks in his integrity
    than he who is perverse in his lips and is a fool.
It isn't good to have zeal without knowledge,
    nor being hasty with one's feet and missing the way.
The foolishness of man subverts his way;
    his heart rages against YHWH.
Wealth adds many friends,
    but the poor is separated from his friend.
A false witness shall not be unpunished.
    He who pours out lies shall not go free.
Many will entreat the favor of a ruler,
    and everyone is a friend to a man who gives gifts.
All the relatives of the poor shun him:
    how much more do his friends avoid him!
    He pursues them with pleas, but they are gone.
He who gets wisdom loves his own soul.
    He who keeps understanding shall find good.
A false witness shall not be unpunished.
    He who utters lies shall perish.
Delicate living is not appropriate for a fool,
    much less for a servant to have rule over princes.
The discretion of a man makes him slow to anger.
    It is his glory to overlook an offense.
The king's wrath is like the roaring of a lion,
    but his favor is like dew on the grass.
A foolish son is the calamity of his father.
    A wife's quarrels are a continual dripping.
House and riches are an inheritance from fathers,
    but a prudent wife is from YHWH.
Slothfulness casts into a deep sleep.
    The idle soul shall suffer hunger.
He who keeps the commandment keeps his soul,

but he who is contemptuous in his ways shall die.
He who has pity on the poor lends to YHWH;
  he will reward him.
Discipline your son, for there is hope;
  don't be a willing party to his death.
A hot-tempered man must pay the penalty,
  for if you rescue him, you must do it again.
Listen to counsel and receive instruction,
  that you may be wise in your latter end.
There are many plans in a man's heart,
  but YHWH's counsel will prevail.
That which makes a man to be desired is his kindness.
  A poor man is better than a liar.
The fear of YHWH leads to life, then contentment;
  he rests and will not be touched by trouble.
The sluggard buries his hand in the dish;
  he will not so much as bring it to his mouth again.
Flog a scoffer, and the simple will learn prudence;
  rebuke one who has understanding, and he will gain knowl-
  edge.
He who robs his father and drives away his mother,
  is a son who causes shame and brings reproach.
If you stop listening to instruction, my son,
  you will stray from the words of knowledge.
A corrupt witness mocks justice,
  and the mouth of the wicked gulps down iniquity.
Penalties are prepared for scoffers,
  and beatings for the backs of fools.

....

Wine is a mocker and beer is a brawler.
  Whoever is led astray by them is not wise.
The terror of a king is like the roaring of a lion.
  He who provokes him to anger forfeits his own life.
It is an honor for a man to keep aloof from strife,
  but every fool will be quarreling.
The sluggard will not plow by reason of the winter;
  therefore he shall beg in harvest, and have nothing.
Counsel in the heart of man is like deep water,

but a man of understanding will draw it out.
Many men claim to be men of unfailing love,
  but who can find a faithful man?
A righteous man walks in integrity.
  Blessed are his children after him.
A king who sits on the throne of judgment
  scatters away all evil with his eyes.
Who can say, "I have made my heart pure.
  I am clean and without sin?"
Differing weights and differing measures,
  both of them alike are an abomination to YHWH.
Even a child makes himself known by his doings,
  whether his work is pure, and whether it is right.
The hearing ear, and the seeing eye,
  YHWH has made even both of them.
Don't love sleep, lest you come to poverty.
  Open your eyes, and you shall be satisfied with bread.
"It's no good, it's no good," says the buyer;
  but when he is gone his way, then he boasts.
There is gold and abundance of rubies,
  but the lips of knowledge are a rare jewel.
Take the garment of one who puts up collateral for a stranger;
  and hold him in pledge for a wayward woman.
Fraudulent food is sweet to a man,
  but afterwards his mouth is filled with gravel.
Plans are established by advice;
  by wise guidance you wage war!
He who goes about as a tale-bearer reveals secrets;
  therefore don't keep company with him who opens wide his
  lips.
Whoever curses his father or his mother,
  his lamp shall be put out in blackness of darkness.
An inheritance quickly gained at the beginning,
  won't be blessed in the end.
Don't say, "I will pay back evil."
  Wait for YHWH, and he will save you.
YHWH detests differing weights,
  and dishonest scales are not pleasing.
A man's steps are from YHWH;
  how then can man understand his way?

It is a snare to a man to make a rash dedication,
  then later to consider his vows.
A wise king winnows out the wicked,
  and drives the threshing wheel over them.
The spirit of man is YHWH's lamp,
  searching all his innermost parts.
Love and faithfulness keep the king safe.
  His throne is sustained by love.
The glory of young men is their strength.
  The splendor of old men is their gray hair.
Wounding blows cleanse away evil,
  and beatings purge the innermost parts.

....

The king's heart is in YHWH's hand like the watercourses.
  He turns it wherever he desires.
Every way of a man is right in his own eyes,
  but YHWH weighs the hearts.
To do righteousness and justice
  is more acceptable to YHWH than sacrifice.
A high look and a proud heart,
  the lamp of the wicked, is sin.
The plans of the diligent surely lead to profit;
  and everyone who is hasty surely rushes to poverty.
Getting treasures by a lying tongue
  is a fleeting vapor for those who seek death.
The violence of the wicked will drive them away,
  because they refuse to do what is right.
The way of the guilty is devious,
  but the conduct of the innocent is upright.
It is better to dwell in the corner of the housetop
  than to share a house with a contentious woman.
The soul of the wicked desires evil;
  his neighbor finds no mercy in his eyes.
When the mocker is punished, the simple gains wisdom.
  When the wise is instructed, he receives knowledge.
The Righteous One considers the house of the wicked,
  and brings the wicked to ruin.
Whoever stops his ears at the cry of the poor,

he will also cry out, but shall not be heard.
A gift in secret pacifies anger,
*   and a bribe in the cloak, strong wrath.*
It is joy to the righteous to do justice;
*   but it is a destruction to the workers of iniquity.*
The man who wanders out of the way of understanding
*   shall rest in the assembly of the departed spirits.*
He who loves pleasure will be a poor man.
*   He who loves wine and oil won't be rich.*
The wicked is a ransom for the righteous,
*   the treacherous for the upright.*
It is better to dwell in a desert land,
*   than with a contentious and fretful woman.*
There is precious treasure and oil in the dwelling of the wise;
*   but a foolish man swallows it up.*
He who follows after righteousness and kindness
*   finds life, righteousness, and honor.*
A wise man scales the city of the mighty,
*   and brings down the strength of its confidence.*
Whoever guards his mouth and his tongue
*   keeps his soul from troubles.*
The proud and arrogant man—"Scoffer" is his name—
*   he works in the arrogance of pride.*
The desire of the sluggard kills him,
*   for his hands refuse to labor.*
There are those who covet greedily all day long;
*   but the righteous give and don't withhold.*
The sacrifice of the wicked is an abomination—
*   how much more, when he brings it with a wicked mind!*
A false witness will perish.
*   A man who listens speaks to eternity.*
A wicked man hardens his face;
*   but as for the upright, he establishes his ways.*
There is no wisdom nor understanding
*   nor counsel against* YHWH.
The horse is prepared for the day of battle;
*   but victory is with* YHWH.

....

A good name is more desirable than great riches,
and loving favor is better than silver and gold.
The rich and the poor have this in common:
YHWH is the maker of them all.
A prudent man sees danger and hides himself;
but the simple pass on, and suffer for it.
The result of humility and the fear of YHWH
is wealth, honor, and life.
Thorns and snares are in the path of the wicked:
whoever guards his soul stays from them.
Train up a child in the way he should go,
and when he is old he will not depart from it.
The rich rule over the poor.
The borrower is servant to the lender.
He who sows wickedness reaps trouble,
and the rod of his fury will be destroyed.
He who has a generous eye will be blessed;
for he shares his food with the poor.
Drive out the mocker, and strife will go out;
yes, quarrels and insults will stop.
He who loves purity of heart and speaks gracefully
is the king's friend.
YHWH's eyes watch over knowledge;
but he frustrates the words of the unfaithful.
The sluggard says, "There is a lion outside!
I will be killed in the streets!"
The mouth of an adulteress is a deep pit.
He who is under YHWH's wrath will fall into it.
Folly is bound up in the heart of a child:
the rod of discipline drives it far from him.
Whoever oppresses the poor for his own increase and whoever gives
to the rich,
both come to poverty.

Turn your ear, and listen to the words of the wise.
Apply your heart to my teaching.
For it is a pleasant thing if you keep them within you,
if all of them are ready on your lips.
I teach you today, even you,
So that your trust may be in YHWH.

Haven't I written to you thirty excellent things
of counsel and knowledge,
To teach you truth, reliable words,
to give sound answers to the ones who sent you?

Don't exploit the poor, because he is poor;
and don't crush the needy in court;
for YHWH will plead their case,
and plunder the life of those who plunder them.

Don't befriend a hot-tempered man,
and don't associate with one who harbors anger:
lest you learn his ways,
and ensnare your soul.

Don't you be one of those who strike hands,
of those who are collateral for debts.
If you don't have means to pay,
why should he take away your bed from under you?

Don't move the ancient boundary stone
which your fathers have set up.

Do you see a man skilled in his work?
He will serve kings.
He won't serve obscure men.

....

When you sit to eat with a ruler,
consider diligently what is before you;
put a knife to your throat,
if you are a man given to appetite.
Don't be desirous of his dainties,
since they are deceitful food.
Don't weary yourself to be rich.
In your wisdom, show restraint.
Why do you set your eyes on that which is not?
For it certainly sprouts wings like an eagle and flies in the sky.
Don't eat the food of him who has a stingy eye,

and don't crave his delicacies:
    for as he thinks about the cost, so he is.
    "Eat and drink!" he says to you,
    but his heart is not with you.
The morsel which you have eaten you shall vomit up,
    and lose your good words.

Don't speak in the ears of a fool,
    for he will despise the wisdom of your words.

Don't move the ancient boundary stone.
    Don't encroach on the fields of the fatherless,
for their Defender is strong.
    He will plead their case against you.

Apply your heart to instruction,
    and your ears to the words of knowledge.
Don't withhold correction from a child.
    If you punish him with the rod, he will not die.
Punish him with the rod,
    and save his soul from Sheol.

My son, if your heart is wise,
    then my heart will be glad, even mine.
Yes, my heart will rejoice
    when your lips speak what is right.
Don't let your heart envy sinners,
    but rather fear YHWH all day long.
Indeed surely there is a future hope,
    and your hope will not be cut off.
Listen, my son, and be wise,
    and keep your heart on the right path!
Don't be among ones drinking too much wine,
    or those who gorge themselves on meat:
for the drunkard and the glutton shall become poor;
    and drowsiness clothes them in rags.
Listen to your father who gave you life,
    and don't despise your mother when she is old.
Buy the truth, and don't sell it.
    Get wisdom, discipline, and understanding.

The father of the righteous has great joy.
    Whoever fathers a wise child delights in him.
Let your father and your mother be glad!
    Let her who bore you rejoice!
My son, give me your heart;
    and let your eyes keep in my ways.
For a prostitute is a deep pit;
    and a wayward wife is a narrow well.
Yes, she lies in wait like a robber,
    and increases the unfaithful among men.

Who has woe?
    Who has sorrow?
    Who has strife?
    Who has complaints?
    Who has needless bruises?
    Who has bloodshot eyes?
Those who stay long at the wine;
    those who go to seek out mixed wine.
Don't look at the wine when it is red,
    when it sparkles in the cup,
    when it goes down smoothly.
In the end, it bites like a snake,
    and poisons like a viper.
Your eyes will see strange things,
    and your mind will imagine confusing things.
Yes, you will be as he who lies down in the middle of the sea,
    or as he who lies on top of the rigging:
"They hit me, and I was not hurt!
    They beat me, and I don't feel it!
    When will I wake up? I can do it again.
    I can find another."

....

Don't be envious of evil men,
    neither desire to be with them;
for their hearts plot violence
    and their lips talk about mischief.
Through wisdom a house is built;

by understanding it is established;
by knowledge the rooms are filled
　　with all rare and beautiful treasure.
A wise man has great power;
　　and a knowledgeable man increases strength;
for by wise guidance you wage your war;
　　and victory is in many advisors.
Wisdom is too high for a fool.
　　He doesn't open his mouth in the gate.
One who plots to do evil
　　will be called a schemer.
The schemes of folly are sin.
　　The mocker is detested by men.
If you falter in the time of trouble,
　　your strength is small.
Rescue those who are being led away to death!
　　Indeed, hold back those who are staggering to the slaughter!
If you say, "Behold, we didn't know this,"
　　doesn't he who weighs the hearts consider it?
He who keeps your soul, doesn't he know it?
　　Shall he not render to every man according to his work?
My son, eat honey, for it is good,
　　the droppings of the honeycomb, which are sweet to your taste;
so you shall know wisdom to be to your soul.
　　If you have found it, then there will be a reward:
　　Your hope will not be cut off.
Don't lay in wait, wicked man, against the habitation of the
righteous.
　　Don't destroy his resting place;
for a righteous man falls seven times and rises up again;
　　but the wicked are overthrown by calamity.
Don't rejoice when your enemy falls.
　　Don't let your heart be glad when he is overthrown,
lest YHWH see it, and it displease him,
　　and he turn away his wrath from him.
Don't fret yourself because of evildoers,
　　neither be envious of the wicked;
for there will be no reward to the evil man.
　　The lamp of the wicked will be snuffed out.
My son, fear YHWH and the king.

Don't join those who are rebellious;
for their calamity will rise suddenly.
Who knows what destruction may come from them both?

These also are sayings of the wise.

To show partiality in judgment is not good.
He who says to the wicked, "You are righteous,"
peoples will curse him, and nations will abhor him—
but it will go well with those who convict the guilty,
and a rich blessing will come on them.
An honest answer
is like a kiss on the lips.
Prepare your work outside,
and get your fields ready.
Afterwards, build your house.
Don't be a witness against your neighbor without cause.
Don't deceive with your lips.
Don't say, "I will do to him as he has done to me;
I will repay the man according to his work."
I went by the field of the sluggard,
by the vineyard of the man void of understanding:
Behold, it was all grown over with thorns.
Its surface was covered with nettles,
and its stone wall was broken down.
Then I saw, and considered well.
I saw, and received instruction:
a little sleep, a little slumber,
a little folding of the hands to sleep,
so your poverty will come as a robber
and your want as an armed man.

....

These also are proverbs of Solomon, which the men of Hezekiah
king of Judah copied out.
It is the glory of God to conceal a thing,
but the glory of kings is to search out a matter.
As the heavens for height, and the earth for depth,
so the hearts of kings are unsearchable.
Take away the dross from the silver,

and material comes out for the refiner;
Take away the wicked from the king's presence,
    and his throne will be established in righteousness.
Don't exalt yourself in the presence of the king,
    or claim a place among great men;
for it is better that it be said to you, "Come up here,"
        than that you should be put lower in the presence of the prince,
        whom your eyes have seen.
Don't be hasty in bringing charges to court.
    What will you do in the end when your neighbor shames you?
Debate your case with your neighbor,
        and don't betray the confidence of another,
        lest one who hears it put you to shame,
        and your bad reputation never depart.

A word fitly spoken
    is like apples of gold in settings of silver.
As an earring of gold, and an ornament of fine gold,
    so is a wise reprover to an obedient ear.
As the cold of snow in the time of harvest,
    so is a faithful messenger to those who send him;
    for he refreshes the soul of his masters.
As clouds and wind without rain,
    so is he who boasts of gifts deceptively.
By patience a ruler is persuaded.
    A soft tongue breaks the bone.
Have you found honey?
    Eat as much as is sufficient for you,
    lest you eat too much, and vomit it.
Let your foot be seldom in your neighbor's house,
    lest he be weary of you, and hate you.
A man who gives false testimony against his neighbor
    is like a club, a sword, or a sharp arrow.
Confidence in someone unfaithful in time of trouble
    is like a bad tooth or a lame foot.
As one who takes away a garment in cold weather,
    or vinegar on soda,
    so is one who sings songs to a heavy heart.
If your enemy is hungry, give him food to eat.
    If he is thirsty, give him water to drink;

for you will heap coals of fire on his head,
     and YHWH will reward you.
The north wind produces rain;
     so a backbiting tongue brings an angry face.
It is better to dwell in the corner of the housetop
     than to share a house with a contentious woman.
Like cold water to a thirsty soul,
     so is good news from a far country.
Like a muddied spring and a polluted well,
     so is a righteous man who gives way before the wicked.
It is not good to eat much honey,
     nor is it honorable to seek one's own honor.
Like a city that is broken down and without walls
     is a man whose spirit is without restraint.

....

Like snow in summer, and as rain in harvest,
     so honor is not fitting for a fool.
Like a fluttering sparrow,
     like a darting swallow,
     so the undeserved curse doesn't come to rest.
A whip is for the horse,
     a bridle for the donkey,
     and a rod for the back of fools!
Don't answer a fool according to his folly,
     lest you also be like him.
Answer a fool according to his folly,
     lest he be wise in his own eyes.
One who sends a message by the hand of a fool
     is cutting off feet and drinking violence.
Like the legs of the lame that hang loose,
     so is a parable in the mouth of fools.
As one who binds a stone in a sling,
     so is he who gives honor to a fool.
Like a thorn bush that goes into the hand of a drunkard,
     so is a parable in the mouth of fools.
As an archer who wounds all,
     so is he who hires a fool
     or he who hires those who pass by.
As a dog that returns to his vomit,

so is a fool who repeats his folly.
Do you see a man wise in his own eyes?
　There is more hope for a fool than for him.
The sluggard says, "There is a lion in the road!
　A fierce lion roams the streets!"
As the door turns on its hinges,
　so does the sluggard on his bed.
The sluggard buries his hand in the dish.
　He is too lazy to bring it back to his mouth.
The sluggard is wiser in his own eyes
　than seven men who answer with discretion.
Like one who grabs a dog's ears
　is one who passes by and meddles in a quarrel not his own.
Like a madman who shoots torches, arrows, and death,
　is the man who deceives his neighbor and says, "Am I not
　joking?"
For lack of wood a fire goes out.
　Without gossip, a quarrel dies down.
As coals are to hot embers,
　and wood to fire,
　so is a contentious man to kindling strife.
The words of a whisperer are as dainty morsels,
　they go down into the innermost parts.
Like silver dross on an earthen vessel
　are the lips of a fervent one with an evil heart.
A malicious man disguises himself with his lips,
　but he harbors evil in his heart.
When his speech is charming, don't believe him,
　for there are seven abominations in his heart.
His malice may be concealed by deception,
　but his wickedness will be exposed in the assembly.
Whoever digs a pit shall fall into it.
　Whoever rolls a stone, it will come back on him.
A lying tongue hates those it hurts;
　and a flattering mouth works ruin.

....

Don't boast about tomorrow;
　for you don't know what a day may bring.
Let another man praise you,

and not your own mouth;
  a stranger, and not your own lips.
A stone is heavy,
  and sand is a burden;
  but a fool's provocation is heavier than both.
Wrath is cruel,
  and anger is overwhelming;
  but who is able to stand before jealousy?
Better is open rebuke
  than hidden love.
The wounds of a friend are faithful,
  although the kisses of an enemy are profuse.
A full soul loathes a honeycomb;
  but to a hungry soul, every bitter thing is sweet.
As a bird that wanders from her nest,
  so is a man who wanders from his home.
Perfume and incense bring joy to the heart;
  so does earnest counsel from a man's friend.
Don't forsake your friend and your father's friend.
    Don't go to your brother's house in the day of your disaster.
    A neighbor who is near is better than a distant brother.
Be wise, my son,
  and bring joy to my heart,
  then I can answer my tormentor.
A prudent man sees danger and takes refuge;
  but the simple pass on, and suffer for it.
Take his garment when he puts up collateral for a stranger.
    Hold it for a wayward woman!
He who blesses his neighbor with a loud voice early in the morning,
  it will be taken as a curse by him.
A continual dropping on a rainy day
  and a contentious wife are alike:
restraining her is like restraining the wind,
  or like grasping oil in his right hand.

Iron sharpens iron;
  so a man sharpens his friend's countenance.
Whoever tends the fig tree shall eat its fruit.
  He who looks after his master shall be honored.

Like water reflects a face,
    so a man's heart reflects the man.
Sheol and Abaddon are never satisfied;
    and a man's eyes are never satisfied.
The crucible is for silver,
    and the furnace for gold;
    but man is refined by his praise.
Though you grind a fool in a mortar with a pestle along with grain,
    yet his foolishness will not be removed from him.

Know well the state of your flocks,
    and pay attention to your herds:
for riches are not forever,
    nor does the crown endure to all generations.
The hay is removed, and the new growth appears,
    the grasses of the hills are gathered in.
The lambs are for your clothing,
    and the goats are the price of a field.
There will be plenty of goats' milk for your food,
    for your family's food,
    and for the nourishment of your servant girls.

....

The wicked flee when no one pursues;
    but the righteous are as bold as a lion.
In rebellion, a land has many rulers,
    but order is maintained by a man of understanding and
    knowledge.
A needy man who oppresses the poor
    is like a driving rain which leaves no crops.
Those who forsake the law praise the wicked;
    but those who keep the law contend with them.
Evil men don't understand justice;
    but those who seek YHWH understand it fully.
Better is the poor who walks in his integrity,
    than he who is perverse in his ways, and he is rich.
Whoever keeps the law is a wise son;
    but he who is a companion of gluttons shames his father.
He who increases his wealth by excessive interest

gathers it for one who has pity on the poor.
He who turns away his ear from hearing the law,
even his prayer is an abomination.
Whoever causes the upright to go astray in an evil way,
he will fall into his own trap;
but the blameless will inherit good.
The rich man is wise in his own eyes;
but the poor who has understanding sees through him.
When the righteous triumph, there is great glory;
but when the wicked rise, men hide themselves.
He who conceals his sins doesn't prosper,
but whoever confesses and renounces them finds mercy.
Blessed is the man who always fears;
but one who hardens his heart falls into trouble.
As a roaring lion or a charging bear,
so is a wicked ruler over helpless people.
A tyrannical ruler lacks judgment.
One who hates ill-gotten gain will have long days.
A man who is tormented by life blood will be a fugitive until death;
no one will support him.
Whoever walks blamelessly is kept safe;
but one with perverse ways will fall suddenly.
One who works his land will have an abundance of food;
but one who chases fantasies will have his fill of poverty.
A faithful man is rich with blessings;
but one who is eager to be rich will not go unpunished.
To show partiality is not good;
yet a man will do wrong for a piece of bread.
A stingy man hurries after riches,
and doesn't know that poverty waits for him.
One who rebukes a man will afterward find more favor
than one who flatters with the tongue.
Whoever robs his father or his mother and says, "It's not wrong,"
is a partner with a destroyer.
One who is greedy stirs up strife;
but one who trusts in YHWH will prosper.
One who trusts in himself is a fool;
but one who walks in wisdom is kept safe.
One who gives to the poor has no lack;

but one who closes his eyes will have many curses.
When the wicked rise, men hide themselves;
   but when they perish, the righteous thrive.

....

He who is often rebuked and stiffens his neck
   will be destroyed suddenly, with no remedy.
When the righteous thrive, the people rejoice;
   but when the wicked rule, the people groan.
Whoever loves wisdom brings joy to his father;
   but a companion of prostitutes squanders his wealth.
The king by justice makes the land stable,
   but he who takes bribes tears it down.
A man who flatters his neighbor
   spreads a net for his feet.
An evil man is snared by his sin,
   but the righteous can sing and be glad.
The righteous care about justice for the poor.
   The wicked aren't concerned about knowledge.
Mockers stir up a city,
   but wise men turn away anger.
If a wise man goes to court with a foolish man,
   the fool rages or scoffs, and there is no peace.
The bloodthirsty hate a man of integrity;
   and they seek the life of the upright.
A fool vents all of his anger,
   but a wise man brings himself under control.
If a ruler listens to lies,
   all of his officials are wicked.
The poor man and the oppressor have this in common:
   YHWH gives sight to the eyes of both.
The king who fairly judges the poor,
   his throne shall be established forever.
The rod of correction gives wisdom,
   but a child left to himself causes shame to his mother.
When the wicked increase, sin increases;
   but the righteous will see their downfall.
Correct your son, and he will give you peace;
   yes, he will bring delight to your soul.
Where there is no revelation, the people cast off restraint;

but one who keeps the law is blessed.
A servant can't be corrected by words.
    Though he understands, yet he will not respond.
Do you see a man who is hasty in his words?
    There is more hope for a fool than for him.
He who pampers his servant from youth
    will have him become a son in the end.
An angry man stirs up strife,
    and a wrathful man abounds in sin.
A man's pride brings him low,
    but one of lowly spirit gains honor.
Whoever is an accomplice of a thief is an enemy of his own soul.
    He takes an oath, but dares not testify.
The fear of man proves to be a snare,
    but whoever puts his trust in YHWH is kept safe.
Many seek the ruler's favor,
    but a man's justice comes from YHWH.
A dishonest man detests the righteous,
    and the upright in their ways detest the wicked.

....

The words of Agur the son of Jakeh; the revelation:
the man says to Ithiel,
    to Ithiel and Ucal:
"Surely I am the most ignorant man,
    and don't have a man's understanding.
I have not learned wisdom,
    neither do I have the knowledge of the Holy One.
Who has ascended up into heaven, and descended?
    Who has gathered the wind in his fists?
    Who has bound the waters in his garment?
    Who has established all the ends of the earth?
    What is his name, and what is his son's name, if you know?

"Every word of God is flawless.
    He is a shield to those who take refuge in him.
Don't you add to his words,
    lest he reprove you, and you be found a liar.

"Two things I have asked of you.

Don't deny me before I die.
Remove far from me falsehood and lies.
 Give me neither poverty nor riches.
 Feed me with the food that is needful for me,
lest I be full, deny you, and say, 'Who is YHWH?'
 or lest I be poor, and steal,
 and so dishonor the name of my God.

"Don't slander a servant to his master,
 lest he curse you, and you be held guilty.

There is a generation that curses their father,
 and doesn't bless their mother.
There is a generation that is pure in their own eyes,
 yet are not washed from their filthiness.
There is a generation, oh how lofty are their eyes!
 Their eyelids are lifted up.
There is a generation whose teeth are like swords,
 and their jaws like knives,
 to devour the poor from the earth, and the needy from among
 men.

"The leech has two daughters:
 'Give, give.'

"There are three things that are never satisfied;
 four that don't say, 'Enough:'
 Sheol,
 the barren womb;
 the earth that is not satisfied with water;
 and the fire that doesn't say, 'Enough.'

"The eye that mocks at his father,
 and scorns obedience to his mother:
 the ravens of the valley shall pick it out,
 the young eagles shall eat it.

"There are three things which are too amazing for me,
 four which I don't understand:
 The way of an eagle in the air,

the way of a serpent on a rock,
the way of a ship in the middle of the sea,
and the way of a man with a maiden.

"So is the way of an adulterous woman:
She eats and wipes her mouth,
and says, 'I have done nothing wrong.'

"For three things the earth trembles,
and under four, it can't bear up:
For a servant when he is king,
a fool when he is filled with food,
for an unloved woman when she is married,
and a servant who is heir to her mistress.

"There are four things which are little on the earth,
but they are exceedingly wise:
The ants are not a strong people,
yet they provide their food in the summer.
The hyraxes are but a feeble folk,
yet make they their houses in the rocks.
The locusts have no king,
yet they advance in ranks.
You can catch a lizard with your hands,
yet it is in kings' palaces.

"There are three things which are stately in their march,
four which are stately in going:
The lion, which is mightiest among animals,
and doesn't turn away for any;
the greyhound;
the male goat;
and the king against whom there is no rising up.

"If you have done foolishly in lifting up yourself,
or if you have thought evil,
put your hand over your mouth.
For as the churning of milk produces butter,
and the wringing of the nose produces blood;
so the forcing of wrath produces strife."

....

The words of king Lemuel; the revelation which his mother taught him.

"Oh, my son!
    Oh, son of my womb!
    Oh, son of my vows!
Don't give your strength to women,
    nor your ways to that which destroys kings.
It is not for kings, Lemuel,
    it is not for kings to drink wine,
    nor for princes to say, 'Where is strong drink?'
lest they drink, and forget the law,
    and pervert the justice due to anyone who is afflicted.
Give strong drink to him who is ready to perish,
    and wine to the bitter in soul.
Let him drink, and forget his poverty,
    and remember his misery no more.
Open your mouth for the mute,
    in the cause of all who are left desolate.
Open your mouth, judge righteously,
    and serve justice to the poor and needy."

Who can find a worthy woman?
    For her price is far above rubies.
The heart of her husband trusts in her.
    He shall have no lack of gain.
She does him good, and not harm,
    all the days of her life.
She seeks wool and flax,
    and works eagerly with her hands.
She is like the merchant ships.
    She brings her bread from afar.
She rises also while it is yet night,
    gives food to her household,
    and portions for her servant girls.
She considers a field, and buys it.
    With the fruit of her hands, she plants a vineyard.
She arms her waist with strength,

and makes her arms strong.
She perceives that her merchandise is profitable.
    Her lamp doesn't go out by night.
She lays her hands to the distaff,
    and her hands hold the spindle.
She opens her arms to the poor;
    yes, she extends her hands to the needy.
She is not afraid of the snow for her household;
    for all her household are clothed with scarlet.
She makes for herself carpets of tapestry.
    Her clothing is fine linen and purple.
Her husband is respected in the gates,
    when he sits among the elders of the land.
She makes linen garments and sells them,
    and delivers sashes to the merchant.
Strength and dignity are her clothing.
    She laughs at the time to come.
She opens her mouth with wisdom.
    Kind instruction is on her tongue.
She looks well to the ways of her household,
    and doesn't eat the bread of idleness.
Her children rise up and call her blessed.
    Her husband also praises her:
"Many women do noble things,
    but you excel them all."
Charm is deceitful, and beauty is vain;
    but a woman who fears YHWH, she shall be praised.
Give her of the fruit of her hands!
    Let her works praise her in the gates!

THE BOOK OF

ECCLESIASTES

28 MIN

The words of the Preacher, the son of David, king in Jerusalem:

"Vanity of vanities," says the Preacher; "Vanity of vanities, all is vanity." What does man gain from all his labor in which he labors under the sun? One generation goes, and another generation comes; but the earth remains forever. The sun also rises, and the sun goes down, and hurries to its place where it rises. The wind goes toward the south, and turns around to the north. It turns around continually as it goes, and the wind returns again to its courses. All the rivers run into the sea, yet the sea is not full. To the place where the rivers flow, there they flow again. All things are full of weariness beyond uttering. The eye is not satisfied with seeing, nor the ear filled with hearing. That which has been is that which shall be; and that which has been done is that which shall be done: and there is no new thing under the sun. Is there a thing of which it may be said, "Behold, this is new?" It has been long ago, in the ages which were before us. There is no memory of the former; neither shall there be any memory of the latter that are to come, among those that shall come after.

I, the Preacher, was king over Israel in Jerusalem. I applied my heart to seek and to search out by wisdom concerning all that is done under the sky. It is a heavy burden that God has given to the sons of men to be afflicted with. I have seen all the works that are done under the sun; and behold, all is vanity and a chasing after wind. That which is crooked can't be made straight; and that which is lacking can't be counted. I said to myself, "Behold, I have obtained for myself great wisdom above all who were before me in Jerusalem. Yes, my heart has had great experience of wisdom and knowledge." I applied my heart to know wisdom, and to know madness and folly. I perceived that this also was a chasing after wind. For in much wisdom is much grief; and he who increases knowledge increases sorrow.

....

I said in my heart, "Come now, I will test you with mirth: therefore enjoy pleasure;" and behold, this also was vanity. I said of laughter, "It is foolishness;" and of mirth, "What does it accomplish?"

I searched in my heart how to cheer my flesh with wine, my heart yet guiding me with wisdom, and how to lay hold of folly, until I might see what it was good for the sons of men that they should do under heaven all the days of their lives. I made myself great works. I built myself houses. I planted myself vineyards. I made myself gardens and parks, and I planted trees in them of all kinds of fruit. I made myself pools of water, to water from it the forest where trees were grown. I bought male servants and female servants, and had servants born in my house. I also had great possessions of herds and flocks, above all who were before me in Jerusalem. I also gathered silver and gold for myself, and the treasure of kings and of the provinces. I got myself male and female singers, and the delights of the sons of men: musical instruments, and that of all sorts. So I was great, and increased more than all who were before me in Jerusalem. My wisdom also remained with me. Whatever my eyes desired, I didn't keep from them. I didn't withhold my heart from any joy, for my heart rejoiced because of all my labor, and this was my portion from all my labor. Then I looked at all the works that my hands had worked, and at the labor that I had labored to do; and behold, all was vanity and a chasing after wind, and there was no profit under the sun.

I turned myself to consider wisdom, madness, and folly; for what can the king's successor do? Just that which has been done long ago. Then I saw that wisdom excels folly, as far as light excels darkness. The wise man's eyes are in his head, and the fool walks in darkness— and yet I perceived that one event happens to them all. Then I said in my heart, "As it happens to the fool, so will it happen even to me; and why was I then more wise?" Then I said in my heart that this also is vanity. For of the wise man, even as of the fool, there is no memory forever, since in the days to come all will have been long forgotten. Indeed, the wise man must die just like the fool!

So I hated life, because the work that is worked under the sun was grievous to me; for all is vanity and a chasing after wind. I hated all my labor in which I labored under the sun, because I must leave it to the man who comes after me. Who knows whether he will be a wise man or a fool? Yet he will have rule over all of my labor in which I have labored, and in which I have shown myself wise under the sun. This also is vanity.

Therefore I began to cause my heart to despair concerning all the labor in which I had labored under the sun. For there is a man whose labor is with wisdom, with knowledge, and with skillfulness; yet he shall leave it for his portion to a man who has not labored for it. This also is vanity and a great evil. For what does a man have of all his labor and of the striving of his heart, in which he labors under the sun? For all his days are sorrows, and his travail is grief; yes, even in the night his heart takes no rest. This also is vanity. There is nothing better for a man than that he should eat and drink, and make his soul enjoy good in his labor. This also I saw, that it is from the hand of God. For who can eat, or who can have enjoyment, more than I? For to the man who pleases him, God gives wisdom, knowledge, and joy; but to the sinner he gives travail, to gather and to heap up, that he may give to him who pleases God. This also is vanity and a chasing after wind.

....

For everything there is a season, and a time for every purpose under heaven:
> *a time to be born,*
>> *and a time to die;*
> *a time to plant,*
>> *and a time to pluck up that which is planted;*
> *a time to kill,*
>> *and a time to heal;*
> *a time to break down,*
>> *and a time to build up;*
> *a time to weep,*
>> *and a time to laugh;*
> *a time to mourn,*
>> *and a time to dance;*
> *a time to cast away stones,*
>> *and a time to gather stones together;*
> *a time to embrace,*
>> *and a time to refrain from embracing;*
> *u time to seek,*
>> *and a time to lose;*
> *a time to keep,*
>> *and a time to cast away;*
> *a time to tear,*
>> *and a time to sew;*
> *a time to keep silence,*
>> *and a time to speak;*
> *a time to love,*
>> *and a time to hate;*
> *a time for war,*
>> *and a time for peace.*

What profit has he who works in that in which he labors? I have seen the burden which God has given to the sons of men to be afflicted with. He has made everything beautiful in its time. He has also set eternity in their hearts, yet so that man can't find out the work that God has done from the beginning even to the end. I know that there is nothing better for them than to rejoice, and to do good as long as they live. Also that every man should eat and drink, and enjoy good in all his labor, is the gift of God. I know that whatever God does, it shall be forever. Nothing can be added to it, nor anything taken from it; and God has done it, that men should fear before him. That which is has been long ago, and that which is to be has been long ago. God seeks again that which is passed away.

Moreover I saw under the sun, in the place of justice, that wickedness was there; and in the place of righteousness, that wickedness was there. I said in my heart, "God will judge the righteous and the wicked; for there is a time there for every purpose and for every work." I said in my heart, "As for the sons of men, God tests them, so that they may see that they themselves are like animals. For that which happens to the sons of men happens to animals. Even one thing happens to them. As the one dies, so the other dies. Yes, they have all one breath; and man has no advantage over the animals; for all is vanity. All go to one place. All are from the dust, and all turn to dust again. Who knows the spirit of man, whether it goes upward, and the spirit of the animal, whether it goes downward to the earth?"

Therefore I saw that there is nothing better than that a man should rejoice in his works; for that is his portion: for who can bring him to see what will be after him?

....

Then I returned and saw all the oppressions that are done under the sun: and behold, the tears of those who were oppressed, and they had no comforter; and on the side of their oppressors there was power; but they had no comforter. Therefore I praised the dead who have been long dead more than the living who are yet alive. Yes, better than them both is him who has not yet been, who has not seen the evil work that is done under the sun. Then I saw all the labor and achievement that is the envy of a man's neighbor. This also is vanity and a striving after wind.

The fool folds his hands together and ruins himself. Better is a handful, with quietness, than two handfuls with labor and chasing after wind.

Then I returned and saw vanity under the sun. There is one who is alone, and he has neither son nor brother. There is no end to all of his labor, neither are his eyes satisfied with wealth. "For whom then, do I labor and deprive my soul of enjoyment?" This also is vanity. Yes, it is a miserable business.

Two are better than one, because they have a good reward for their labor. For if they fall, the one will lift up his fellow; but woe to him who is alone when he falls, and doesn't have another to lift him up. Again, if two lie together, then they have warmth; but how can one keep warm alone? If a man prevails against one who is alone, two shall withstand him; and a threefold cord is not quickly broken.

Better is a poor and wise youth than an old and foolish king who doesn't know how to receive admonition any more. For out of prison he came out to be king; yes, even in his kingdom he was born poor. I saw all the living who walk under the sun, that they were with the youth, the other, who succeeded him. There was no end of all the people, even of all them over whom he was—yet those who come after shall not rejoice in him. Surely this also is vanity and a chasing after wind.

....

Guard your steps when you go to God's house; for to draw near to listen is better than to give the sacrifice of fools, for they don't know that they do evil. Don't be rash with your mouth, and don't let your heart be hasty to utter anything before God; for God is in heaven, and you on earth. Therefore let your words be few. For as a dream comes with a multitude of cares, so a fool's speech with a multitude of words. When you vow a vow to God, don't defer to pay it; for he has no pleasure in fools. Pay that which you vow. It is better that you should not vow, than that you should vow and not pay. Don't allow your mouth to lead you into sin. Don't protest before the messenger that this was a mistake. Why should God be angry at your voice, and destroy the work of your hands? For in the multitude of dreams there are vanities, as well as in many words; but you must fear God.

If you see the oppression of the poor, and the violent taking away of justice and righteousness in a district, don't marvel at the matter, for one official is eyed by a higher one, and there are officials over them. Moreover the profit of the earth is for all. The king profits from the field.

He who loves silver shall not be satisfied with silver; nor he who loves abundance, with increase: this also is vanity. When goods increase, those who eat them are increased; and what advantage is there to its owner, except to feast on them with his eyes?

The sleep of a laboring man is sweet, whether he eats little or much; but the abundance of the rich will not allow him to sleep.

There is a grievous evil which I have seen under the sun: wealth kept by its owner to his harm. Those riches perish by misfortune, and if he has fathered a son, there is nothing in his hand. As he came out of his mother's womb, naked shall he go again as he came, and shall take nothing for his labor, which he may carry away in his hand. This also is a grievous evil, that in all points as he came, so shall he go. And what profit does he have who labors for the wind? All his days he also eats in darkness, he is frustrated, and has sickness and wrath.

Behold, that which I have seen to be good and proper is for one to eat and to drink, and to enjoy good in all his labor, in which he labors under the sun, all the days of his life which God has given him; for this is his portion. Every man also to whom God has given riches and wealth, and has given him power to eat of it, and to take his portion, and to rejoice in his labor—this is the gift of God. For he shall not often reflect on the days of his life; because God occupies him with the joy of his heart.

....

There is an evil which I have seen under the sun, and it is heavy on men: a man to whom God gives riches, wealth, and honor, so that he lacks nothing for his soul of all that he desires, yet God gives him no power to eat of it, but an alien eats it. This is vanity, and it is an evil disease.

If a man fathers a hundred children, and lives many years, so that the days of his years are many, but his soul is not filled with good, and moreover he has no burial; I say, that a stillborn child is better than he: for it comes in vanity, and departs in darkness, and its name is covered with darkness. Moreover it has not seen the sun nor known it. This has rest rather than the other. Yes, though he live a thousand years twice told, and yet fails to enjoy good, don't all go to one place? All the labor of man is for his mouth, and yet the appetite is not filled. For what advantage has the wise more than the fool? What has the poor man, that knows how to walk before the living? Better is the sight of the eyes than the wandering of the desire. This also is vanity and a chasing after wind. Whatever has been, its name was given long ago; and it is known what man is; neither can he contend with him who is mightier than he. For there are many words that create vanity. What does that profit man? For who knows what is good for man in life, all the days of his vain life which he spends like a shadow? For who can tell a man what will be after him under the sun?

....

A good name is better than fine perfume; and the day of death better than the day of one's birth. It is better to go to the house of mourning than to go to the house of feasting; for that is the end of all men, and the living should take this to heart. Sorrow is better than laughter; for by the sadness of the face the heart is made good. The heart of the wise is in the house of mourning; but the heart of fools is in the house of mirth. It is better to hear the rebuke of the wise than for a man to hear the song of fools. For as the crackling of thorns under a pot, so is the laughter of the fool. This also is vanity. Surely extortion makes the wise man foolish; and a bribe destroys the understanding. Better is the end of a thing than its beginning.

The patient in spirit is better than the proud in spirit. Don't be hasty in your spirit to be angry, for anger rests in the bosom of fools. Don't say, "Why were the former days better than these?" For you do not ask wisely about this.

Wisdom is as good as an inheritance. Yes, it is more excellent for those who see the sun. For wisdom is a defense, even as money is a defense; but the excellency of knowledge is that wisdom preserves the life of him who has it.

Consider the work of God, for who can make that straight, which he has made crooked? In the day of prosperity be joyful, and in the day of adversity consider; yes, God has made the one side by side with the other, to the end that man should not find out anything after him.

All this I have seen in my days of vanity: there is a righteous man who perishes in his righteousness, and there is a wicked man who lives long in his evildoing. Don't be overly righteous, neither make yourself overly wise. Why should you destroy yourself? Don't be too wicked, neither be foolish. Why should you die before your time? It is good that you should take hold of this. Yes, also don't withdraw your hand from that; for he who fears God will come out of them all. Wisdom is a strength to the wise man more than ten rulers who are in a city. Surely there is not a righteous man on earth who does good and doesn't sin. Also don't take heed to all words that are spoken, lest you hear your servant curse you; for often your own heart knows that you yourself have likewise cursed others. All this I have proved in wisdom. I said, "I will be wise;" but it was far from me. That which is, is far off and exceedingly deep. Who can find it out? I turned around, and my heart sought to know and to search out, and to seek wisdom and the scheme of things, and to know that wickedness is stupidity, and that foolishness is madness.

I find more bitter than death the woman whose heart is snares and traps, whose hands are chains. Whoever pleases God shall escape from her; but the sinner will be ensnared by her.

"Behold, I have found this," says the Preacher, "to one another, to find out the scheme which my soul still seeks, but I have not found. I have found one man among a thousand, but I have not found a woman among all those. Behold, I have only found this: that God made man upright; but they search for many schemes."

....

Who is like the wise man? And who knows the interpretation of a thing? A man's wisdom makes his face shine, and the hardness of his face is changed. I say, "Keep the king's command!" because of the oath to God. Don't be hasty to go out of his presence. Don't persist in an evil thing, for he does whatever pleases him, for the king's word is supreme. Who can say to him, "What are you doing?" Whoever keeps the commandment shall not come to harm, and his wise heart will know the time and procedure. For there is a time and procedure for every purpose, although the misery of man is heavy on him. For he doesn't know that which will be; for who can tell him how it will be? There is no man who has power over the spirit to contain the spirit; neither does he have power over the day of death. There is no discharge in war; neither shall wickedness deliver those who practice it.

All this I have seen, and applied my mind to every work that is done under the sun. There is a time in which one man has power over another to his hurt. So I saw the wicked buried. Indeed they came also from holiness. They went and were forgotten in the city where they did this. This also is vanity. Because sentence against an evil work is not executed speedily, therefore the heart of the sons of men is fully set in them to do evil. Though a sinner commits crimes a hundred times, and lives long, yet surely I know that it will be better with those who fear God, who are reverent before him. But it shall not be well with the wicked, neither shall he lengthen days like a shadow, because he doesn't fear God.

There is a vanity which is done on the earth, that there are righteous men to whom it happens according to the work of the wicked. Again, there are wicked men to whom it happens according to the work of the righteous. I said that this also is vanity. Then I commended mirth, because a man has no better thing under the sun, than to eat, and to drink, and to be joyful: for that will accompany him in his labor all the days of his life which God has given him under the sun.

When I applied my heart to know wisdom, and to see the business that is done on the earth (even though eyes see no sleep day or night), then I saw all the work of God, that man can't find out the work that is done under the sun, because however much a man labors to seek it out, yet he won't find it. Yes even though a wise man thinks he can comprehend it, he won't be able to find it.

....

For all this I laid to my heart, even to explore all this: that the righteous, and the wise, and their works, are in the hand of God; whether it is love or hatred, man doesn't know it; all is before them. All things come alike to all. There is one event to the righteous and to the wicked; to the good, to the clean, to the unclean, to him who sacrifices, and to him who doesn't sacrifice. As is the good, so is the sinner; he who takes an oath, as he who fears an oath. This is an evil in all that is done under the sun, that there is one event to all: yes also, the heart of the sons of men is full of evil, and madness is in their heart while they live, and after that they go to the dead. For to him who is joined with all the living there is hope; for a living dog is better than a dead lion. For the living know that they will die, but the dead don't know anything, neither do they have any more a reward; for their memory is forgotten. Also their love, their hatred, and their envy has perished long ago; neither do they any longer have a portion forever in anything that is done under the sun.

Go your way—eat your bread with joy, and drink your wine with a merry heart; for God has already accepted your works. Let your garments be always white, and don't let your head lack oil. Live joyfully with the wife whom you love all the days of your life of vanity, which he has given you under the sun, all your days of vanity, for that is your portion in life, and in your labor in which you labor under the sun. Whatever your hand finds to do, do it with your might; for there is no work, nor plan, nor knowledge, nor wisdom, in Sheol, where you are going.

I returned and saw under the sun that the race is not to the swift, nor the battle to the strong, neither yet bread to the wise, nor yet riches to men of understanding, nor yet favor to men of skill; but time and chance happen to them all. For man also doesn't know his time. As the fish that are taken in an evil net, and as the birds that are caught in the snare, even so are the sons of men snared in an evil time, when it falls suddenly on them.

I have also seen wisdom under the sun in this way, and it seemed great to me. There was a little city, and few men within it; and a great king came against it, besieged it, and built great bulwarks against it. Now a poor wise man was found in it, and he by his wisdom delivered the city; yet no man remembered that same poor man. Then I said, "Wisdom is better than strength." Nevertheless the poor man's wisdom is despised, and his words are not heard. The words of the wise heard in quiet are better than the cry of him who rules among fools. Wisdom is better than weapons of war; but one sinner destroys much good.

....

Dead flies cause the oil of the perfumer to produce an evil odor;
so does a little folly outweigh wisdom and honor.
A wise man's heart is at his right hand,
but a fool's heart at his left. Yes also when the fool walks by the
way, his understanding fails him, and he says to everyone that
he is a fool. If the spirit of the ruler rises up against you, don't
leave your place; for gentleness lays great offenses to rest.

There is an evil which I have seen under the sun, the sort of error which proceeds from the ruler. Folly is set in great dignity, and the rich sit in a low place. I have seen servants on horses, and princes walking like servants on the earth. He who digs a pit may fall into it; and whoever breaks through a wall may be bitten by a snake. Whoever carves out stones may be injured by them. Whoever splits wood may be endangered by it. If the ax is blunt, and one doesn't sharpen the edge, then he must use more strength; but skill brings success.

If the snake bites before it is charmed, then is there no profit for the charmer's tongue. The words of a wise man's mouth are gracious; but a fool is swallowed by his own lips. The beginning of the words of his mouth is foolishness; and the end of his talk is mischievous madness. A fool also multiplies words.

Man doesn't know what will be; and that which will be after him, who can tell him? The labor of fools wearies every one of them; for he doesn't know how to go to the city.

> *Woe to you, land, when your king is a child,*
>> *and your princes eat in the morning!*
> *Happy are you, land, when your king is the son of nobles,*
>> *and your princes eat in due season,*
>> *for strength, and not for drunkenness!*
> *By slothfulness the roof sinks in;*
>> *and through idleness of the hands the house leaks.*
> *A feast is made for laughter,*
>> *and wine makes the life glad;*
>> *and money is the answer for all things.*
> *Don't curse the king, no, not in your thoughts;*
>> *and don't curse the rich in your bedroom:*
>> *for a bird of the sky may carry your voice,*
>> *and that which has wings may tell the matter.*

....

Cast your bread on the waters;
> *for you shall find it after many days.*
> *Give a portion to seven, yes, even to eight;*
>> *for you don't know what evil will be on the earth.*
> *If the clouds are full of rain, they empty themselves on the earth;*
>> *and if a tree falls toward the south, or toward the north,*
>> *in the place where the tree falls, there shall it be.*
> *He who observes the wind won't sow;*
>> *and he who regards the clouds won't reap.*
> *As you don't know what is the way of the wind,*
>> *nor how the bones grow in the womb of her who is with child;*
>> *even so you don't know the work of God who does all.*
> *In the morning sow your seed,*
>> *and in the evening don't withhold your hand;*
>> *for you don't know which will prosper, whether this or that,*
>> *or whether they both will be equally good.*
> *Truly the light is sweet,*

and it is a pleasant thing for the eyes to see the sun.
Yes, if a man lives many years, let him rejoice in them all;
    but let him remember the days of darkness, for they shall be
    many.
    All that comes is vanity.
Rejoice, young man, in your youth,
    and let your heart cheer you in the days of your youth,
    and walk in the ways of your heart,
    and in the sight of your eyes;
    but know that for all these things God will bring you into
    judgment.
Therefore remove sorrow from your heart,
    and put away evil from your flesh;
    for youth and the dawn of life are vanity.

Remember also your Creator in the days of your youth,
    before the evil days come, and the years draw near,
    when you will say, "I have no pleasure in them;"
Before the sun, the light, the moon, and the stars are darkened,
    and the clouds return after the rain;
in the day when the keepers of the house shall tremble,
    and the strong men shall bow themselves,
    and the grinders cease because they are few,
    and those who look out of the windows are darkened,
and the doors shall be shut in the street;
    when the sound of the grinding is low,
    and one shall rise up at the voice of a bird,
    and all the daughters of music shall be brought low;
yes, they shall be afraid of heights,
    and terrors will be on the way;
    and the almond tree shall blossom,
    and the grasshopper shall be a burden,
    and desire shall fail;
    because man goes to his everlasting home,
    and the mourners go about the streets:
before the silver cord is severed,
    or the golden bowl is broken,
    or the pitcher is broken at the spring,
    or the wheel broken at the cistern,

and the dust returns to the earth as it was,
and the spirit returns to God who gave it.
"Vanity of vanities," says the Preacher.
"All is vanity!"

Further, because the Preacher was wise, he still taught the people knowledge. Yes, he pondered, sought out, and set in order many proverbs. The Preacher sought to find out acceptable words, and that which was written blamelessly, words of truth. The words of the wise are like goads; and like nails well fastened are words from the masters of assemblies, which are given from one shepherd. Furthermore, my son, be admonished: of making many books there is no end; and much study is a weariness of the flesh.

This is the end of the matter. All has been heard. Fear God and keep his commandments; for this is the whole duty of man. For God will bring every work into judgment, with every hidden thing, whether it is good, or whether it is evil.

THE

SONG OF SONGS

15 MIN

The Song of songs, which is Solomon's.

Beloved

Let him kiss me with the kisses of his mouth;
  for your love is better than wine.
Your oils have a pleasing fragrance.
  Your name is oil poured out,
  therefore the virgins love you.
Take me away with you.
  Let's hurry.
  The king has brought me into his rooms.

Friends

We will be glad and rejoice in you.
  We will praise your love more than wine!

Beloved

They are right to love you.
I am dark, but lovely,
  you daughters of Jerusalem,
  like Kedar's tents,
  like Solomon's curtains.
Don't stare at me because I am dark,
  because the sun has scorched me.
My mother's sons were angry with me.
  They made me keeper of the vineyards.
  I haven't kept my own vineyard.
Tell me, you whom my soul loves,
  where you graze your flock,
  where you rest them at noon;
  for why should I be as one who is veiled
  beside the flocks of your companions?

Lover

If you don't know, most beautiful among women,
  follow the tracks of the sheep.
  Graze your young goats beside the shepherds' tents.

I have compared you, my love,
  to a steed in Pharaoh's chariots.
Your cheeks are beautiful with earrings,
  your neck with strings of jewels.

Friends

We will make you earrings of gold,
with studs of silver.
Beloved
While the king sat at his table,
my perfume spread its fragrance.
My beloved is to me a sachet of myrrh,
that lies between my breasts.
My beloved is to me a cluster of henna blossoms
from the vineyards of En Gedi.
Lover
Behold, you are beautiful, my love.
Behold, you are beautiful.
Your eyes are like doves.
Beloved
Behold, you are beautiful, my beloved, yes, pleasant;
and our couch is verdant.
Lover
The beams of our house are cedars.
Our rafters are firs.

....

Beloved
I am a rose of Sharon,
a lily of the valleys.
Lover
As a lily among thorns,
so is my love among the daughters.
Beloved
As the apple tree among the trees of the wood,
so is my beloved among the sons.
I sat down under his shadow with great delight,
his fruit was sweet to my taste.
He brought me to the banquet hall.
His banner over me is love.
Strengthen me with raisins,
refresh me with apples;
for I am faint with love.
His left hand is under my head.
His right hand embraces me.
I adjure you, daughters of Jerusalem,

by the roes, or by the hinds of the field,
 that you not stir up, nor awaken love,
 until it so desires.

The voice of my beloved!
 Behold, he comes,
 leaping on the mountains,
 skipping on the hills.
My beloved is like a roe or a young deer.
 Behold, he stands behind our wall!
He looks in at the windows.
 He glances through the lattice.

My beloved spoke, and said to me,
 "Rise up, my love, my beautiful one, and come away.
For behold, the winter is past.
 The rain is over and gone.
The flowers appear on the earth.
 The time of the singing has come,
 and the voice of the turtledove is heard in our land.
The fig tree ripens her green figs.
 The vines are in blossom.
 They give out their fragrance.
Arise, my love, my beautiful one,
 and come away."
Lover
 My dove in the clefts of the rock,
 in the hiding places of the mountainside,
 let me see your face.
 let me hear your voice;
 for your voice is sweet and your face is lovely.
 Catch for us the foxes,
 the little foxes that plunder the vineyards;
 for our vineyards are in blossom.
Beloved
 My beloved is mine, and I am his.
 He browses among the lilies.
 Until the day is cool, and the shadows flee away,
 turn, my beloved,
 and be like a roe or a young deer on the mountains of Bether.

....

By night on my bed,
    I sought him whom my soul loves.
    I sought him, but I didn't find him.
  I will get up now, and go about the city;
    in the streets and in the squares I will seek him whom my soul
    loves.
    I sought him, but I didn't find him.
  The watchmen who go about the city found me;
    "Have you seen him whom my soul loves?"
  I had scarcely passed from them,
    when I found him whom my soul loves.
  I held him, and would not let him go,
    until I had brought him into my mother's house,
    into the room of her who conceived me.

I adjure you, daughters of Jerusalem,
    by the roes, or by the hinds of the field,
    that you not stir up nor awaken love,
    until it so desires.

Who is this who comes up from the wilderness like pillars of
smoke,
    perfumed with myrrh and frankincense,
    with all spices of the merchant?
Behold, it is Solomon's carriage!
    Sixty mighty men are around it,
    of the mighty men of Israel.
They all handle the sword, and are expert in war.
    Every man has his sword on his thigh,
    because of fear in the night.

King Solomon made himself a carriage
    of the wood of Lebanon.
He made its pillars of silver,
    its bottom of gold, its seat of purple,
    the middle of it being paved with love,
    from the daughters of Jerusalem.
Go out, you daughters of Zion, and see king Solomon,

with the crown with which his mother has crowned him,
in the day of his weddings,
in the day of the gladness of his heart.

....

Lover
Behold, you are beautiful, my love.
Behold, you are beautiful.
Your eyes are like doves behind your veil.
Your hair is as a flock of goats,
that descend from Mount Gilead.
Your teeth are like a newly shorn flock,
which have come up from the washing,
where every one of them has twins.
None is bereaved among them.
Your lips are like scarlet thread.
Your mouth is lovely.
Your temples are like a piece of a pomegranate behind your
veil.
Your neck is like David's tower built for an armory,
on which a thousand shields hang,
all the shields of the mighty men.
Your two breasts are like two fawns
that are twins of a roe,
which feed among the lilies.

Until the day is cool, and the shadows flee away,
I will go to the mountain of myrrh,
to the hill of frankincense.

You are all beautiful, my love.
There is no spot in you.
Come with me from Lebanon, my bride,
with me from Lebanon.
Look from the top of Amana,
from the top of Senir and Hermon,
from the lions' dens,
from the mountains of the leopards.

You have ravished my heart, my sister, my bride.

You have ravished my heart with one of your eyes,
with one chain of your neck.
How beautiful is your love, my sister, my bride!
How much better is your love than wine,
the fragrance of your perfumes than all kinds of spices!
Your lips, my bride, drip like the honeycomb.
Honey and milk are under your tongue.
The smell of your garments is like the smell of Lebanon.
My sister, my bride, is a locked up garden;
a locked up spring,
a sealed fountain.
Your shoots are an orchard of pomegranates, with precious fruits,
henna with spikenard plants,
spikenard and saffron,
calamus and cinnamon, with every kind of incense tree;
myrrh and aloes, with all the best spices,
a fountain of gardens,
a well of living waters,
flowing streams from Lebanon.

Beloved
Awake, north wind, and come, you south!
Blow on my garden, that its spices may flow out.
Let my beloved come into his garden,
and taste his precious fruits.

....

Lover
I have come into my garden, my sister, my bride.
I have gathered my myrrh with my spice;
I have eaten my honeycomb with my honey;
I have drunk my wine with my milk.

Friends
Eat, friends!
Drink, yes, drink abundantly, beloved.

Beloved
I was asleep, but my heart was awake.
It is the voice of my beloved who knocks:
"Open to me, my sister, my love, my dove, my undefiled;
for my head is filled with dew,
and my hair with the dampness of the night."

I have taken off my robe. Indeed, must I put it on?
  I have washed my feet. Indeed, must I soil them?
My beloved thrust his hand in through the latch opening.
  My heart pounded for him.
I rose up to open for my beloved.
  My hands dripped with myrrh,
  my fingers with liquid myrrh,
  on the handles of the lock.
I opened to my beloved;
  but my beloved left, and had gone away.
My heart went out when he spoke.
  I looked for him, but I didn't find him.
  I called him, but he didn't answer.
The watchmen who go about the city found me.
  They beat me.
  They bruised me.
  The keepers of the walls took my cloak away from me.

I adjure you, daughters of Jerusalem,
  If you find my beloved,
  that you tell him that I am faint with love.

Friends
  How is your beloved better than another beloved,
    you fairest among women?
  How is your beloved better than another beloved,
  that you do so adjure us?

Beloved
  My beloved is white and ruddy.
    The best among ten thousand.
  His head is like the purest gold.
    His hair is bushy, black as a raven.
  His eyes are like doves beside the water brooks,
    washed with milk, mounted like jewels.
  His cheeks are like a bed of spices with towers of perfumes.
    His lips are like lilies, dropping liquid myrrh.
  His hands are like rings of gold set with beryl.
    His body is like ivory work overlaid with sapphires.
  His legs are like pillars of marble set on sockets of fine gold.
    His appearance is like Lebanon, excellent as the cedars.
  His mouth is sweetness;

yes, he is altogether lovely.
This is my beloved, and this is my friend,
    daughters of Jerusalem.

....

Friends
Where has your beloved gone, you fairest among women?
    Where has your beloved turned, that we may seek him with
    you?
Beloved
My beloved has gone down to his garden,
    to the beds of spices,
    to pasture his flock in the gardens, and to gather lilies.
I am my beloved's, and my beloved is mine.
    He browses among the lilies.

Lover
You are beautiful, my love, as Tirzah,
    lovely as Jerusalem,
    awesome as an army with banners.
Turn away your eyes from me,
    for they have overcome me.
Your hair is like a flock of goats,
    that lie along the side of Gilead.
Your teeth are like a flock of ewes,
    which have come up from the washing,
    of which every one has twins;
    not one is bereaved among them.
Your temples are like a piece of a pomegranate behind your veil.

There are sixty queens, eighty concubines,
    and virgins without number.
My dove, my perfect one, is unique.
    She is her mother's only daughter.
    She is the favorite one of her who bore her.
The daughters saw her, and called her blessed.
    The queens and the concubines saw her, and they praised her.

Who is she who looks out as the morning,
    beautiful as the moon,

clear as the sun,
and awesome as an army with banners?

I went down into the nut tree grove,
to see the green plants of the valley,
to see whether the vine budded,
and the pomegranates were in flower.
Without realizing it,
my desire set me with my royal people's chariots.
Friends
Return, return, Shulammite!
Return, return, that we may gaze at you.
Lover
Why do you desire to gaze at the Shulammite,
as at the dance of Mahanaim?

....

How beautiful are your feet in sandals, prince's daughter!
Your rounded thighs are like jewels,
the work of the hands of a skillful workman.
Your body is like a round goblet,
no mixed wine is wanting.
Your waist is like a heap of wheat,
set about with lilies.
Your two breasts are like two fawns,
that are twins of a roe.
Your neck is like an ivory tower.
Your eyes are like the pools in Heshbon by the gate of Bathrab-
bim.
Your nose is like the tower of Lebanon which looks toward
Damascus.
Your head on you is like Carmel.
The hair of your head like purple.
The king is held captive in its tresses.
How beautiful and how pleasant you are,
love, for delights!
This, your stature, is like a palm tree,
your breasts like its fruit.
I said, "I will climb up into the palm tree.
I will take hold of its fruit."

Let your breasts be like clusters of the vine,
    the smell of your breath like apples.
Your mouth is like the best wine,
    that goes down smoothly for my beloved,
    gliding through the lips of those who are asleep.

Beloved
I am my beloved's.
    His desire is toward me.
Come, my beloved! Let's go out into the field.
    Let's lodge in the villages.
Let's go early up to the vineyards.
    Let's see whether the vine has budded,
    its blossom is open,
    and the pomegranates are in flower.
    There I will give you my love.
The mandrakes produce fragrance.
    At our doors are all kinds of precious fruits, new and old,
    which I have stored up for you, my beloved.

....

Oh that you were like my brother,
    who nursed from the breasts of my mother!
If I found you outside, I would kiss you;
    yes, and no one would despise me.
I would lead you, bringing you into the house of my mother,
    who would instruct me.
I would have you drink spiced wine,
    of the juice of my pomegranate.
His left hand would be under my head.
    His right hand would embrace me.

I adjure you, daughters of Jerusalem,
    that you not stir up, nor awaken love,
    until it so desires.

Friends
Who is this who comes up from the wilderness,
    leaning on her beloved?

Beloved
Under the apple tree I aroused you.

There your mother conceived you.
There she was in labor and bore you.

Set me as a seal on your heart,
as a seal on your arm;
for love is strong as death.
Jealousy is as cruel as Sheol.
Its flashes are flashes of fire,
a very flame of YHWH.
Many waters can't quench love,
neither can floods drown it.
If a man would give all the wealth of his house for love,
he would be utterly scorned.

Brothers
We have a little sister.
She has no breasts.
What shall we do for our sister
in the day when she is to be spoken for?

If she is a wall,
we will build on her a turret of silver.
If she is a door,
we will enclose her with boards of cedar.

Beloved
I am a wall, and my breasts like towers,
then I was in his eyes like one who found peace.
Solomon had a vineyard at Baal Hamon.
He leased out the vineyard to keepers.
Each was to bring a thousand shekels of silver for its fruit.
My own vineyard is before me.
The thousand are for you, Solomon,
two hundred for those who tend its fruit.

Lover
You who dwell in the gardens, with friends in attendance,
let me hear your voice!

Beloved
Come away, my beloved!
Be like a gazelle or a young stag on the mountains of spices!

APPENDICES

GLOSSARY

The following words used in the World English Bible are not very common, either because they refer to ancient weights, measures, or money, or because they are in some way unique to the Bible.

Abaddon *Abaddon is Hebrew for destruction.*

Abba *Abba is a Chaldee word for father, used in a respectful, affectionate, and familiar way, like papa, dad, or daddy. Often used in prayer to refer to our Father in Heaven.*

adultery *Adultery is having sexual intercourse with someone besides your own husband or wife. In the Bible, the only legitimate sexual intercourse is between a man and a woman who are married to each other.*

alpha *Alpha is the first letter of the Greek alphabet. It is sometimes used to mean the beginning or the first.*

amen *Amen means "so be it" or "it is certainly so."*

angel *"Angel" literally means "messenger" or "envoy," and is usually used to refer to spiritual beings who normally are invisible to us, but can also appear as exceedingly strong creatures or as humans.*

Apollyon *Apollyon is Greek for destroyer.*

apostle *"Apostle" means a delegate, messenger, or one sent forth with orders. This term is applied in the New Testament in both a general sense connected with a ministry of establishing and strengthening church fellowships, as well as in a specific sense to "The*

12 Apostles of the Lamb" (Revelation 21:14). The former category applies to a specific ministry that continues in the Church (Ephesians 4:11-13) and which includes many more than 12 people, while the latter refers to the apostles named in Matthew 10:2-4, except with Judas Iscariot replaced by Matthias (Acts 1:26).

Armageddon   See Har-magedon.

assarion   An assarion is a small Roman copper coin worth one tenth of a drachma, or about an hour's wages for an agricultural laborer.

aureus   An aureus is a Roman gold coin, worth 25 silver denarii. An aureus weighed from 115 to 126.3 grains (7.45 to 8.18 grams).

baptize   Baptize means to immerse in, or wash with something, usually water. Baptism in the Holy Spirit, fire, the Body of Christ, and suffering are also mentioned in the New Testament, along with baptism in water. Baptism is not just to cleanse the body, but as an outward sign of an inward spiritual cleansing and commitment. Baptism is a sign of repentance, as practiced by John the Baptizer, and of faith in Jesus Christ, as practiced by Jesus' disciples.

bath   A bath is a liquid measure of about 22 liters, 5.8 U. S. gallons, or 4.8 imperial gallons.

batos   A batos is a liquid measure of about 39.5 liters, 10.4 U. S. gallons, or 8.7 imperial gallons.

Beelzebul   literally, lord of the flies. A name used for the devil.

Beersheba *Beersheba is Hebrew for "well of the oath" or "well of the seven." A city in Israel.*

behold *Look! See! Wow! Notice this! Lo!*

cherub *A cherub is a kind of angel with wings and hands that is associated with the throne room of God and guardian duty. See Ezekiel 10.*

cherubim *Cherubim means more than one cherub or a mighty cherub.*

choenix *A choenix is a dry volume measure that is a little more than a liter (which is a little more than a quart). A choenix was the daily ration of grain for a soldier in some armies.*

concubine *a woman who is united to a man for the purpose of providing him with sexual pleasure and children, but not being honored as a full partner in marriage; a second-class wife. In Old Testament times (and in some places now), it was the custom of middle-eastern kings, chiefs, and wealthy men to marry multiple wives and concubines, but God commanded the Kings of Israel not to do so (Deuteronomy 17:17) and Jesus encouraged people to either remain single or marry as God originally intended: one man married to one woman (Matthew 19:3-12; 1 Corinthians 7:1-13).*

cor *A cor is a dry measure of about 391 liters, 103 U. S. gallons, or 86 imperial gallons.*

corban *Corban is a Hebrew word for an offering devoted to God.*

crucify *Crucify means to execute someone by nailing them to a cross with metal spikes. Their hands are stretched out on the crossbeam with spikes driven through their wrists or hands. Their feet or ankles are attached to a cross with a metal spike. The weight of the victim's body tends to force the air out of his lungs. To rise up to breathe, the victim has to put weight on the wounds, and use a lot of strength. The victim is nailed to the cross while the cross is on the ground, then the cross is raised up and dropped into a hole, thus jarring the wounds. Before crucifixion, the victim was usually whipped with a Roman cat of nine tails, which had bits of glass and metal tied to its ends. This caused chunks of flesh to be removed and open wounds to be placed against the raw wood of the cross. The victim was made to carry the heavy crossbeam of his cross from the place of judgment to the place of crucifixion, but often was physically unable after the scourging, so another person would be pressed into involuntary service to carry the cross for him. Roman crucifixion was generally done totally naked to maximize both shame and discomfort. Eventually, the pain, weakness, dehydration, and exhaustion of the muscles needed to breathe make breathing impossible, and the victim suffocates.*

cubit *A cubit is a unit of linear measure, from the elbow to the tip of the longest finger of a man. This unit is commonly converted to 0.46 meters or 18 inches, although that varies with height of the man doing the measurement. There is also a "long" cubit that is longer than a regular cubit by a handbreadth. (Ezekiel 43:13)*

cummin *Cummin is an aromatic seed from Cuminum cyminum, resembling caraway in flavor and appearance. It is used as a spice.*

darnel *Darnel is a weed grass (probably bearded darnel or Lolium temulentum) that looks very much like wheat until it is mature, when the seeds reveal a great difference. Darnel seeds aren't good for much except as chicken feed or to burn to prevent the spread of this weed.*

denarii *denarii: plural form of denarius, a silver Roman coin worth about a day's wages for a laborer.*

denarius *A denarius is a silver Roman coin worth about a day's wages for an agricultural laborer. A denarius was worth 1/25th of a Roman aureus.*

devil *The word "devil" comes from the Greek "diabolos," which means "one prone to slander; a liar." "Devil" is used to refer to a fallen angel, also called "Satan," who works to steal, kill, destroy, and do evil. The devil's doom is certain, and it is only a matter of time before he is thrown into the Lake of Fire, never to escape.*

didrachma *A didrachma is a Greek silver coin worth 2 drachmas, about as much as 2 Roman denarii, or about 2 days wages. It was commonly used to pay the half-shekel temple tax.*

distaff *part of a spinning wheel used for twisting threads.*

drachma *A drachma is a Greek silver coin worth about one Roman denarius, or about a day's wages for an agricultural laborer.*

El-Elohe-Israel *El-Elohe-Israel means "God, the God of Israel" or "The God of Israel is mighty."*

ephah *An ephah is a measure of volume of about 22 liters, 5.8 U. S. gallons, 4.8 imperial gallons, or a bit more than half a bushel.*

Gehenna *Gehenna is one word used for Hell. It comes from the Hebrew Gey-Hinnom, literally "valley of Hinnom." This word originated as the name for a place south of the old city of Jerusalem where the city's rubbish was burned. At one time, live babies were thrown crying into the fire under the arms of the idol, Moloch, to die there. This place was so despised by the people after the righteous King Josiah abolished this hideous practice that it was made into a garbage heap. Bodies of diseased animals and executed criminals were thrown there and burned.*

gittith *Gittith is a musical term possibly meaning "an instrument of Gath."*

goad *a sharp, pointed prodding device used to motivate reluctant animals (such as oxen and mules) to move in the right direction.*

gospel *Gospel means "good news" or "glad tidings," specifically the Good News of Jesus' life, death, and resurrection for our salvation, healing, and provision; and the hope of eternal life that Jesus made available to us by God's grace.*

Hades *Hades: The nether realm of the disembodied spirits. Also known as "hell."*

Har-magedon *Har-magedon, also called Armegeddon, is most likely a reference to hill ("har") of Megiddo, near the Carmel Range in Israel. This area has a large valley plain with plenty of room for armies to maneuver.*

hin *A hin was about 6.5 liters or 1.7 gallons.*

homer *One homer is about 220 liters, 6.2 U. S. bushels, 6.1 imperial bushels, 58 U. S. gallons, or 48.4 imperial gallons.*

hypocrite *a stage actor; someone who pretends to be someone other than who they really are; a pretender; a dissembler*

Ishmael *Ishmael is the son of Abraham and Hagar. Ishmael literally means, "God hears."*

Jehovah *See "YAHWEH."*

Jesus *"Jesus" is Greek for the Hebrew name "Yeshua," which is a short version of "Yehoshua," which comes from "Yoshia," which means "He will save."*

kodrantes *A kodrantes is a small coin worth one half of an Attic chalcus or two lepta. It is worth less than 2% of a day's wages for an agricultural laborer.*

lepta *Lepta are very small, brass, Jewish coins worth half a Roman quadrans each, which is worth a quarter of the copper assarion. Lepta are worth less than 1% of an agricultural worker's daily wages.*

leviathan *Leviathan is a poetic name for a large aquatic creature, posssibly a crocodile or a dinosaur.*

mahalath *Mahalath is the name of a tune or a musical term.*

manna *Name for the food that God miraculously provided to the Israelites while they were wandering in the wilderness between Egypt and the promised land.*

From Hebrew *man-hu* (*What is that?*) or *manan* (*to allot*). See Exodus 16:14-35.

marriage   *the union of a husband and a wife for the purpose of cohabitation, procreation, and to enjoy each other's company. God's plan for marriage is between one man and one woman (Mark 10:6-9; 1 Corinthians 7). Although there are many cases of a man marrying more than one woman in the Old Testament, being married to one wife is a requirement to serve in certain church leadership positions (1 Timothy 3:2,12; Titus 1:5-6).*

maschil   *Maschil is a musical and literary term for "contemplation" or "meditative psalm."*

michtam   *A michtam is a poem.*

mina   *A mina is a Greek coin worth 100 Greek drachmas (or 100 Roman denarii), or about 100 day's wages for an agricultural laborer.*

myrrh   *Myrrh is the fragrant substance that oozes out of the stems and branches of the low, shrubby tree commiphora myrrha or comiphora kataf native to the Arabian deserts and parts of Africa. The fragrant gum drops to the ground and hardens into an oily yellowish-brown resin. Myrrh was highly valued as a perfume, and as an ingredient in medicinal and ceremonial ointments.*

Nicolaitans   *Nicolaitans were most likely Gnostics who taught the detestable lie that the physical and spiritual realms were entirely separate and that immorality in the physical realm wouldn't harm your spiritual health.*

omega   *Omega is the last letter of the Greek alphabet. It is sometimes used to mean the last or the end.*

Peniel *Peniel is Hebrew for "face of God."*

phylactery *a leather container for holding a small scroll containing important Scripture passages that is worn on the arm or forehead in prayer. These phylacteries (tefillin in Hebrew) are still used by orthodox Jewish men. See Deuteronomy 6:8.*

Praetorium *Praetorium: the Roman governor's residence and office building, and those who work there.*

quadrans *A quadrans is a Roman coin worth about 1/64 of a denarius. A denarius is about one day's wages for an agricultural laborer.*

rabbi *Rabbi is a transliteration of the Hebrew word for "my teacher," used as a title of respect for Jewish teachers.*

Rahab *Rahab is either (1) The prostitute who hid Joshua's 2 spies in Jericho (Joshua 2,6) and later became an ancestor of Jesus (Matthew 1:5) and an example of faith (Hebrews 11:31; James 2:25); or (2) Literally, "pride" or "arrogance" — possibly a reference to a large aquatic creature (Job 9:13; 26:12; Isaiah 51:9) or symbolically referring to Egypt (Psalm 87:4; 89:10; Isaiah 30:7).*

repent *to change one's mind; turn away from sin and turn towards God; to abhor one's past sins and determine to follow God.*

Rhabboni *Rhabboni: a transliteration of the Hebrew word for "great teacher."*

Sabbath *The seventh day of the week, set aside by God for* *man to rest.*

saints *The Greek word for "saints" literally means "holy ones." Saints are people set apart for service to God as holy and separate, living in righteousness. Used in the Bible to refer to all Christians and to all of those who worship* YHWH *in Old Testament times.*

Samaritan *A Samaritan is a resident of Samaria. The Samaritans and the Jews generally detested each other during the time that Jesus walked the Earth.*

sata *a dry measure of capacity approximately equal to 13 liters or 1.5 pecks.*

Satan *Satan means "accuser." This is one name for the devil, an enemy of God and God's people.*

scribe *A scribe is one who copies God's law. They were often respected as teachers and authorities on God's law.*

selah *Selah is a musical term indicating a pause or instrumental interlude for reflection.*

seraphim *Seraphim are 6-winged angels. See Isaiah 6:2-6.*

sexual immorality *The term "sexual immorality" in the New Testament comes from the Greek "porneia," which refers to any sexual activity besides that between a husband and his wife. In other words, prostitution (male or female), bestiality, homosexual activity, any sexual intercourse outside of marriage, and the production and consumption of pornography all are included in this term.*

shekel *A measure of weight, and when referring to that weight in gold, silver, or brass, of money. A shekel is approximately 16 grams, about a half an ounce, or 20 gerahs (Ezekiel 45:12).*

Sheol *Sheol is the place of the dead.*

Shibah *Shibah is Hebrew for "oath" or "seven." See Beersheba.*

shigionoth *Victorious music.*

soul *"Soul" refers to the emotions and intellect of a living person, as well as that person's very life. It is distinguished in the Bible from a person's spirit and body. (1 Thessalonians 5:23, Hebrews 4:12)*

span *A span is the length from the tip of a man's thumb to the tip of his little finger when his hand is stretched out (about half a cubit, or 9 inches, or 22.8 cm.)*

spirit *Spirit, breath, and wind all derive from the same Hebrew and Greek words. A person's spirit is the very essence of that person's life, which comes from God, who is a Spirit being (John 4:24, Genesis 1:2; 2:7). The Bible distinguishes between a person's spirit, soul, and body (1 Thessalonians 5:23, Hebrews 4:12). Some beings may exist as spirits without necessarily having a visible body, such as angels and demons (Luke 9:39, 1 John 4:1-3).*

stadia *stadia: plural for "stadion," a linear measure of about 184.9 meters or 606.6 feet (the length of the race course at Olympia).*

stater *A stater is a Greek silver coin equivalent to four Attic or two Alexandrian drachmas, or a Jewish shekel: just exactly enough to cover the half-shekel Temple Tax for two people.*

tabernacle *a dwelling place or place of worship, usually a tent.*

talent *A measure of weight or mass of 3000 shekels.*

Tartarus   *Tartarus is the Greek name for an underworld for the wicked dead; another name for Gehenna or Hell.*

teraphim   *Teraphim are household idols that may have been associated with inheritance rights to the household property.*

Yah   *"Yah" is a shortened form of "Yahweh," which is God's proper name. This form is used occasionally in the Old Testament, mostly in the Psalms. See "Yahweh."*

YHWH (Yahweh)   *"Yahweh" is God's proper name. In Hebrew, the four consonants roughly equivalent to YHWH were considered too holy to pronounce, so the Hebrew word for "Lord" (Adonai) was substituted when reading it aloud. When vowel points were added to the Hebrew Old Testament, the vowel points for "Adonai" were mixed with the consonants for "Yahweh," which if you pronounced it literally as written, would be pronounced "Yehovah" or "Jehovah." When the Old Testament was translated to Greek, the tradition of substituting "Lord" for God's proper name continued in the translation of God's name to "Lord" (Kurios). Some English Bibles translate God's proper name to "LORD" or "GOD" (usually with small capital letters), based on that same tradition. This can get really confusing, since two other words ("Adonai" and "Elohim") translate to "Lord" and "God," and they are sometimes used together. The ASV of 1901 (and some other translations) render YHWH as "Jehovah." The most probable pronunciation of God's proper name is "Yahweh." In Hebrew, the name "Yahweh" is related to the active declaration "I AM." See Exodus 3:13-14. Since Hebrew has no tenses, the declaration "I AM" can also be interpreted as "I WAS" and "I WILL BE." Compare Revelation 1:8.*

VOLUMES IN THIS SERIES

Volume 1: The Pentateuch

- Genesis
- Exodus
- Leviticus
- Numbers
- Deuteronomy

Volume 2: History

- Joshua
- Judges
- Ruth
- 1 & 2 Samuel
- 1 & 2 Kings
- 1 & 2 Chronicles
- Ezra
- Nehemiah
- Esther

Volume 3: Poetry & Wisdom

- Job
- Psalms
- Proverbs
- Ecclesiastes
- Song of Songs

Volume 4: The Prophets

- Isaiah
- Jeremiah
- Lamentations
- Ezekiel
- Daniel

- Hosea
- Joel
- Amos
- Obadiah
- Jonah
- Micah
- Nahum
- Habakkuk
- Zephaniah
- Haggai
- Zechariah
- Malachi

Volume 5: New Testament

- Matthew
- Mark
- Luke
- John
- Acts
- Romans
- 1 & 2 Corinthians
- Galatians
- Ephesians
- Philippians
- Colossians
- 1 & 2 Thessalonians
- 1 & 2 Timothy
- Titus
- Philemon
- Hebrews
- James
- 1 & 2 Peter
- 1, 2, and 3 John
- Jude
- Revelation

Volume 6: Deuterocanon, Apocrypha, and Pseudepigrapha

- Tobit
- Judith
- Additions to Esther (additions found in the LXX namely Esther 10:4 – 16:24)
- Wisdom (also known as the Wisdom of Solomon)
- Ecclesiasticus (or Sirach)
- Baruch
- Epistle of Jeremy
- Prayer of Azarias (Daniel 3:24–97 in the LXX & Vulgate)
- Susanna (Daniel 13 in the LXX & Vulgate)
- Bel and the Dragon (Daniel 14 in the LXX & Vulgate)
- I Maccabees
- II Maccabees
- 1 Esdras
- Prayer of Manasses
- Psalm 151
- III Maccabees
- IV Maccabees
- 2 Esdras

FURTHER STUDY

Reader's Bibles are great, but if you want to learn more get a good study Bible. It will help you really dig into the text. Also, check out this stuff that I have found helpful:

 TheBibleProject.com

These guys are awesome. They make 5-10 minute explainer videos on every book of the Bible as well as common Biblical themes. Their "Read Scripture" series are little power lectures that get you into the main themes of each book and point you in some directions to explore in your own study.

 BillHull.net

This is my Dad. He's pretty rad. He writes books on discipleship and church leadership. This is where I would link you to Amazon if I could, but you will have to look them up yourself. If you are a pastor make sure to check out this thing he started at *TheBonhoefferProject.com*

 DownloadYouthMinistry.com

Are you a youth worker? God bless your over-worked and under-paid soul! DYM has a shocking array of resources to make your life easier and your ministry more effective. It was co-founded by Doug Fields. Doug also has some great books on marriage and parenting on his personal website *DougFields.com*